31177

DATE			

WITHDRAWN

WITHDRAWN

© THE BAKER & TAYLOR CO.

Books by Harold Clurman

THE FERVENT YEARS (1945)

LIES LIKE TRUTH (1958)

THE NAKED IMAGE (1966)

ON DIRECTING (1972)

THE DIVINE PASTIME (1974)

ALL PEOPLE ARE FAMOUS (1974)

Harold Clurman

(instead of

HARCOURT BRAC

PEOPLE

FAMOUS

an autobiography)

JOVANOVICH   NEW YORK AND LONDON

Library of Congress Cataloging in Publication Data

Clurman, Harold, 1901-
   All people are famous.

   1. Clurman, Harold, 1901- I. Title.
PN2287.C548A33   792'.0233'0924 [B]   74-13820
ISBN 0-15-104775-8

First edition
B C D E

For Aaron Copland

Contents

Preface

I have never kept a diary. Once, during a visit to the Soviet Union in 1935, I put some words into a notebook, mostly about the plays I was seeing there and the stage folk I was meeting. But my acquaintances and friends have always extended well beyond the narrow circle of the theatre.

Perhaps because I have known so many famous and extraordinary people, I am always being asked to write an autobiography. I rejected the idea a long time ago, on the grounds that it is impossible to tell the truth about oneself because one does not know it. The person who undertakes to write an account of his life often ends up boasting as much about his vices as about his virtues. Didn't Rousseau confess to misdeeds he had never committed? It is through their "fictions" that most artists tell the truth about themselves.

Then too, one's life is not entirely one's own: there are the "others." The "other," Jean Paul Sartre notwithstanding, does not constitute hell (his famous aphorism applies chiefly to schizoid personalities). Thought is created in solitude, said Goethe, character in society. Having always rejoiced in company and in companionship, I decided to write a book devoted to some of the others in my life. Henry James said that although a writer must never put himself in a book, he cannot possibly keep himself out. This book is therefore about myself through others.

The others I write about are all people who have influenced me, directly or indirectly, and not a few of them have also influenced the world. I associate many of them with certain salient points of contemporary history: the old Lower East Side of Manhattan, Paris in the twenties, the Depression of the thirties, Hollywood before and during the war, Moscow, Tokyo, and other storied scenes and times. My book is about people in their places.

They are of many kinds and climes. Though a theatre man by profession, fascinated from early boyhood by all manner of spectacle, I didn't choose to make a career of the theatre till I was twenty-three. Before that, and ever after, it was not just the theatre but all the arts that attracted me. Aaron Copland, who has played an important role in my life, said to me when we were very young, "Art is your religion." I was troubled by the statement at the time, because I realized it contained an element of truth, but today I could go so far as to deny it. Art for me is the bearer of an essence far more profound even than religion. Brecht called this essence "the art of life," but even that is inadequate. Perhaps it would be best not to name it at all. Names are prone to vulgarization, to obsolescence (think of what has happened to "God," to "law and order"). But whatever that essence may be—and it is surely a holy spirit—I seek it in some of the people around me, that is, in their actions. And the artist's most worthy action is usually his creation.

Acknowledgments

The first eleven chapters of this book were written at the American Academy in Rome during the spring of 1972; the last five in New York and Los Angeles during the fall of 1973.

The manuscript was typed by Joan Ungaro. In view of my wretched penmanship, this was no easy task. Miss Ungaro also contributed valuable editorial advice.

I also wish to acknowledge the invaluable aid of my editor, Steven M. L. Aronson.

What I possess I see as in the distance,
and what vanished becomes my reality.

—Goethe, *Faust*

If I am not for myself, who will be for me? And if I am only
for myself, what am I?

—Hillel (Hebrew sage)

Young Alexander conquered India.
He alone?
Caesar beat the Gauls.
Was there not even a cook in his army?
Philip of Spain wept as his fleet
Was sunk and destroyed. Were there no other tears?
Frederick the Great triumphed in the Seven Years War. Who
Triumphed with him?

> —Brecht, *A Worker Reads History,* translated by
> H. R. Hays

CHAPTER

1

Father's Day

When I was asked in a recent interview who among all the people I've ever known has been most influential in shaping my character or mode of thought, I answered without hesitation, "My father."

He was born in Kamenetz, in the Ukraine, close to the borders of Poland and Romania. In 1888, when he was only nineteen, he left the Ukraine, in "steerage" on the S.S. *Chicago*, with my mother, who was somewhat older than he, and their four-year-old son Morris, "Moe." By the time I was born, in 1901, my father was a New York physician who had studied medicine at Yale and received his degree from New York University.

When I was about nineteen, a family friend—Billy Rose's mother—told me, to what purpose I was never able to discover, that Moe was only my half brother. This information did not disturb me in the least: Moe was my brother, no matter to what degree, and I loved him dearly. Only a year ago my nephew Richard Clurman, the ex-New York parks commissioner, assured me that the "secret" information I had received more than fifty years ago was correct. But I did not want to hear the details.

From the day my father left for America, he never wrote to or received a single letter from his parents. So I never knew any of my grandparents (somewhere I remember seeing a photo of my mother's parents). It was an extremely bitter generation gap that separated my father from his, a man so learned in Hebrew lore and so fanatically strict in ritual practice that the Jewish community of Kamenetz practically worshiped him and undertook to support him.

It was said that whenever my grandfather entered a room and saw a "graven image," even if it was only a photo of a member of his family, he struck it down with his cane. I used to hear how he had thrashed my father for reading a book in Russian, which was, as far as he was concerned, the language of the "heathen." My father was forbidden to read such books, but he read them anyway; he also read such daring writers as Plekhanov, the leader of the Menshevik segment of the Social Democratic party. But if my father was something of a Marxist, his Marxism was diluted by a complex emotionalism.

One night—I was about nine—my father came into my bedroom just as I was falling asleep, and stood quietly by my bed for a few moments in the dark, as if he were struggling to bring himself to speak. He told me that he had just received a letter announcing his father's death and that, although they had quarreled bitterly and had in fact become totally estranged, he had been weeping. Despite all the discord between them, he was still bound to his father and to the life he had abjured. Of his mother, my father never spoke a word. She must have been one of those women who are overshadowed by their commanding husbands, one of those women whom tyranny makes weak.

The Lower East Side of Manhattan was a great disappointment to my father. He had to take any work he could find: in a hat factory, for a start. Later on, he took a job selling insurance. A childless widow he tried to persuade to insure herself was stubborn in her refusal. "But if you don't have insurance," he argued, "you won't be properly buried." "If they don't bury me out of love," she countered, "they'll do it because of the stink."

My mother recognized that he would never succeed in business and at some point suggested that he become a doctor. How, my father asked, was he going to become a doctor? There was a second son to feed now. My mother had her answer prepared: they would open a candy-and-newspaper store in New Haven, of all places, and she would take care of the store while he studied at Yale!

And, sure enough, by the time I was born on the corner of Rivington and Essex streets on the old Lower East Side, my father was a doctor. A couple of years later, the family (I had three older brothers: Moe, Albert, and Will) moved two blocks away to Rivington Street near Suffolk, to a three-story house opposite P.S. 160—my first school. Ours was one of the few private houses in the neighborhood; with its two electric torches atop long steel columns flanking a short flight of steps that led to the front door, it was in fact considered something of a mansion.

When I was six, my father took me to see Jacob Adler, the greatest Yiddish-speaking actor of the day, in a translation from the German called *Uriel Acosta* (Uriel Acosta was a disciple of Spinoza), and a while later to see Adler play Shylock.

I could not possibly have understood a word of either of these plays, for I knew no Yiddish. Although my parents spoke mostly Yiddish and Russian to each other and to some of their relatives and close friends, they never spoke anything but English to us children.

I learned to understand Yiddish by hearing it spoken on the stage, and by overhearing conversations between my father and his immigrant patients, and, still later, by listening to my father as he read me the stories of Sholom Aleichem and Peretz. My father wanted me to know I was a Jew. Yet, for him, knowing one was a Jew had very little to do with religion. He was anything but religious; I once heard him soberly declare, "There are two things I don't believe in: God and the afterlife," which, to my amusement, shocked the American-born wife of one of my brothers.

For all that, my father believed that every man should reap sustenance from his tradition. It was a heritage that one handed down to one's children for them to carry on, broadened and heightened by their own experience, learning, and knowledge. This, he said, was the root of culture.

So my father had me learn Hebrew, but he also made certain that I read the works of Mark Twain! And he saw to it that I studied the ancient language not at an old-fashioned Hebrew school but with teachers who had a modern outlook and used modern methods.

He gave me the Old Testament to read and he explained the history and meaning of the Jewish holidays to me. But he also encouraged me to read Shakespeare aloud to him. When I finished a passage or a scene, he asked if I had really understood it. And when I answered yes, he challenged me in a kindly manner to say what I had gathered from the reading.

He observed the Jewish holidays in a rather desultory fashion. He would have matzos served at Passover, with hardly any accompanying ritual. He would describe the nature of the traditional "Four Questions" the youngest son was required to ask of his father at the Seder, but the explanation was totally without dogma; it sought to communicate a sentiment, a sense of the legendary but still vital past. That was how he imparted a knowledge of "Jewishness" to me. He never fasted, or asked any of his sons to fast, on Yom Kippur. My *bar mitzvah* was more a gesture of instruction than anything else. There was no solemnity about it at all. A cultural attitude was implied; I could use it if I were so inclined.

I devoured Horatio Alger when I was ten. This worried my brothers, who had concluded that Alger's rags-to-riches stories were trash. Al said to Will, "He'll get over it when he grows up." My growing up in this respect was rapid. One of my proudest memories—the one I still summon up when friends ask me what sort of man my father was—is of the day my father brought me Turgenev's *Fathers and Sons*. He also urged Thomas Hardy on me, and Dostoevski. He knew I would read Dickens and the like at school. His literary selections were formidable stuff for a boy, but one of the results was that, insofar as I could help it, I never again read trash.

On the walls of my father's waiting room in the Bronx, there were portraits of Shelley and of Moses Mendelssohn, the model for Ephraim Lessing's play *Nathan the Wise* and the translator of the Old Testament into German. Our library at home contained all Heine's poety in German, all Maupassant's stories in English, all of Byron, Buckle's *History of Civilization,* James Huneker's *Iconoclasts,* a book about modern dramatists, Schopenhauer's *The World as Will and Idea,* and the poetry of Pushkin and Lermontov in Russian.

One wonderful evening, my father read Ibsen's *Ghosts* in Russian to my mother. I didn't know Russian; what struck me was the care and seriousness with which my father explained the play to my much less well educated mother. He was preparing for a visit to the theatre at which a then famous Russian actor, Paul Orlenev, was appearing together with the then still unknown Nazimova, who was said to be his mistress as well as his leading lady. Orlenev was a drunkard and a "routine" anti-Semite who supposedly called Nazimova his *zhidovka,* an insulting Russian term for a Jewess. (This strikes me as odd, because in all the years of Nazimova's success on the American stage and screen, I never heard anything about her being Jewish.) My father told me that Orlenev, whom he considered a great actor, had given all of Ibsen's *Brand* in two evenings—at a time when Ibsen was rarely played on the New York stage, and, when played, reviled. (As late as 1918, on the opening night of *Hedda Gabler* at the Plymouth Theatre, with Nazimova in the title role, I heard the theatre critic of the New York *American,* Alan Dale, acknowledge that if the play were ever accepted, it would only be as a study in neurosis.)

My father gave me Shaw's *Dramatic Criticism and Essays* for my sixteenth birthday, inscribed: "To my son, Harold, because of his special interest in dramatic literature." That visit to *Uriel Acosta* had "taken," and I never ceased imploring, insisting, crying out to be taken again and again to the theatre. I was "hooked."

The plays I was seeing were all rather sophisticated— one of them was a version of Daudet's *Sappho!* The Yiddish theatre of those days, much admired by the "Victorian"

Hapgood family, offered plays by Gorki, Ibsen, Hauptmann, and Tolstoi. Jacob Adler was the first actor in America to play Tolstoi's *Living Corpse,* which was not presented in English until 1918 with John Barrymore. Adler had also played Shylock in Yiddish, on Broadway, in 1903.

As a minor, I was permitted to share, for an extra twenty-five cents, the single orchestra seat my father bought for a dollar. When his lively practice kept him from satisfying my obstreperous demands to see still one more play, he asked my brother Moe, then a medical student and also an avid theatregoer, to take me.

Some of my father's friends suggested that I might have a talent for the theatre. My father was skeptical. When he spoke of my future—which he did not do very often—he predicted that I would become a teacher. Every member of the family liked going to the theatre, but none of them dreamed of embarking on a career in it. I alone chose to do so—but that was a long time later and something of an afterthought.

My father was my first friend. We had intimate and joyous talks about ideas and emotions. He personified the very life of the spirit for me.

Our home resounded with argument. There was much talk of politics. But this was not merely palaver about candidates, elections, and topical issues: philosophy was involved. There was a kind of loftiness in all the discussions. I listened attentively, rarely understanding the substance of these conversations but fascinated by the fireworks, the drama, the show.

Religion too was a subject of debate. Even the Orthodox were occasionally represented; my father was always respectful of them. He doubted the efficacy of Zionism: the Arabs, he maintained, would never allow the Jews to live peacefully in Palestine. In 1917 he was strongly anti-Bolshevik. None of these subjects were matters of casual after-dinner talk; they were all considerations of great moment.

He was much occupied with literature: American, English, Russian, French, German. He was perhaps the first person to write about Mark Twain in a Yiddish-language publication. He also wrote the first review in Yiddish of Tolstoi's *Kreutzer Sonata*. For him, literature was not an adornment; it was personally important. Hearing him speak about it, I felt that the "good life" could be achieved only through an understanding of the greatest books. I rarely heard him talk of "art"—only of the heart, blood, and brain that went into the making of it. His tastes were formed by the nineteenth-century masters: the Russian realists; the English as well as the Russian romantic poets; Hardy, Balzac, and Flaubert. He also read William Dean Howells, Arnold Bennett, and Galsworthy, but these for him were light stuff.

When my brother Moe, after he became a doctor, spoke enthusiastically about some Broadway hit he had just seen—such as *On Trial* by Elmer Reizenstein, who was to become Elmer Rice—my father was contemptuous. Such plays had no merit, he told him, and no serious person would occupy himself with such trivia. My brothers came to think of his attitude as arrogant and disconcertingly *old world*.

The Lower East Side of my father's day, though bristling with Al Smith's kind of Irish, with Italians, with Poles and others of Slavic strain, was predominantly Jewish. Most literary accounts, like Mike Gold's *Jews Without Money,* emphasize the ghetto poverty; the scrubby, the raggedly provincial, the raucous, the shabbily "exotic." Thrown in for good measure are gleams of laughter, warmth, a hangdog pathos.

There is verisimilitude in all this, to be sure. But missing too often is a recognition of a deeper vein of spiritual fortitude, a fount of lyricism, a nobility of aspiration, an irrepressible idealism. Respect for learning and humane accomplishment shone through the crude surface and fostered not only composers, Irving Berlin and George Gershwin among them, but also actors, artists, writers, musical virtuosi, scientists, and political and social leaders who today are recognized as part of the American heritage. The first person in America to be elected to Congress on the Socialist ticket, Meyer London, represented the district of my birth. And the first Socialist judge, Jacob Panken, officiated there. Stella Adler, my first wife, who was born in upper Manhattan when it was very much like a park, once told an interviewer: "I worked my way *up* to the Lower East Side." I know what she means.

The ambiance, vivid in color, rife with struggle, pulsating with action of every kind from the highest reaches of intellectual and spiritual aspiration to the rawest forays into gangsterdom, was preternaturally theatrical. From time to time I heard pistol shots shatter the silence of the night, the indolence of a summer afternoon. The front part of our house, which served also as my father's office, swarmed with strangers whenever anybody was brought in beaten or cut up by thugs in the nearby poolroom. Still a boy, I witnessed victims of street accidents and fires, children half dead from falls from windows, as they were carried in to my father's office.

At night the streets blazed with a special incandescence. One side of Rivington Street was lined with pushcarts loaded with fruit, vegetables, clothing, and household utensils. The vendors noisily sang the virtues of their wares: a bazaar! The kerosene-fed torches attached to the carts not only illuminated what was in them but glared as if in celebrant conflagration. . . . There were many drugstores where my father as a medical man had privileged entry but which he used to visit not so much to discuss professional matters as to carry on his intellectual debates in an arena other than the family gatherings.

What made those East Side drugstores emblematically vivid for me were the containers in the front windows resembling huge hourglasses filled with varicolored liquids and given added brightness by the electric lights projected through them. They had something of the glamorous vibration of a stage setting. As I think back to that time and place—the old Lower East Side—I see it as a glow dispelling all drabness, healing many wounds.

If the streets were loud with cries of outrage, they also sang. The cantors whose chants could somehow be heard through the portals of the synagogues had excellent voices. (It is perhaps no coincidence that Jan Peerce and Richard Tucker began their careers as cantors.) My love of this and other vocal music spilled over to a delight in opera. Although my father had no musical knowledge, he used to speak enthusiastically of a wonderful Italian tenor named Bonci. I made my father buy me a Victrola, and night after night I played the records of Caruso and Zimbalist and Elman.

At seventeen, I began attending the Met regularly by myself, and shortly after reading *Jean Christophe*, which, naturally, my father had given me, I became an incorrigible concertgoer. I began to read books on the visual arts and to visit exhibitions of the "moderns": Matisse, Picasso, Duchamp.

For all the aches and pains it echoed, the hurly-burly of the old Lower East Side never struck me as depressing. On the contrary, I found its atmosphere affectionate and somehow gay—Italians often speak of Naples in the same way. Some of our great comics and minstrels—Eddie Cantor, Al Jolson, Groucho Marx—in their brash energy, general mockery, and sentimentality are a product of that vanished day and place.

Those early days of the twentieth century—my recollection of them goes back to about 1906—were my father's best time. But though good-humored, witty, eager for the pleasures of the table as well as of the mind, he was not an altogether happy man and toward the end of his life, in the forties, he was a thoroughly distressed one.

During my childhood, my parents had quarreled violently. Often, at night, hearing their voices reach a terrible pitch of exasperation, I cringed under the blankets and covered my ears with the pillow. To this day, I flinch in extreme uneasiness when a scene of marital dispute is recreated on the stage.

It took me years to fathom the cause of my parents' discord, which I instinctively knew was different from the ordinary husband-and-wife misunderstanding. The breach between them seemed fundamental and insoluble.

My mother had seen in my father a clearly superior person, thoughtful, educated, lofty. But although she never fully realized it, hers was the nature at once more adventurous and more practical. I recognized in her as she grew older a somber regret, almost a resentment, that she had been restricted to being the caretaker of the home—of her husband and four sons—and that she had never been permitted to widen the scope of her instruction. She felt—and she was right to feel—that if she had been encouraged to study and learn more, she could have accomplished as much as anyone in the family.

My father was intimidated by the America of pragmatic aims and decisive action. My mother wanted them to buy a house in a peaceful neighborhood in Brooklyn, and he objected. But then he changed his mind, he was at the point of yielding to my mother's pressure. A day later he backed off from the purchase.

During the twenties, when everybody was plunging headlong into Wall Street speculation, my mother grew impatient with my father's reluctance to follow suit. He did not "understand" money; he was fearful of any but the simplest means of acquiring it. When he finally consented to buy stock, he asked my brother Moe to handle the transactions, with the result that even before the Wall Street crash a good part of our family's investments were lost; Moe, as guileless as my father, had bought securities through a broker who proceeded to abscond with all his clients' funds.

Father was a good doctor but he was really a writer at heart; I believe that he could have developed into a first-rate critic. Through the criticism he did write, he offended his editors and his journalist friends by his forthrightness and sarcasm. He scored his greatest success with a series of popular articles on medical subjects which he contributed to a Jewish newspaper. There was charm in the writing, common sense in the substance, and the same blunt honesty that had alienated so many of his patients. Kind, even tenderhearted, as he was, he never did cultivate a "bedside manner."

My mother did not appreciate my father's quandary, the fact that he was at ease only with books, with ideas, and in deep conversation on what to her were totally abstract topics. At times his shyness seemed sheer perversity to her, a desire and an excuse not to take part in the real world

Indeed, he feared the world outside the place he had worked so hard to create for himself among relatives and like-minded European comrades: physicians, dentists, pharmacists, writers, teachers, poets. He was ill at ease with folk from other spheres. He would tremble like a timid boy when confronted by a bank clerk who was transacting a loan for him. He always felt that he was an alien in the harsh new world. He who had read and understood Mark Twain, Emerson, and Thoreau did not feel at home in America. It was years before he would consent to apply for citizenship. Perhaps he harbored the hope of returning someday to Russia, which more and more he spoke of with a nostalgia born of deep uneasiness. The Bolshevik revolution erased that dream, and in 1919 he legally became an American.

He was suspicious of America because he believed, as Coolidge is supposed to have put it, that "the business of America is business," and he detested business. He found

America spiritually and culturally raw. He remained skeptical when, first-generation chauvinist that I was, I pointed out the remarkable advances in the arts that America was making through its new novelists, poets, critics, composers, painters, playwrights, men like Sherwood Anderson, Edgar Lee Masters, Edmund Wilson, Ernest Bloch, Max Weber, and Eugene O'Neill. America to him was so materialistic that he took to referring to our civilization as "syphilization."

My brothers opposed him fiercely in his view of America. They always sided with my mother; at times they were almost conspiratorial. Though I too often thought him wrong-headed and misguided in this rationalization of his own timidity, I was sorry for him. He felt isolated not only within his country but also within his own family. Yet I could not help quarreling with him, and since we were both passionate believers—though differently motivated—our disagreements were often acrimonious. Through them all, he sensed my underlying sympathy for him and respected me more than he did any of my brothers. We fought about Joyce, for example—Joyce was too much for him—but it was not really Joyce we were fighting about!

The Lower East Side was beginning to lose its creative thrust. Its successful citizens were moving away. With some trepidation, and, as always, at my mother's bidding, my father followed. In 1913 we moved to the Bronx—it was almost sylvan then—and presently my father opened an office there. My theatregoing was now absorbing more time than any of my school studies; it had, in fact, assumed the proportions of an addiction.

When World War I broke out the next year, my father was determinedly pro-Ally. I remember how vehemently he used to argue with his friend, a German newspaper vendor and something of a street-corner philosopher, who was pro-German and referred to the Russians as "barbarians." Father countered in praise of Russian soulfulness as reflected in Turgenev, Tolstoi, Chekhov, and the early revolutionary thinkers—Herzen, for example. Above all, Father despised Prussian militarism.

After the war, his practice boomed. The frantic days of the influenza epidemic made him prosperous, but they also exhausted and disheartened him. He was a soft man, and the suffering he saw among the poor who were his patients took such a terrible toll that he determined to give up general medicine and to specialize in the diseases of the heart and lungs. Past fifty, he set out for Vienna to spend a year studying.

Not long before, I had made a turning-point decision myself—to interrupt my studies at Columbia and go to Paris. I proposed the idea to my father and he immediately gave it his blessing. The thought of my becoming a student in what he considered the center of European culture appealed to him. My brothers Al and Will were worried that at my vulnerable age—twenty!—I might contract one of those ailments for which Paris was infamous. My father brushed the warning aside: Harold, he said, was a "good boy," chiefly interested in the theatre and learning, a reader, a concertgoer, a visitor to art galleries and the opera. This was true, though at all times I have been acutely aware of the other sex.

As the S.S. *Paris* was being pulled out from the pier and I waved good-by to my family—this was to be our first long separation—I noticed that my father was having the utmost difficulty in holding back tears. I saw him press his hand to his mouth, possibly to stifle a sob. But it would not be long before he would be sailing to Europe himself.

During a visit I paid my parents in Vienna, I had a crisis of conscience. I had completed my formal education and yet I was doing nothing at all to support myself. I spent all my time in Vienna reading German—I remember sitting in the Volksgarten, bent over *Death in Venice;* I also went to concerts and visited Salzburg for the first Modern Music Festival. At the library of the University of Vienna, I caught up with the study of English literature I had neglected at the Sorbonne. It had never occurred to me before that all this education was not "productive." I had even had the temerity, at the age of twenty-two, to propose to my parents that I return to Paris for another pleasant, aimless year.

It suddenly struck me that my disregard of a practical goal, of the necessity to earn money, was downright shameful. "I can't go on living like this," I blurted out one day to my mother, "being supported by you and doing nothing." The violence of this statement surprised us both. She looked at me, as shocked as if I had just uttered an obscenity. I was not to think of "such things." I was to do as I pleased because, for one thing, what I did always had merit and, for another, I was her son. My family did not have much money. But money-mindedness was foreign to them. I never regretted not being more interested in money, but as for my parents, they were to pay dearly for their innocence.

In 1924, we were all settled back in New York, and after a few months of shuttling between publishers' offices and theatrical managements I finally obtained a job as an extra in a play called *The Saint,* written by Stark Young and produced by Kenneth MacGowan, Robert Edmond Jones, and Eugene O'Neill at the Greenwich Village Theatre on Sheridan Square. Although I was paid only ten dollars a week and the play ran only two weeks, my parents never questioned the advisability of my choice of employment. Then, as ever, they were confident that I would find my way.

Every Friday night, my brothers and I gathered for dinner at my parents' apartment. Often my brothers' children were there too: Al's sons, Morton and Larry, Will's sons, Bobby and Dick, and occasionally Moe and his daughter Irma and his son Stanley, who lived in "distant" Borough Park. There were the usual feverish debates about politics, with everyone shouting at the same time and telling stories. A basic conviviality and warmth bound us together. We were living the good life.

Years passed in this way. My father, a heart specialist

now, moved to a big new office on the Grand Concourse, then an "elite" section of the Bronx. Somewhere along the line I moved, to the Hotel Shelton on Forty-eighth Street. I continued to do a variety of odd acting jobs. I landed the job of stage manager for Rodgers and Hart's first hit, *The Garrick Gaieties.* I was appointed the playreader for the Theatre Guild. And then my father lost the rest of his savings in the stock-market crash.

When the money crisis of the thirties began to affect my father's practice, my brother Will, the family's only "businessman," suggested they move to a smaller apartment. My father said, "Before I move to such a place, you'll have to carry me out in a coffin." He was nevertheless obliged, by plain and simple facts, to follow Will's advice.

I speak of Will as a businessman. He had little aptitude for formal study; he lacked the patience of Al, his senior, who was a real plugger and became, first, a bacteriologist and later a lawyer for the state of New York. (For all that, he had no special talent and seemed all his life an effaced person, a follower; he must have been assailed by the sense that despite his sober abilities and good will he was being overlooked.)

Will might have been happier if his ambition had been confined to business. He was the only Clurman not to attend a university, the only one not given to assiduous reading. But he was better-looking and dressed more nattily than the rest of us. He had, moreover, a facility for dealing with those outside the small family circle. Still, he was envious, perhaps in awe, of the cultural stamp that was the mark of our home. He therefore wanted not only to "show" us—to make a lot of money, in short to become an American success—but also to achieve some distinction that none of the rest of us had. He raised funds to build a synagogue, he worked tirelessly to establish an imposing hospital on Long Island. But, having more imagination and daring than executive and commercial skill, he overextended himself—and thus ended by getting calamitously into debt, a fact he managed, with something like genius, to conceal from almost everyone. I believe that these worries contributed to the cancer that caused his early death.

In the middle thirties, my father grew more and more depressed. All the tensions of his nature had been aggravated by family circumstances. His decline was barely perceptible for a time, but then, every Friday night when I returned to the Bronx for the ritual gathering, I could see his festering bitterness.

About this time, my mother was stricken with Parkinson's disease. My father pronounced it incurable. But another doctor in the apartment house my parents lived in told my mother that he could administer a treatment to arrest and possibly even cure the disease. My mother naturally wished to undergo the treatment. My father objected—he was never a good "psychologist" when it came to my mother—insisting that the neighboring doctor was a quack. From this my mother deduced that my father did not wish her to get well.

This wounded him deeply. It was not just the implied slur that hurt him, but the insult to his abilities as a physician in which he had always taken such pride. He was now being impugned by his own wife and, indirectly, by other members of the family. I was asked to "hold court" on the matter. I told my father that it was natural for my mother to try any remedy and that her "accusation" was a symptom of her extreme anxiety and nothing more. I told my mother that my father feared the new remedy might prove more harmful than the disease.

My father regarded me as the son who understood him best. He had, he confessed, neglected his three older sons to some extent. They had grown up while he was struggling to establish himself. But as a doctor with a practice already large by the time I was born, he was able to devote himself to me, even to educate me. He once told me that as a baby I had called *him* Mama. I had access to his office even when he was seeing patients, and I often watched him perform minor operations: the lancing of abscesses, tonsillectomies, and the like. The result was that I conceived a permanent horror of seeing anyone bleed, though I have never been alarmed when I myself bled.

He confided his most intimate thoughts to me, his misgivings as well as his ideals. He struck me only twice, and in both cases I deserved it. The first time was when I overslept outrageously; the second, when I failed to help him put up the top of his car when it was pouring (he used to let me drive his car for him when he made his calls). He regarded me as the sage, the Solomon of the family! He had been mightily impressed when at the age of seventeen I said, in response to some complaint of his about my mother's unfairness to him, "But Papa, you think of Mother only as your wife. You must remember that she is first of all a *woman*." He was silent, but a little later he said, "Harold, that was wise."

When I founded the Group Theatre and began producing and directing plays, my father not only respected me, he revered me. He worried about the Group almost as much as I did. He saw that my efforts on its behalf were often excruciating. Then, uncharacteristically, indeed perhaps for the first time in his life, he began to warn me to assure myself of financial security. He would say over and over again, "You don't know how terrible it is to be without money." He himself was still suffering from the effects of the crash. His warning was taken up by my brother Moe, who cherished me and was proud of me. Though I understood the reasons for these admonitions and appreciated the love and concern that prompted them, they irritated me. For, as I told Moe one day, too arrogantly, I'm afraid, I may have been poor but I was living a life of freedom and adventure, while he was constricting and diminishing himself in his attempt to emulate those whose fortunes he spoke of with such abject envy. "I am interested," I said, as certain as I had ever been certain, "only in creating a humane life for myself and for those around me." This of course was my father speaking through me, about a pattern of life which he had set for me by his example.

These recriminations were to become most pronounced in the letters I exchanged with my family a few years later, when I went to Hollywood. My father's and Moe's pleas for me not to lose sight of the economics of living were exacerbated by a letter I wrote home saying that I planned to return to New York and the theatre.

One day in 1942, while working in Hollywood—for a long time my work consisted chiefly of watching other people make movies and of reading a good many books totally unrelated to my job—I received word that my father had died. I reached New York just in time for the funeral services and burial. I was impassive and cool all the while: tears came to my eyes only when the officiating rabbi uttered the words "Samuel Michael Clurman *was* a man. . . ." He was gone, but for me he would remain ever present. I still have dreams about him, pitiful dreams in which I try to atone for not having been kind enough to him.

The only member of the family I saw weeping that day was Moe, who, if what Billy Rose's mother had told me long before was true, was not even my father's son. Moe had always been the softest, the most loving of my brothers, indeed the most loving person in the whole family.

The afternoon after the funeral, Moe took me aside to tell me that our father had taken his life by means of a drug readily available to him as a doctor. On several occasions, I had heard my father say that he believed suicide was acceptable and understandable when life could no longer be borne with self-respect. He left a note, which Moe had discovered and not shown to anyone, begging our forgiveness for his deed. He wrote that he had quarreled with my brother Al, who had cried out at him, "You're a fool!" Late that night, my mother had called to my father in the bed alongside hers to bring her a glass of water. When he did not answer, she got up, walked to Al's bedroom, and said directly, "I think Papa is dead."

My father's life had become for him a burden too onerous to bear, and my brother's insult must have been the last straw. In a letter he had written me while I was in Hollywood, he mentioned in passing that he was in danger of going blind. I suspected that more than anything else my father felt that he had lost face in the eyes of the family and the world; that he had become useless.

Suicide is deemed sinful, but I could not help feeling that, in my father's case, it was heroic. There was something lyrically life-loving in him, and it was only right that when he had lost the joy of life, he should no longer wish to live. My mother died a year later. I was still in Hollywood and the news reached me in a letter from my wife, Stella Adler.

To think of my father in a sad way would be to break faith with who and what he was. He believed in the essential values most of the religions and humanities teach: the sacred ness of life, compassion for one's fellow man, a reverence for honesty, courage, learning, life-enhancing action, humility in the face of the universal mystery.

He could never overcome his limitations. He did not take sufficient advantage of America. He was not daring enough to risk close contact with the unfamiliar. Hence his unreadiness to lend sympathetic attention to or even to accept contemporary developments in the arts, sciences, modes of thought, and behavior. He was entirely rooted in the cultural atmosphere of the nineteenth century.

The apparent triumph of Nazism contributed a great deal to his devitalization and ultimate despair; he feared an extreme political and social reaction throughout Western society. He was profoundly shaken by Stefan Zweig's suicide in Brazil, which he attributed to the collapse of Zweig's humanist dream; for this he, like many others, blamed Hitler.

My father taught me to maintain high standards of conduct and taste. Here he was absolute—too much so, perhaps. He was given to blurting out truths to people whose appreciation of literature and theatre was glib or merely fashionable. He warned me not to overlook the lessons of the past; those who dwell entirely in the present, he said, are pigs.

From the first he knew something it took me years to realize: that Stalin was a monster. Yet he acknowledged that the Soviet Union had accomplished much that was valuable. He was always on the side of the good. Although he had great commiseration for the poor, there was something unwaveringly aristocratic about him: he would tolerate only the best. He insisted on the best food, within limits set by the diet of his parental home; and he dressed elegantly, to the point of carrying a cane, as did most of the gentlemen of his day. He once quoted the Talmud to the tune that a spot on a person's clothes is a spot on his soul! I laughed at this, and was impressed. For the past twenty years I have gone everywhere sporting a cane—though I do not need one. I am not surprised nowadays to hear myself answer the question "What are your politics?" with "I'm a left-wing royalist." It is meant as a joke, and yet I do subscribe to Ibsen's dictum that "I am for democracy, but I wish it to be aristocratic." There were other maxims my father passed on to me. He often quoted Flaubert's advice to Maupassant: "To express what one wishes one must look at things with enough attention to discover in them what has never before been seen (or said) by anyone else. . . . That is what is meant by originality."

My father considered himself a philosophical materialist. In our discussions about history, politics, or art (discussions that as often as not turned into torrid disagreements) I sometimes pointed out the contradictions of his nature, and he always remarked: "You don't understand the divided soul." Today I believe I do, though for a long time I was perhaps even more dogmatic than he. Even now, despite a considerable quotient of skepticism—which strikes many as cynicism, though it is chiefly a means of keeping balance—I am, like my father, a person of strong convictions.

Friends in the City of Light

I was born in New York's Lower East Side in the first year of the century; I was reborn in Paris during the twenties.

Planning to make the voyage to the French capital, I could speak of little else. My sister-in-law Elsie, Moe's wife, told me that her cousin was planning a similar trip—to study composition. His name was Aaron Copland. She thought we ought to meet.

I had caught a glimpse of him at Moe's engagement party in Brooklyn; Elsie's family and the Coplands were Brooklynites. I also remember seeing him in the standing-room section of the balcony of Carnegie Hall. But I was inordinately shy in those days and did not even say hello.

Through Elsie, we arranged to meet at Brentano's book-store, then at Fifth Avenue and Twenty-seventh Street. From there we went down to the Battery, where Aaron had to pick up his passport. Knowing that he was a musician, I began talking about Paul Rosenfeld, then the music critic of the *Dial*, whose new book, *Musical Portraits*, I had just read with pleasure. This was in June, 1921. When we got to know each other better, Aaron told me that he had gone home after our first conversation and told his mother that he had met a fellow—Elsie's brother-in-law, no less—who read both George Jean Nathan *and* Paul Rosenfeld—for I had gone on to speak about the two critics who most fascinated me at the time, the editors of the monthly *Smart Set:* Nathan and H. L. Mencken. Mencken, I maintained, was the more important of the two. (I still hold to that opinion. Ironically, in 1958, I was the first winner of the George Jean Nathan Award for dramatic criticism.) Aaron was due to sail immediately for France, where he had enrolled in the newly established summer school of music at Fontainebleau. And in September I would matriculate at the Faculty of Letters of the University of Paris—the Sorbonne. We agreed to correspond in the meantime.

Two months later, aboard the S.S. *Paris,* I received a telegram from Aaron saying that an apartment was being prepared for us at 207 *bis* Boulevard Raspail, across from both the Dôme and the Rotonde.

Fresh to the delights of Paris, I stopped for a few days at the Hôtel de Vaugirard, now long gone, opposite the Senate building and the Luxembourg Gardens, at one time the home of Jules Janin, the renowned theatre critic who in the 1830s had been the first to recognize the genius of Rachel and Deburau.

That first day, roaming Paris in a daze, I noticed a poster announcing a concert at the Salle Gaveau at which students of the Fontainebleau school were to have their compositions played. Aaron Copland was one of them.

The following morning Aaron burst into my room. He had hardly said hello before he announced that he had just sold a short piano piece he called *The Cat and the Mouse* to the French music publisher Durand for five hundred francs, about thirty-five dollars then, and that this was one of two compositions of his that were to be played at the Salle Gaveau.

The great day came, and an old professor of music introduced Copland as *"un jeune compositeur de tendance moderne."* I had been in Paris only a week and already I was able to write a letter home saying that I had heard Elsie's cousin's music and that I believed he would become America's leading composer. In 1970, at a concert given at Alice Tully Hall in honor of Copland's seventieth birthday, I told my nephew Richard Clurman about my prophecy of 1921. "Find that letter," he said, "and you'll be a famous man!"

At twenty-one, Copland was already mature. He has grown since then, to be sure, but he has not changed. He seems to have been born balanced. His character has a classic stamp: there is deep feeling in him, good sense, an unfailing justness. He is generous to his friends and colleagues, gracious and considerate to everyone. Nadia Boulanger, with whom he studied composition in Fontainebleau and for three years in Paris, had told him, "You will make your way in the world because you never offend."

Paul Rosenfeld called Copland a "practical poet." Many years later, when I suggested that Aaron engage a business manager, a friend of his said, "If Aaron could find a person who is a better businessman than he is, he would hire him."

During our first walks around Paris, I was amused and perhaps slightly irritated when I heard Aaron murmur every time he passed a store that was going out of business, "Couldn't make it pay." Finally I snapped, "Why do you always repeat that silly phrase?" "Oh," he said, "it's what my folks used to say about every shop in our neighborhood that closed." They had run a small department store in Brooklyn.

Virgil Thomson has said of Copland that, musically, he knows how to make five cents perform the services of a dollar. He never spent more than was necessary on anything; but his economy was a sign not of parsimony but of an almost instinctive sense of measure. When we ate out together, I was puzzled to see that his checks always came to much less than mine.

I am of a much more extravagant, perhaps romantic, nature, given to impulse and passionate overstatement. Aaron accepted this as he always accepts sharp differences of personality. His calm and his sound judgment have had a beneficent effect on me. He never preaches; he instructs through example. He is always perfectly relaxed. In those days I was tense, shy to the point of morbidness; I could communicate only with intimates. Aaron did all the talking for me. I had studied French in high school and college (he never went to college) and knew much more of it than he, but people thought the opposite because I hardly spoke. When I confessed my adolescent sins to Aaron—that I had lied, that I had stolen—he modestly and lucidly explained that they were normal manifestations of adolescent growth.

Without his or my realizing it, he became my mentor. He was only nine months older than I. As time passed, he was to become the mentor to many—especially to young composers whose talents he was quick to recognize and foster.

The secret or source of his wisdom can be traced to his utter acceptance of himself at an early age. He made peace with himself and so could be at peace with the whole world.

His self-assurance is really a sort of stoicism without strain, the expression of the containment or mastery of the suffering caused by his recognition of a fault he suspected in his personality. There is in most of us something to inspire a sense of guilt; a person completely without this sense is either a villain or an oaf. Guilt poisons our moral system unless we are able to operate on it through reason; this is not at all the same thing as excusing it. Aaron faced what disturbed him; by understanding that it was inevitable, he took possession of it—which is what I mean by containing one's suffering, living with or being at home with it. Thus, instead of developing into a lifelong impediment, not to mention a nuisance to others, his suffering became a source of great strength.

Without the least conceit, Copland knew and knows his own value. His modesty has no self-abnegation, just as his self-esteem has not a touch of arrogance. His privately declared motto was from Baudelaire: "What is most important is to be a great man for oneself." Once, a passenger on a transatlantic steamer approached him with "Mr. Copland, I don't like your music." Aaron wrote me: "I didn't think any more highly of him on that account."

In the first days of our friendship, Aaron asked me if I had read Freud. I had not, I said, but I knew something of his theories; he was just then coming into vogue among literary folk. "Have you ever tried to psychoanalyze yourself?" he asked. "No," I replied, "it would be indiscreet."

Aaron already knew himself; I didn't know myself at all. He knew that he was a composer. I had no idea what I was.

Aaron and I became habitués of Shakespeare and Company, Sylvia Beach's famous English lending library on the Rue de l'Odéon; we went for French books to La Maison des Amis des Livres across the street, regally presided over by Adrienne Monnier, Sylvia Beach's friend.

Sylvia Beach's place, chockablock with the latest and best books, was the center for the American literary colony in Paris. Malcolm Cowley, Edmund Wilson, and Paul Rosenfeld had all frequented Shakespeare and Company and had now left for home. But we often saw James Joyce, Ernest Hemingway, and Ford Madox Ford there, and occasionally Ezra Pound, all of whom, except for Hemingway, were familiar names to us. But we were too intimidated to address them. We were, after all, "kids."

The most prominent as well as the most frequent of the visitors was Joyce, whose *Ulysses* was just about to be published by Sylvia Beach; Aaron and I got together the twenty dollars it cost to buy the paper-bound first edition. Joyce cut an unforgettable figure. Sitting beside Miss Beach's desk in the center of the room, with his back to the street, he appeared to be hiding. We did not then know about his eye ailment. His posture bespoke a deliberate avoidance. He said very little, even to Miss Beach. I had the impression that he would be content to sit immovably for hours without uttering a word.

Out of this prolonged silence I once heard him ask Sylvia Beach, "Who is Blasco Ibáñez?" The translation of Blasco Ibáñez's *Four Horsemen of the Apocalypse* had just become a triumphant best seller everywhere. "He's a Spanish novelist," she answered. "Any good?" Joyce asked in a voice so perfunctory I suspected he was not really interested in the reply. Miss Beach answered in a vague murmur.

Day after day, after these silent sessions, Joyce rose, left the shop, and walked slowly down the street toward the Boulevard Saint-Germain, his head slightly tilted, dark glasses over his eyes, a walking stick in his hand. The silence that surrounded him seemed to emanate from his very person. The French, I was told, described him as "a melancholy Jesus."

At Adrienne Monnier's, Aaron and I paid to attend a reading of the Molly Bloom soliloquy in a French translation made by the novelist Valery Larbaud. There were fewer than a hundred people present, all seated on wooden camp chairs. Joyce had characteristically made himself incon- spicuous, averting his eyes from both the reader and the audience. He was practically invisible, but everyone's eyes were fully on him.

One day Aaron got up his nerve and approached Joyce, who was, as usual, beside Sylvia Beach's desk. He asked him, "How did you come by the song whose notes are in your novel?" "My mother sang it to me," Joyce answered.

But in the evening at the Rotonde he would tell jokes and laugh merrily. The laugh I remember best—a laugh that made me laugh—was at the Comédie des Champs-Elysées. I was sitting in the second balcony, Joyce was below in the orchestra. The play was Shaw's *Androcles and the Lion,* with Michel Simon as Caesar. In the French version, little An- drocles keeps addressing Caesar as "Monsieur César," and Caesar, exasperated, exclaims, "Monsieur César, Monsieur César—you'll be calling me 'Jules' next!" It was the only time I saw Joyce's face in something other than grave thought and sadness.

Several times I saw Joyce's wife, son, and daughter come into Shakespeare and Company. They always came sepa- rately, without Joyce: Joyce's wife was not quite pretty and yet she was more than pretty; there was something inde- finably voluptuous about her. This was also true of his daughter, who, though slightly cross-eyed, was both less and more than pretty, with a noticeably lovely skin common to Irish girls. The son wore thick-lensed glasses and had a decidedly studious air.

Hemingway looked a gay blade, mustached, tall, and husky. He wore a kind of fisherman's cap. He spoke in a surprisingly piping voice. I was startled one day to hear him explode with, "Who the hell does he think he is?" I soon realized he was referring to Ford Madox Ford, who was in the habit of offering paternalistic advice to young writers. Hemingway was always bluff and hearty. Aaron told me that one evening at the bar of the Rotonde, Hemingway took him aside and pointed out one of the customers. "A great fellow, that," Hemingway piped. "He's had the clap five times."

The city of light enlightened me. I was fascinated by Jacques Copeau's productions at the Vieux Colombier, and also by the Pitoëff offerings, which remain among the simplest and best I have ever seen. They included in rapid succession the first production outside Italy of Pirandello's *Six Characters in Search of an Author,* and productions of plays by Chekhov, Shaw, Andreyev, and Molnar.

Through Aaron, whom I used to take with me to the theatre, I was invited to concerts, the most notable of which were those given by Koussevitzky at the Opéra. I remember how, at the world premiere of Ravel's orchestral version of Moussorgsky's *Pictures at an Exhibition,* Aaron exclaimed as the first notes were struck, "That's just how *I* orchestrated it!"

After one concert, Aaron asked me if I had liked Schönberg's *Pierrot Lunaire,* which had been the main event. When I said yes, he almost jumped with delight: "You're on our side! You're one of us!" He was referring to the battle for what was then modern music: there were not many devotees of the Viennese twelve-tone composers in those days. Cocteau had called Schönberg a composer for the blackboard, and Stravinsky was the admired master of the young French musicians. The concertgoing and ballet public had just about gotten over the shock of *Le Sacre du Printemps*—and Stravinsky was on the verge of causing new, though milder, shocks of a different sort.

Les Six—Poulenc, Milhaud, Louis Durey, Germaine Taillefere, Honegger, and Auric—were the towering musical innovators in the Paris of the twenties. (Auric was to "sell out"—this is just how he described it himself, sorrowfully, years later—to the movies.) Cocteau was the literary spokesman for the group. They held public meetings to fortify themselves and win adherents to their cause. Like most rebels, they had to murder their fathers. This consisted in belittling the old gods, Debussy and Ravel. In public, Auric was particularly sarcastic about Ravel, whose virtuosity he took care to characterize in the most ridiculous superlatives. Erik Satie, whom *les Six* held in the highest esteem, sat on the platform during Auric's attack on Ravel, beaming the whole while with honeyed malice.

I heard Cocteau lecture at one of the meetings sponsored by *les Six*. It was more an essay than a lecture—all metaphor and paradox—in which he attempted to define the aesthetic of his generation. He saw this aesthetic as being specifically French, in contrast to the German of Wagner and others. He went on to speak of Gallic lightness, clarity, finesse, succinctness. Characteristically playful, he paused every ten minutes to let an American named MacGowan play a jazz piano piece; American jazz was all the rage then with the French.

Copland introduced me to Nadia Boulanger. Stravinsky is reputed to have said to someone who wished to study with him: "You may learn from her everything I could teach you." Every week she invited her favorite pupils to tea at her apartment on the Rue Ballu, right off Place de Clichy.

At the head of the table sat the majestically gracious

and genial Boulanger *mère,* who was Russian-born and spoke with a marked accent. She was gayer, bolder, and more expansive than any of her guests; certainly gayer than her almost severe daughter. The mother had a nice word for everyone. She often turned to me: "You, Clurman, who have read everything, tell me what you think of . . ."

Nadia often asked one of her students to name the exact note coming from a piano in a neighboring apartment. The student would invariably guess wrong, and Nadia would correct him. Once I tried to explain my endless admiration for Chaliapin. When he sang, I said, it seemed like a natural mode of speech, as if there were no other way he could possibly communicate his thoughts and feelings. "You mean," Nadia commented, "he really sings."

One evening after a Casals cello recital we all went to La Régence café, opposite the Comédie-Française. The music played by the house orchestra was most disturbing to Nadia. "Don't listen to it," I suggested. "It's impossible for me not to listen," she answered, and her classic head, the dignity of her bearing, her wonderfully intelligent eyes gazing through her pince-nez, gave her a positively august look.

I was favored by indirect musical instruction from her. After each of his weekly lessons, Copland would give me— as far as he could—a summary of what he had learned that day. When he summed up the key to her instruction in the phrase *"la grande ligne,"* the long line crucial to the construction, understanding, and judgment of a composition, I wondered how that might be applied to the other arts.

Yet for all my abiding regard for her, I could never forget that she had said that Roy Harris, who through Aaron's recommendation and encouragement had come to study with her, would go further than Copland because, unlike Copland, he was not handicapped by being a Jew.

My musical education in Paris took many guises, but

the melody that recurs in my memory as the motto of Aaron's
and my association in the apartment on the Boulevard Raspail is Poulenc's *Mouvements Perpétuels,* which Aaron kept
playing over and over again that first year; it was the home-
work given him by the piano teacher he had chosen, the
Spaniard Ricardo Viñes. Aaron would take time to explain
to me the sonata form as well as the syntax of the symphony,
which to this day I find myself unable to rationalize the
existence of; to speak to me of program music, about which
I was and would remain skeptical. On the other hand, when
Aaron tried to persuade me, according to the "neoclassic"
canon of the day, that a musical composition was a "thing"
with no meaning outside itself, I balked. My argument was
that, in Lucretius's phrase, "nothing comes from nothing."
Though we may speak descriptively and for purposes of con-
venience of "abstract art," there is, I maintained, no such
thing. While words cannot altogether convey the essential
content of any work of art, all art possesses a human meaning which is what gives it its ultimate value.

This was the kind of youthful discussion Aaron and I
engaged in fifty years ago and more. He was not especially
concerned with aesthetic theories, but he thought I was
gifted in sensing the "meaning underlying the notes," though
I couldn't read them.

One summer day, strolling along the Boulevard Raspail,
I saw a long, important-looking funeral procession coming
toward me. This must be the funeral of a *somebody,* I
thought. It was. It was the funeral of Saint-Saëns, who was
to be buried in the Montparnasse cemetery nearby. Being
curious and idle, I decided to join the cortege. I had a special
reason for remembering Saint-Saëns. His *Samson and Delilah*
at the Met, with Caruso as Samson, was the first opera I had
ever attended; I was seventeen and wearing not "knicker-
bockers" but trousers for the first time!

At the burial ground, two men were called upon to

speak in tribute. The first I recognized as Charles Widor—
who had introduced Copland at the Fontainebleau school
concert as *"un jeune compositeur de tendance moderne."*
He mumbled something about Saint-Saëns having been
"the Mozart of France," the sort of rhetoric that always
makes me gag. He was followed by a man of about forty,
who spoke in a manner so unemphatic that what he said
went totally unnoticed by the gathering at the grave. The
octogenarian composer who had just died, he remarked, had
been a deterrent to musical progress; in fact, something of
a reactionary. "But we of the younger generation . . ." (I
believe I was the only truly young person there and I was
neither a musician nor a Frenchman) "we of the younger
generation have to forgive the old codger, who did contribute
something to the repute of French music *in his day.*"

This sort of malice was typical of the musical world in
Paris at the time, though it was not at all, of course, confined
to the musical world. The combative air was another reason
I enjoyed so much going to concerts. When Béla Bartók, new
to the French capital, was given the honor of having an evening at the Sorbonne devoted to his compositions, all was
dignified and respectful. But whenever a concert introduced
a note of the ultramodern, havoc was sure to break out.

The hissing of a Milhaud symphony at the Théâtre des
Champs-Elysées on the Avenue Montaigne—scene of the
scandalous *Sacre du Printemps* premiere eight years before
—was comparatively tame, but when the young pianist Jean
Wiener followed a Bach concerto with a piece of jazz, there
were catcalls climaxed by shouts of "Play music! Play music!
Music!"

George Antheil, puffed by Ezra Pound as a genius, had
his *Ballet Mécanique* played at the Théâtre des Champs-
Elysées—only to hear the piece, which was clearly derivative
of Stravinsky's *Les Noces* (Antheil used eight pianos instead
of Stravinsky's four), roundly hissed. Pound rose in a box,

a strikingly tall, lean figure with a great shock of red hair and a trim Vandyke beard, and shouted, *"Taisez-vous, imbéciles!"*

After the first act of the first performance of his *Christophe Colombe* at the Opéra, Milhaud was walking up the aisle toward the foyer, when Florent Schmitt, a bitter, witty composer of secondary rank (also a chauvinist and an anti-Semite), leaned out of his box and called out, "What, you're leaving already!" On meeting Copland backstage after a Koussevitzky concert, Schmitt lashed out at him with "You Americans are geniuses in business, what do you mean by engaging in such foreign pursuits as musical composition?" Aaron took this as a joke and laughed. But Schmitt was not joking.

In 1927 I witnessed a near riot at the Châtelet during the Paris premiere by the Ballet Russe of *Romeo and Juliet,* a ballet by the young English composer Constant Lambert. The sets were by Max Ernst, who had been what might be called a card-carrying member of the surrealist group. A number of young men, all very elegant in dress and bearing, stood up in one of the first-tier boxes and began shouting unintelligible invective indiscriminately. From the upper balconies, as if on cue, leaflets were flung down on the audience to protest Ernst's collaboration with so damnably bourgeois an institution as the Ballet Russe! (The surrealists were at that time veering politically toward the left.) Poor Constant Lambert, whose piece, if it could be judged at all under the circumstances, was light enough, tried in innocent horror to silence the demonstrators. For at least five minutes, not a note of music could be heard. The band of aesthetic fops in the box held their ground, arms akimbo, as if defying a military assault, until the arrival of the gendarmes. In the audience that evening close by me sat e. e. cummings, wholly unperturbed by the fracas.

I can add an interesting footnote here to the history of dance. During the melee the company's stage manager ordered the curtain lowered. As it was about to come down from the two sides of the proscenium, a dancer leaped out and, holding on to the curtain with his hands, prevented it from closing. His name was George Balanchine.

On the sidewalk, after the performance, I saw André Breton, the literary spokesman for the surrealists, who had no doubt instigated the *putsch* and, like a general, was waiting to hear a report of it from his handsomely attired minions. He too was in evening dress. "No one hurt?" he asked.

Copland's receptiveness and understanding of almost every new trend in music were impeccable. I was therefore a little astonished at the 1926 International Modern Music Festival in Zurich to hear him ask Anton Webern to explain why he, Copland, had failed to comprehend the latest Schönberg quartet. Webern, mild in manner, speaking a markedly Viennese German, answered, "You must hear the work many more times. One can't hope to understand Kant at a first reading." This still seems to me a good answer, as was Faulkner's to someone who complained of having read one of his novels three times without having understood it: "Read it four times!"

When Copland asked Webern what he thought of a certain piece that had been played the night before, he replied that it smacked of Korngold, a schmaltzy Viennese composer. Copland, surprised and delighted, exclaimed, "That's what my friend Clurman here said at the concert—and he can't read a note." Webern waved this aside with "One has a feeling for music or one hasn't." I was pleased; like Max Beerbohm, I can't abide flattery—unless it be fulsome.

Through Aaron I met Roger Sessions and George Antheil, who were both in Paris then. Roger Sessions was then, as always, a scholarly man of resolute probity and deliberate speech. George Antheil, a "natural-born" composer, struck me as both cocky and infantile. . . . Many years later he wrote an anguished article in *Tomorrow* (a magazine, now defunct, to which, for six years, I contributed a monthly column on the arts), bemoaning the fact that Copland was the only serious American composer who could make a living at it.

Also living in Paris was Virgil Thomson. What a personality! I first met him in the lobby of the Salle Gaveau before a concert of which I have no recollection apart from his presence. I speak of a first meeting, but in a sense, though we were introduced, we did not really meet. People in general paid little attention to me because I was simply a student, and in the musical world I had no identity except as Copland's friend.

I remember a casual remark Thomson made on this occasion—Thomson's remarks are always casual, and all the sharper for it—about a certain conductor. "When he plays Debussy, there's not a dry seat in the house," he said.

Thomson's rapid-fire speech, his arid, high-pitched voice and nasal Midwestern accent brook no contradiction. Whatever he says appears to be the last word. He once challenged Marc Blitzstein's affirmation that there was much to be hoped for in Prokofiev's future with "I'm not interested in his future, because I don't like his present."

Thomson has changed very little since those early Paris days, except that he is now much stouter and given to cat naps in company (even at the concerts he once reviewed so bitingly, he has been known to indulge in intervals of sleep). His conversation is still celebrated for being always this or that side of outrageous—the more outrageous, the more he himself enjoys it; there is no theme he considers too portentous to make the most saucy sexual allusions to. He has prejudices that he maintains against all comers as if they were incontrovertible truths; the grace is that they make him funny rather than disconcerting. He is basically just, ever eager to be fair, but there is no use denying he can be nasty. At a luncheon in honor of Aaron's receiving a decoration from the German government in 1970, at which the German cultural attaché in New York toasted Aaron's good health, Thomson cried, *"Vive la France!"*

Sundays were our days of ranging over Paris, our holy days when neither Aaron nor I had work to do. Some Sunday mornings, we attended Mass at Notre-Dame. The chief attraction was Marcel Dupré, who played the organ there. One morning, on my way out, just before the great portal I put on my hat. "For God's sake, Harold," Aaron whispered in amused shock, "you're not in a theatre!"

I visited the Louvre frequently and went to many exhibitions of painting at the private galleries—alone, since Aaron was admittedly insensible to graphic art. I knew nothing about the art world as a business. I was attracted by Chagall's work when I first saw it in 1922, but it was years before I realized that the "green rabbis" I liked so much could then have been bought for a song. Apart from the fact that I had not much money (I could live decently enough on the twenty-five dollars a week sent me from home), it never occurred to me that pictures were merchandise to be bought or sold.

My education in painting and music was the very opposite of normal. Most people develop their tastes by contact with accredited examples. I, on the contrary, had some difficulty in appreciating the standard models. I didn't "get" them. I found myself in accord with Alfred Stieglitz, who told me that the old masters first struck him as so much "old leather." I was in no way disconcerted when in 1919 I saw for the first time Duchamp's *Nude Descending a Staircase,* and I took great pleasure in Picasso, Matisse, Rouault, not to speak of Cézanne and the impressionists, who had already found favor even among those of conservative disposition. But I could not fathom the value of Giotto, Leonardo, Rembrandt, and other giants.

So too with music. Stravinsky, Webern, and Schönberg

seemed to me to be speaking a language that was almost vernacular. But Bach, even much of Beethoven—those were the hard nuts to crack!

During my student days in Paris I tried to write a bit. I translated some critical pieces by Gide, the writer then most fashionable among the young. Nothing came of this. Later I tried translating Gide's book on Dostoevski. I submitted my translation of one chapter to Gide's representative, Victor Llona, the French translator of Dreiser, who presently reported back to me that Gide had approved the translation but that the English publisher had not.

I succeeded only once in getting myself published. In 1923 Van Wyck Brooks, then editor of the *Freeman,* wrote me that he liked a piece of mine about the Modern Music Festival in Salzburg but that the Scottish critic Edwin Muir had already submitted a creditable account of the event. However, Brooks did accept an article I had written sitting in the Luxembourg Gardens—a pen portrait of Maurice Boissard, the theatre critic for the mighty *Nouvelle Revue Française.* He was not what I would now call a sound theatre critic, but he was devastatingly funny—an eccentric old curmudgeon of the sort that Paris needed very badly in those days when most of the other critics were positively venal.

I was paid twenty-five dollars for the piece. I was proud that it had been accepted by Van Wyck Brooks. The wire Moe sent with the news said, "Atta boy!"

Aaron not only encouraged me to write, he also influenced my writing. When he heard me say something he considered particularly noteworthy, he said, "You must write or you'll talk your talent away." And just as his mind is extremely rational and his orchestration clean and unfussy, so his criticism of my writing was aimed at making my prose simple and terse.

It would be an absurd extravagance, would it not, to compare Paris with Manhattan's Lower East Side? Yet I found a peculiar similarity between them. When the family moved from the Lower East Side to a then much less crowded section of the Bronx, I told my astonished parents that I preferred the Lower East Side with all its dirt, confusion, and noise. The Bronx had less character, it was bland and dull—one might say castrated. But Paris, for all its broad avenues, trim gardens, and leisurely pace, teemed with life. It bubbled, even festered in places, with strange juices. Its very corruption struck me as generative. The streets were a show, there was drama everywhere; the people were characters in a pullulating parade, part festival, part criminal plot. These are the environments, rich in conflict and contradiction, manured by ambitions and angers both base and exalted, that produce the art, the wild politics, the epic madness of our times.

The characters one encountered! Grotesque, delirious, wounded, eloquent! Everyone seemed to harbor a special secret, a sin that sprouted flowers of evil or of a miraculous healing. It was a world that gave us the bombs of both Dadaism and the militant reactionaries. Minds were at work, plotting havoc or rich with the promises of discovery. Old Europe had gone to seed, indeed was rotten, but the decay somehow eradiated light. Paris was above all adventure, rank and exciting. *Ouvert la nuit!*

Every metropolis has its uncharted personalities. Some are merely glimpsed in passing—like the imperious vagrant, a "Bonapartist" who could be seen very early in the morning all alone on the deserted Place Saint-Michel, dressed in the fashion of the Empire, a frayed nobleman standing upon his dignity. No one knew who he was, except perhaps the police. He was decorative and harmless.

I found my own private type. One day as I sat reading at the round table in the American Library, then located near the Elysée Palace, I looked up from my book and noticed a young man with curly brown hair, large intense eyes, and the swarthy skin of a Yemenite Jew.

He was so markedly different in appearance from everyone else who frequented the library that I was moved to do something altogether uncharacteristic. I leaned across the table and asked, "Are you an American?" When he answered "Yes," I said, "Come out into the hall. You have an interesting face. I'd like to talk to you."

He was my age, twenty, or perhaps a little younger. He had worked his way across the sea as a stoker on a coal-propelled steamer, because as a boy in Buffalo he had read *The Count of Monte Cristo* and conceived a passion for Paris. On the boat, the muscular Aussies in the hold soon realized that he was much too frail for the job. They pitied the poor little bugger and told him just to sit by on the side and rest, they would do the work for him. His pay was the free passage.

He had not a sou when he got to Paris. Not a single sou. He spoke no French, knew no one, and had no clothes apart from what he was wearing. He must have passed bewildered and wide-eyed through the busy traffic of the Gare Saint-Lazare. A French laborer going by was apparently as much struck by his looks as I had been. The worker engaged him in conversation, asked him home, let him sleep on the floor, and the next day got him a job as a dishwasher in a bistro.

Living literally from hand to mouth, he still found time to stop in at the American Library. Moved by his poverty, which he carried lightly, and captivated by his candor, I asked him to lunch, then to dinner, and made plans to see him again in a few days.

He had just enough money to buy meals for himself at a hostelry for Jewish students. They cost two francs each. When he invited me, I went, curious about the hostelry, but I couldn't eat the food. I was sorry that he had to make do with this meager fare, not that he seemed to mind it. The meals I gave him cost about seven francs, and were lavish by his standards.

On several occasions I asked my new friend—his name was Israel Sonnabend, but I never called him anything but "Sonny"—to the theatre. The first of the plays we saw was *Six Characters in Search of an Author*. We often sat at cafés together with a bearded student whom we had befriended, arguing loudly about politics or aesthetics. At these arguments the bearded student was the most adept, Sonny the funniest, and I the loudest. The people at other tables stared at us as if we were lunatics about to jump at one another's throats. These friendly jousts went on for the whole three years I was in Paris.

I never corresponded with Sonny after 1924, when I left France. But when in 1926 I came back to Paris for a summer holiday with the money I had saved from my job as stage manager of *The Garrick Gaieties*, I ran into him almost at once. From that time on, whenever I was in Paris, I was always certain I would encounter him somewhere.

On one visit, I found that he and a Spanish friend of his had built themselves a ramshackle house in someone's courtyard. Sonny had earned a bit of money as a tourist guide by now. He had become fluent in French and seemed to know every bus boy, porter, and pimp in Montmartre. He worked in the spring and summer only. In the winter, he loafed, read, went to political gatherings (he had no special interest in politics, but he enjoyed the rhetoric, the heat of debate, the thrusts, the counterthrusts), and made a host of friends. He magnetized everyone he met, just as he had magnetized me. There was an odd panache about him.

One day during the thirties, Stella Adler and I were sitting at lunch on the *terrasse* of a restaurant close by the Louvre. A tourist bus about to pass suddenly stopped at an unwarranted junction mere inches from us. The guide, who we now recognized was Sonny, jumped from his position at the head of the bus and greeted us joyously. He did more than that, he joined us at the table, and carried on a happy conversation while the startled tourists waited.

Again I took him to meals at the best restaurants. He made reservations for the three of us at the smart night clubs where he was well known. . . . Years later, on a stopover in Paris on my way to Moscow with my Group Theatre colleague Cheryl Crawford, Sonny turned up again, magically. I gave him dinner at a great restaurant, which I was pleased to see he now knew intimately. For some whimsical reason, he took to calling Cheryl Crawford "McCarthy."

He had come a long way since that day in the American Library. He had learned Spanish and hiked through Spain on practically no money. A picaresque character out of a novel, he had roamed Europe doing all sorts of odd jobs, often sleeping on park benches and in other public places. When Stella asked him years later if he did not suffer from his hard life, he replied at once, "No more than from a mosquito bite!" In Spain, pretending he was an expert on French literature, he had been invited to lecture at a university. When asked to speak about Cocteau, of whose work he knew nothing, he dismissed the request as unworthy of him. "Cocteau," he said, "is old hat now. He's through," and proceeded to invent a Parisian literary school he was quite prepared to lecture on. He then agreed to join some adventurer in the circumnavigation of the globe on a small schooner. He did not, of course, get very far. The utter folly of this enchanted me.

I, who was used to his eccentric forays, noticed a special change in him—his ever-increasing knowledge of painting, sculpture, and architecture. I wondered how he had come by it. He explained that on his tourist rounds through Paris, everybody always asked to be shown the Louvre. He had boned up on information supplied by the guidebooks and soon realized that most of it was worthless. The curiosity that had always been his greatest gift impelled him to learn more. He began to follow courses in art history at the Sorbonne given by Henri Foçillon and other savants. He had not officially matriculated, and one professor who noticed him sitting day after day in class called him "the dark listener." Inspired by these learned men, Sonny had gone on to make a close study of the paintings and sculptures at the Louvre, which the guidebooks had described in ways that were utterly meaningless to him. In doing so, he pursued no end except pleasure. Everything was a game to him. He recounted his exploits with the most infectious laugh.

"Paris," Sonny said, as, shortly before the war, we contemplated the city from the heights of Montmartre, "is the ideal spot in which to spend one's exile." He had been away from America for nearly twenty years now. He remained in Paris through the declaration of hostilities. But then, with the curfews and other restrictions of the phony war, free movement was limited. He knew that he had to leave; that, hard as it was, he was going to have to exile himself from Paris.

In 1940, when he returned to America, he was as poor as when he had left. Again, he owned little more than his shirt, which, however, he took care to wash every morning. Having no place to stay, he sought me out. I was living in the apartment of Clifford Odets, who was away in Hollywood, and I invited Sonny to sleep on the commodious living-room couch. I supplied him with a pillow and blankets. When I came in to the living room after his first night's stay, I found that he had not used either. He didn't need them, he explained; he was used to sleeping in his clothes.

I offered him a job as a receptionist in the Group Theatre office, which he accepted gladly. His conduct at the desk was unusual. When an actor came to audition for me and was obliged to wait, Sonny would question him. "Why do you want to be an actor? It's a terrible life," etc., etc. When a theatre notable called me—someone associated with, say, Katharine Cornell—he took it upon himself to decide whether the person was qualified to speak to me. I did not have to fire him. The job bored him and he quit.

I did not hear from him for a long time after that, but

one day when I was out of the office, he came to the desk asking for Cheryl Crawford. When he was told that she was busy, he scribbled a note, handed it to the secretary, and left. When I returned, my secretary said, "There was a little man here who came to see Cheryl. He left a note." I opened it. "Dear McCarthy," it read, "I came to see you. You were busy. I have no time for busy people."

But Sonny came back into my life again, knowing Italian as well as French and Spanish. He got a job in New York reading (and censoring) letters for some government department. Many of my friends found him charmingly original. Elia Kazan told me that he had met him one day in the theatre district. "Come to see my new show [*Café Crown*]," Kazan said. "Just tell me what night you want to go and I'll leave tickets." "You don't have to leave tickets," Sonny replied. "I'll buy them." Kazan insisted that Sonny accept free tickets. "No, no," he rejoined, "I have more money now than I know what to do with; I'm working for the cops." He was making all of thirty-five dollars a week.

After the war, as blithe as ever, he spent his summer months working as a waiter and a dishwasher in various holiday resorts. His wages and tips sufficed to keep him going through the winters. It was his old formula, and it still worked.

During his leisure time he became a dark listener again, this time at Meyer Schapiro's art classes at Columbia. He told me later that Schapiro knew more and had better taste than any of the famed art professors he had "studied" with at the Sorbonne.

Years passed—I was never sure now just how he spent them—then one day I discovered that everyone in the art world knew him. We began to see each other more or less regularly again. Not only had he read everything by now in all the languages he knew (to which he had recently added German), but he spent whole days in museums and galleries. When I accompanied him to the Metropolitan he would stand before a painting and speak deeply, and endlessly, about it. As his voice was not exactly subdued, people would gather around him in a kind of astonishment. This pleased him; in his own way, he was an actor.

He was still quite poor. One day I heard him say to someone, "If I had money, I'd pay Harold a good sum just to sit around to talk to me." For I too had become a long-distance talker. His conversations about art, and through it about history, were so rich and stimulating that the fascinated guests at my house would ask him, "Who are you? What do you do?" His answer was always the same. "I am a consumer," he declared. "I consume art."

Ralph Alswang, the scene designer, lighting expert, and theatre architect, who had designed two of my productions, was at one point making a documentary film about Michelangelo, to be called *The Titan*. He was looking for someone to write the commentary, which Fredric March was to speak. I told Alswang I knew just the man for the job.

I called Sonny, suggesting that he ask for five hundred dollars. After Alswang had been satisfied that Sonnabend was indeed the right person, he asked him how much he expected to be paid. Dutifully, he answered, "Five hundred dollars." The others gasped, about to reject the price, when Sonnabend added, "That's what Harold told me to ask for." His candor won them, and they consented to pay him the whole sum. "And I was ready to do the job for nothing," Sonny told me, laughing that most infectious laugh.

Some time later, I asked Alswang how my friend was doing. "He knows too much," Alswang answered. "He practically knows what Michelangelo's laundry bill amounted to!" This led me, for the first time, to give Sonny some advice. "Why," I asked him, "must you struggle all the time and have to depend on windfalls like the Michelangelo film when you can get a degree and become a professor of art history at some college? You'd be one of the best." He had in fact once thought of writing a thesis on Paul Klee, but gave up on the idea because he felt he couldn't write. "But you talk so well," I countered. "Yes, but when I write, it all becomes so flat." And with that, he passed out of my life for a while again.

Then I heard from someone that he had married Ileana, who had been Leo Castelli's wife. And when we next met, Sonnabend was running a gallery on the Quai des Grands-Augustins. He and his wife were showing the work of Jasper Johns, Andy Warhol, James Rosenquist, Claes Oldenburg, and others, whom the Sonnabends had bought for modest sums and were now selling at prices that were simply staggering. I went to see him at the gallery. I now insisted that *he* invite *me* to the finest restaurants in Paris. It gave him great pleasure to be able to repay me in gourmet meals for the seven-franc meals I had once given him.

At the last of these semibanquets, I jokingly recalled the time when he had been a *clochard*. "I valued you in those days," I twitted him. "Now that you're a successful trader of fashionable artifacts to rich South Americans, Germans, and Spaniards [the French never buy art when it's expensive], I have no use for you!" "Oh," he protested, "I'm still a *clochard* at heart."

Today, Sonnabend and his wife also have a gallery in London, and two in New York (one on Madison Avenue and another, of which he appears to be even more proud, in the SoHo district on lower Broadway). They own apartments in Paris, Venice, and New York. He navigates between all these places as casually as ever.

Years ago Stella Adler chided me for not seeking out, in fact for deliberately avoiding, people who had "made it." It seemed to her that I cultivated the obscure. "Don't you envy anyone?" she challenged.

"I've envied only one person in my life," I said.

"And who was that?" she asked.

"Sonny."

"Why, for God's sake?" she exploded. "He's a tramp."

"Yes," I said, "but he's *free*."

Sonny was only one of a galaxy of dazzling people I met in Paris. I read so many books, heard so much music, saw so many paintings, attended so many plays. Yet none of all this was as magical or as important to me as what occurred one day as I was merely walking by the Seine.

I hesitate to speak of it, and I set it down here only as a sort of appendix, though I feel that the language of poetry alone might evoke that moment of communion which was my Paris "love story."

One October morning I decided to walk the two or three miles from my apartment on the Left Bank to the American Library on the Right Bank. When I got to the Pont Royal I headed toward the Pont Alexandre III, along the *quais* on the Left Bank.

It was one of those early fall days when the sun hangs low over the river, veiled in a delicate mist like a pearly tissue. The air was soft, the streets quiet. The heavens seemed to hug the city: they were that close. The embrace drew in the bridges that stood in repose under the amazing sky—fragile, patient, and content to be so enfolded.

I felt that I too was part of the wedding of the enchanted city—now no larger than what my eyes could take in—with the protective blue air, sun, and clouds above and all around me. This gentle clasp of the elements of which I had become an intervening fragment was as near as I would ever come to an epiphany of beauty. It was an exaltation making me feel, as never before, entirely myself, then making me forget myself and become larger than myself. I was no longer only in Paris, that capital of the mere world, I was immersed in the very center of life.

Never again was I able to recapture the purity of that marriage with the ineffable; but the moment would stay with me forever, as a perfection of experience by which all other moments were to be measured.

CHAPTER

3

The Homecoming

As my student years in Paris were drawing to an end, I thought of settling there—everything about the city enchanted me—except the winter weather—and I made a few lame efforts to find employment. I applied to the Paris *Herald,* which Ezra Pound and Ford Madox Ford wrote articles for. (Ford once said that Pound's prose was a national disaster.) I soon found that I was fit for nothing but further study. But I needed some experience of regular work and, above all, a craft.

What attracted me to Paris more than anything else was that everyone I met there seemed already to be a historic personage, which indeed many of them later became. At the old Trocadéro, where the Palais de Chaillot now stands, Isadora Duncan was announced to appear for the last time; she declared in a speech following her recital that she was going to the Soviet Union because she could no longer abide "this bourgeois life."

This was 1922, and Isadora was forty-six. She had grown stout, and when her breast slipped out of her bodice, it could not have inspired anyone with the slightest tremor of lust. My parents, who on their way home from Vienna had stopped over in Paris to visit me, were present on this occasion. Their confession of total bewilderment at the spectacle of Isadora's art did not surprise me: they had never before attended a dance recital. But I was shocked to discover that I was just as baffled. I was in the same plight as my friend the composer Hanns Eisler would be many years later, when, after seeing Martha Graham dance, he admitted that he had "not understood one leg."

Still, I could never forget Isadora. Indeed, she has grown on me with time. This has nothing at all to do with her legend. I have seen dancers finer and infinitely more beautiful, but none has left on me the enduring impression of Isadora. She was a seminal force. Nature spoke through her, wild and magnetic. Watching her, I experienced something close to fear and exaltation. Her dancing, without tumult, gave forth a torrent of womanly energy. It commanded something like worship.

Her voice as she addressed the audience after the recital had a certain melancholy, a quiet, plaintive flow from out of a lost sphere. Apart from its spirit, her speech was not altogether coherent. She spoke of her first struggles in Paris. She reminded us of how poor she was and how she had spent her last sous to sit in the gallery to see the fabulous Mounet-Sully in *Oedipus* at the Théâtre Français.

Then she paused to defend herself against her critics. One of them, André Levinson, a portly Russian who had settled in Paris and was a champion of the classical ballet, was particularly antagonistic to her. "There's a certain critic in Paris, André Levinson . . ." she began, upon which a gentleman in evening dress in a first-tier box cried out, "He's a dirty Jew!" "I like Jews," Isadora countered in a subdued, tender tone, and the audience applauded. But she was unable to go on. The touching mood of her farewell to Paris had been broken, and she wandered off stage in a kind of daze.

(André Levinson . . . One day, arriving half an hour early for my four o'clock class at the Sorbonne, I caught sight of an announcement informing students that Levinson would speak that afternoon from 3:30 to 4:30 on Russian literature. I found the lecture room and sat down at the rear, close by the exit so that I could slip discreetly away at four to my regular course.

There were only three other people in the big room: two girls in the middle and a young man in the first row. Levinson arrived late and out of breath, his fat face sweating. This, coupled with his heavy Russian accent, made the two girls giggle. They soon left. Now there were only two of us, the young man in front and me. Levinson continued with his lecture, pausing suddenly to ask if "any of my numerous listeners have ever read the poetry of Henri de Régnier? So few Frenchmen do nowadays." He looked to the student in the first row. "I'm a Norwegian," said the youth. Levinson now looked to me. "And what about you?" "I'm an American." A few minutes later I left Levinson with the Norwegian and hurried to my class.)

Much has been made of Isadora's love life, which she herself was urged for commercial reasons to play up. I believe that her sexuality—like everything else about her—was sustained by a special sort of spirituality. Raymond Petit, the French composer and critic, told me that on one of her visits to Paris, Isadora asked for a pianist to accompany her at rehearsals. A brilliant young musician was recommended. When he appeared, Isadora was on the point of sending him away. "He's too ugly," she explained to her incredulous manager. "I can't possibly work in sight of that ugly face." It was suggested that the pianist play with his back to her. She yielded. The pianist—André Caplet, who was to become a celebrated conductor—played so beautifully that Isadora took him as her lover.

I returned to New York in the spring of 1924, to long days of enforced idleness. At first I looked for a job in publishing, and I went to see Van Wyck Brooks at Harcourt, Brace and Company. He talked so much and so brilliantly of the literary world and the state of American culture (about which he was, by the way, most optimistic) that I proceeded to forget the rather mundane purpose of my visit. But Alfred Knopf's wife, Blanche, well fleshed and extremely pretty in those days, was much more direct. She explained that if I wanted to go into publishing I would have to start at the bottom—the package room, for instance. I, in the package room! To this day I can't wrap a package.

Since publishing didn't seem very promising, I decided to concentrate on finding work in the theatre, and here I was more successful. My first job, as an extra in Stark Young's *The Saint,* led to small parts in several other plays as well as some stage-managing jobs. In 1929 I was appointed playreader for the Theatre Guild.

But my interests ranged beyond the theatre. One day I visited the Anderson Galleries, at Park Avenue and Fifty-ninth Street, and saw paintings by a group of artists I had never heard of: Georgia O'Keeffe, John Marin, Marsden Hartley, Arthur Dove, Charles Demuth. Alfred Stieglitz, who was in charge of the gallery and married to O'Keeffe, I had also never heard of, though he was even then a well-known photographer and contributor to the arts.

What struck me first in Stieglitz, apart of course from his arresting appearance—his disheveled gray hair, his bushy eyebrows, his deep eyes, the tufts growing from his ears—was the intensity of his proselytizing. He was eager to know how each visitor to the gallery reacted to each painting. If he did not actually question everyone, he eavesdropped. He desperately wanted the paintings to be *understood*. He was committed to the artists, not simply as individual talents, but as representatives of something astir in the country, something bigger than the art world—life in America itself. There was a kind of religious exaltation in Stieglitz's speech. He was pleading for the recognition of a new spirit, a new awareness he associated with the coming of age of the American consciousness. America! America! America! The word was sounded over and over again, like an incantation. I was reminded of Walt Whitman, for whom America was more an idea to be cherished and a hope of salvation than a place. I listened to Stieglitz argue with a dignified, elegantly tailored, handsomely trim, gray-haired gentleman with a Vandyke beard, whom he had heard pooh-poohing one of O'Keeffe's flower pieces. He interceded and tried to convert the gentleman to a more enlightened view of the painting. Except for mentioning the "tactility" of O'Keeffe's art, he used hardly any technical terms. Instead, he spoke of the painting's special character, its womanliness. There was a certain afflatus whenever Stieglitz uttered the word "woman." The bearded gentleman, however, would allow for nothing. He could perceive no "drawing," no form or composition, in

O'Keeffe's work. Stieglitz went on and on, rapturously, about O'Keeffe, as if he were reciting a lyric poem. When he realized that he was not convincing his listener, he asked shrewdly, "Are you a painter?" The answer was "Yes." "And whom do you admire?" Stieglitz asked. "Meissonier," the gentleman replied. He was obviously a salon artist, trained in the stuffiest of French academic traditions. But this did not diminish the ardor of Stieglitz's proselytization.

When the haughty visitor left, Stieglitz turned to all within earshot and exclaimed, "Meissonier! What can you expect? If he had said Corot, Courbet, Renoir, Monet, there might have been some use in going on with the discussion. But Meissonier!" Nevertheless, I was certain that if the gentleman had not left, Stieglitz would have persisted in his exhortation to the point of collapse—the gentleman's, certainly not his.

For those who did not share his sentiments, Stieglitz felt sorrow rather than contempt. He wished ardently to absorb everyone into a kind of ideal, soulful embrace. When anyone, a mere passer-by, no matter how humble, said anything at all complimentary about one of his artists—especially about his favorites, O'Keeffe and Marin—he spoke of the fact as an extraordinary event, and would quote the unknown person's remark, however leaden, to everyone he met that day. All such contacts were wonderful experiences to him.

Stieglitz's manner induced cultism. For one thing, he seemed to have total recall. He could transform every incident of his life into something more than a good anecdote; for him it was part of a drama fraught with universal significance, a lesson, a parable for all time. I have never known anyone who could make a more wide-reaching symbol of his own life history.

Stieglitz's work and artistic outlook were decidedly modern. He was one of the first to establish the aesthetic value of photography. He recognized the originality and importance of Matisse, Picasso, "le Douanier" Rousseau, Brancusi, and Gertrude Stein before almost anyone else in America. But for all his critical incisiveness, he was romantic in temperament. The romantic sees everything in terms of his personal self; he conceives the world as if it were his own creation. He tends toward solipsism. On this account he invites irritation and hostility from spirits weaker or more sober. The romantic's voracious ego threatens to swallow them, and they do not wish to be swallowed: they too wish to exist. To save themselves, several of Stieglitz's closest associates felt it necessary to flee from him.

I didn't flee. On the contrary, I visited his gallery at least once a week (it later moved to Madison Avenue and Fifty-second Street and was called An American Place), though it was some time before I was formally introduced to him. The photographer Paul Strand, also a Stieglitz discovery and for years a rapt admirer, invited me to join him on a motor trip through New England. Strand proposed that on the way we stop off to visit Stieglitz at his summer place on Lake George. Stieglitz came gingerly through the door to greet us, Strand introduced me as his friend, and Stieglitz invited us to sit down on the porch, blurting out, "History is a lie!" This cryptic exclamation puzzled me, but I was given little time to ponder it: Stieglitz had entered into a long discourse on life, part lament, part harangue, which lasted literally for eighteen hours. We lunched, we dined, and still he spoke. As we retired for the night, the lights in the house still blazing—Strand said that in view of Stieglitz's excited state we ought not to leave—Stieglitz came to our room with us and stood over our beds, continuing his monologue.

The immediate cause of this verbal flood was jealousy, although Stieglitz would have been appalled to hear such a gross word applied to an emotion that was consuming him so utterly. O'Keeffe had gone to New Mexico for a holiday and there, she wrote him, she had met an Indian; she went on to speak of the physical thrill she felt in the Indian's presence. This struck Stieglitz as tantamount to a confession of infidelity. But this he did not speak about directly. He preferred to recall the past: how O'Keeffe as a Texas schoolteacher had sent him some of her early drawings and how he had brought her to New York because, as he put it, she was the first artist "to put Woman into paint," how he had given her her first show, supported her, championed her, and so on.

This was only the starting point for an account of his whole life. He spoke of his student days in Berlin, his love affairs, his first marriage, his devotion to his colleagues—Steichen and others. He told us—although we felt he was speaking beyond us—how he had raised funds so that Marin could paint without financial worry and how Marin had used the money to buy himself a car. . . . He said that in a letter O'Keeffe mentioned that she had just taken her first airplane ride; on receipt of the letter, Stieglitz went right out and asked to be flown over Lake George!

He wrote O'Keeffe several letters a day and read them to Strand and me. But he was not content with writing to her—he also telephoned her, and after hanging up he would invariably remember an inadvertent remark he had made and write her another letter about *that*. He wept a little and said that the trouble was that he was over sixty and she was more than twenty years younger. There was enough detail in his rambling—which progressed by a process of free association—for a full-scale biography.

Among the seemingly incidental anecdotes that studded his wide-ranging discourse was one about an invitation Stieglitz had received from Shaw to visit him in London. Shaw wanted to inform himself about photography, and Stieglitz, who was then in Paris, thought it would be a good idea if Shaw wrote about photography as he, Stieglitz, conceived of it. But crossing the Channel, Stieglitz caught a cold, which made talking difficult, and took the next boat back without meeting Shaw.

There was another story about how he had studied photography with a German professor whose expertise amazed him—that is, until after only six months of instruction, he himself took a photograph that amazed the professor. Another reminiscence concerned a Berlin prostitute who had been his mistress (there is a beautiful photograph of her in the Metropolitan Museum collection), but before he could finish it he veered off to tell us how disconsolate he had been on his return to America and how one day, having nothing better to do, he had stepped into a theatre advertising the appearance of a "famous Italian actress" and how it was the fact that Duse could be seen in New York that reconciled him to living in this country. He added that when he heard that Duse had returned in 1923 to tour America he predicted, correctly, that she would die here.

There was something absurd as well as poignant in the whirl of words that poured from Stieglitz. Yet I was elated that an old man (I was less than half Stieglitz's age then) could get so wrought up about a woman! I had not yet read about Goethe's perennial amorousness. Here was proof that the ardor of love need not die or even diminish with the passing of the years. Proof also that the good life, indeed the best life, was the life of feeling, where one's experiences could be forever envisioned anew. So one must go on treasuring and reinterpreting what one has lived through, even that which one has deemed wrong or bad.

Stieglitz nearly always spoke in a quasi-prophetic vein. That, like all prophets, he could be annoying, even boring, goes without saying. He was also, like many artists, subject on occasion to professional jealousy. He once said to me, "You would not have written about Strand as you did if you had seen my work first." Each man's work was quite unlike the other's. In his last years he would not admit that there was anything more to his various love affairs than the ethereal. He referred to the sexual relationship as "touch," and everything he "touched" was endowed with instant purity. He failed to see how his relationships could be construed as other than holy.

Artists, like everyone else, are given to elaborate rationalizations of their faults and blunders and sins. In a sense they are even more guilty in this respect than ordinary people: they exonerate themselves of all blame on the grounds that they are artists. They do not often recognize that the only thing that differentiates them from others is their capacity to produce art. It is their redemption.

Most artists I have known or read about were personally obnoxious in one way or another; gratuitously conceited or selfish, or not a little foolish, and Stieglitz was certainly all of these a bit. But I never overlooked the fund of real *wisdom* in him. When I first wrote about him, in 1934, I said at once that I thought him one of the major figures in American cultural history.

No matter how long you had absented yourself from him, he always greeted you as if he had been seeing you all the while. He never asked you how you were feeling; he didn't have to, he knew at a glance. He never asked you what was the matter or what was "wrong"; he didn't have to, you just told him.

"Nothing is true," he said to me, "unless it is true for two people." He told a critic: "You are interested in the fruit, I am interested in the tree." He used to say: "To achieve greatness a man must invite tragedy." "You can afford to be an optimist, as long as the pessimist [he meant himself] pays the bills." "If God were an American, everybody would be stillborn. He would be too impatient to wait nine months." "If an American had the choice between encountering God and attending a lecture on Him, he would choose the lecture." "Clurman, you are attempting the impossible [in the Group Theatre]—to combine Fourteenth Street with Times Square!"

When I asked him how, in 1912, he happened to buy one of Picasso's earliest cubist drawings, I saw there was a lesson lurking in his reply. "I bought it," he said, "because I didn't understand it." Stieglitz hated to be called an "art dealer." He was, he declared, a guardian of art. He hated having his various centers—the early "291" (Fifth Avenue), the room at 91 Park Avenue, and finally An American Place —called "art galleries": to him they were havens of human contact. Though many have written about Stieglitz, he has not yet been given his due. Nor, for that matter, have very many other American artists. As I said once to Clifford Odets (who incorporated the line in his play *Paradise Lost*): "We cancel our experience."

Many towering figures in the world of arts and letters gathered around Stieglitz. He was receptive to them all, and quietly understanding. One had to be very stupid or very gross to incur his overt rejection. A woman who expressed the wish to buy a particular O'Keeffe and who the next day changed her mind because she decided another O'Keeffe was better suited to the color of her bedroom found that Stieglitz was no longer willing to sell her either one.

In or around 1918 a young man of intense countenance had introduced himself to Stieglitz by announcing, "My name is Waldo Frank. I hope to do for literature what you have done for the pictorial arts." Whether Waldo Frank actually spoke these exact words or not, it certainly was in his nature and his vein to have spoken them.

Waldo, a declared conscientious objector during World War I (nothing happened to him as a result), was one of my literary heroes, for having written *Our America,* which in enthusiastic prose proclaimed and chronicled America's coming of age since 1915. Though not uncritical of the raw energy of the period just dawning, the book was distinctly proud and hopeful. It saw the torch of the generation that had produced Emerson, Thoreau, Hawthorne, Melville, Whitman, and Mark Twain being taken up by Sherwood Anderson, Edgar Lee Masters, H. L. Mencken, and others. To these writers and those who were to follow—like Waldo Frank himself—he assigned the task of reawakening the American conscience and of shaping it to a form more compatible with its premises than with those of the 1870–1914 generation. Frank's book could well have been called "America Hurrah!"

With Van Wyck Brooks and several others, Waldo Frank had founded *Seven Arts,* a magazine to which many of the best writers and editors of the years to come would contribute. America's entry into the war shortened the magazine's life considerably, and not alone because some of its small staff were drafted.

I met Waldo in 1928, when I sought permission to use his play *New Year's Eve* as practice work for a number of actors—Morris Carnovsky, Sanford Meisner, Franchot Tone—who were to form the nucleus of the Group Theatre in 1931. Waldo and I soon became friends.

He was brilliant, erudite, fluent in French, Spanish, and German, and knowledgeable in the literature of these countries. He was a first-rate cultural critic, familiar with the entire domain of the arts. As if all this were not enough, he played the cello too. His was an alert and original sensibility. He was also courageous, a man of sound and strong convictions. His friends included Lewis Mumford, Hart Crane, Herbert Croly (founder of the *New Republic*), Sherwood Anderson, and nearly all of the most forward-looking South American, and a good many of the European, intellectuals.

In 1929 Waldo wrote a book—published serially in the *New Republic*—called *The Rediscovery of America,* in which the optimism of *Our America* gave way to alarm at the "jungle" (his word) of competitiveness, aggression, success- and Mammon-worship he saw America turning into. There were many admirable pages of close analysis of the dementia that threatened us, but the book on the whole was marred by messianism, Waldo's cardinal sin. Quite consciously he considered himself a prophet, destined to save America through the wisdom and power of his Word.

His prophetic bent had the most adverse consequences.

It rendered his style, which at its best could be resonant and exhilarating, leaden and turgid. He who in socially precarious situations was capable of finesse and even grace became tactless and very nearly offensive. He suffered from the kind of leadership complex that harms not only those obsessed by it but also those who merely come into contact with it.

Worst of all, Waldo believed himself a good novelist. He had, it is true, great descriptive gifts, psychological insight, and an intellectual capacity and critical intuition of unusual scope, but he was not a storyteller, and most of his novels were failures. He insisted, and pretended to believe, that they would be recognized as important. He assured me that he was already hailed as a major figure in Spain and South America, which he had written books about.

When the critic Paul Rosenfeld, another of the men close to Stieglitz, wrote a piece defining Waldo's limitations as a novelist, he felt personally betrayed. He once flatly stated to me that he was greater than D. H. Lawrence and Thomas Mann. I smiled and replied that though his ideas might have therapeutic value and inspirational force, he was not a novelist at all, whereas Lawrence, whose ideas often struck me as mischievously wrongheaded, was truly a novelist. "You like my ideas," Waldo would say, "but not my art," which I would counter with, "Your art consists in the expression of your ideas." Then he would add, "There are very few people who would tolerate what you have allowed yourself to say to me as I have." Once I ventured the opinion that he might have a greater influence on American life and thought if he simplified his writing style and confined himself to critical essays. "You may be right," he answered, "but I can't give up writing novels. I really can't." I could see that he was telling the truth, and I never again offered him any counsel.

Perhaps I shouldn't speak at such length about a writer remembered only by those who read the literary journals from 1919 to perhaps 1950, as well as his provocative pieces in the

New Yorker, McCall's, and other popular magazines. But I
believe he deserved much better from us. When we discuss
literary or cultural matters with educated Europeans we find
that minor figures far less significant than Waldo Frank was
in America are spoken of with respect and sometimes studied
with care. The slaughter of reputations in the cultural life
of this country is scandalous. (It's funny how, as I write it,
the very phrase "cultural life" strikes me as archaic.) The
fact is, all too few reputations remain intact among us. We
erase history even as we make it—"we cancel our experience." Reverence is rare, even for the most renowned; instead, there is a fundamental indifference toward those
vociferously touted, and the ones who have "made it" are
soon enough unmade.

Waldo Frank, conceited and arrogant as he was, was a
superior man. A good deal of what he wrote is still very
much to the point, and we forget or dismiss him at our peril.
There was a large measure of self-consolation in the things
I heard him say not long before he died, when publishers
were beginning to reject his books. I remember one bitter,
penetrating remark: "If a man does not consider his life a
failure, he is already a failure." He was then writing his autobiography, which was never to be finished. The fragment was
posthumously published, and in 1973 I reviewed it for the
Los Angeles *Times.*

Even closer to Stieglitz than Waldo Frank was Paul
Rosenfeld, who had so generously understood and encouraged
the young generation of American composers of the twenties
and thirties. It was he whom I spoke to Aaron Copland about
on our first walk to the Battery of long ago. Recently, at a
conference on criticism, I heard a writer for one of the great
dailies mock Rosenfeld's style. It could certainly be heavy
with strange syntax and an even stranger vocabulary: it was
a deliberate effort to reproduce in words the impressions and
effects of what he had felt, heard, or seen in the various arts.

What pained me was not the objection to Rosenfeld's manner of writing, but the fact that most of the critics and journalists at the conference did not even know who he was. He, who for years had been the music critic of the prestigious *Dial* and for a time the art critic of the *New Yorker!*

Rosenfeld could interpret music at a first hearing; he could recognize new talent while most of his colleagues were still baffled by the unfamiliar and for the most part hostile to it. He was truly part of the musical scene and not, like most reviewers, a bystander. In short, he was an artist in his own right, as every critic worthy of the name must be.

We often crossed swords, Rosenfeld and I. He appeared to indulge himself almost exclusively in the sensations of art, to immerse himself quasi-erotically in them. Though I agreed with T. S. Eliot that "the first condition of right thought is right sensation," I suspected that the emphasis on the sensory in art bespoke a failure to see that art is also an extension of thought and sentiment born of a particular social matrix. Criticism that neglected this interrelationship, I believed, perhaps too dogmatically, was the product of critics cushioned by private incomes. But the Wall Street crash and the Depression that followed shattered their aestheticism along with their incomes, battered their talent, and made them seem sadly irrelevant even to themselves, prematurely obsolescent. It was no longer easy, in many cases it was no longer possible, to proceed along the comfortable lines prosperity had traced.

The people around Stieglitz constituted a clan of live spirits dwelling on a blessed island in a fevered world. John Marin, who looked like a shrewd hayseed philosopher, painted water colors in which the Maine landscape and the Manhattan skyline were equal in their electric energy, equal in his perception of their gladness. Immovable Marsden Hartley sat isolated, as if gazing into unfathomable emptiness. O'Keeffe dressed with nunlike severity, her face austerely matching though hinting that a smile was hidden in it somewhere which might bloom into laughter. All these and others

in the cool retrea: of An American Place were wonderful
oddities, messengers from a world quite apart from the circus
around it. With few exceptions the painters of the Stieglitz
circle were country rather than city people, whose America
lay outside New York. Stieglitz's American Place was a true
oasis.

The twenties were a jumping time. In an article about
a Paul Whiteman concert at Carnegie Hall, I described jazz
as the Coney Island of music. Everything seemed to be
enveloped and consumed by jazz. Musicians, and even artists
and writers, began to use the jargon of jazz as a vernacular.
Copland and many others felt that in doing this they were
not only reflecting but also affirming America. Everyone
seemed effervescently, hysterically proud of America, or gaily
contemptuous of it. New York was bursting with a vitality
that exhilarated as many as it frightened. It was difficult to
tell whether the exhilaration was the product of fear or
whether it was the other way around. There were sixty
theatres on Broadway. And everyone was having a swell time.

In Europe immediately after the war the Dada movement puzzled, annoyed, attracted, and amused most people.
It was an expression of a jocose nihilism, an attempt at clear-
ing the air of inherited poisons—the old traditions and fake
reverence for culture—by its outrageously nonsensical blasphemy. On his way to Europe for the first time, in 1921,
Aaron Copland met Marcel Duchamp on the *France*. Duchamp asked him what he was going to do in Paris. When
Aaron said that he proposed to continue his study of composition, Duchamp was most discouraging. "What do you
want to do that for? That sort of thing is finished. America
is a place of business. Your father is a businessman. Become a
businessman and forget art." It sounded like the truth, and
Aaron was depressed.

Some months later, Aaron told me about his encounter
with Duchamp on the high seas. "It's all very well for a

Frenchman to talk that way," I said. I was angry. "The French are surfeited with culture; they are sick of a culture that did nothing to prevent the disastrous war. But we Americans are *new;* we need art, which, to begin with, is simply the conscious embodiment of our experience. Culture serves as self-realization for us as individuals and as a community." Aaron was satisfied, and Duchamp's irony dispelled, by this passionate outburst.

In retrospect I see that these forces—the perpetual state of exaltation of the Stieglitz circle, the business boom, the merry-go-round confidence as well as the nervousness it inspired, the scathing criticism of America and the prophesies of doom sounded in the writings and conversation of a few intellectuals, the rest of the country's blatant trumpeting of our prosperity as a sign of American virtue and superiority to a collapsing Europe—these were all reflections of the growing pains of our society and, in a way, of its health. America did not need to import Dadaism or to imitate it, though some sophomoric intellectuals thought it the thing to do—America *was* Dada: flighty, vulgar, impudent, crazy, brash. At the same time it was desperate and eager in its quest for sound values. This very chaos made the twenties a period of generative ferment.

There were the concerts of Paul Whiteman and Vincent Lopez, the compositions of George Gershwin, the League of Composers concerts that introduced the music of Varèse; there were Ruggles, the new Stravinsky style, the Ziegfeld Follies, the musicals of Jerome Kern, Vincent Youmans, and Cole Porter, the young Eugene O'Neill. It was a time of vogue for Spengler's *Decline of the West,* of prominence for Sinclair Lewis's *Babbitt,* of relative obscurity for William Faulkner, an era of raids on "radicals," of the rediscovery of Whitman and Melville, of eager interest in Sandburg, Frost, and Eliot, Lardner, Hemingway, and Fitzgerald, the era of the Algonquin circle, the speakeasies, the racketeers,

31177

the Tennessee "monkey trial," the Valentino funeral, the warm attractions of Harlem, Jed Harris's four concurrent Broadway hits. This for me was the twenties, in all its clashing multifariousness.

CHAPTER

4

Early Theatre
Encounters

I was lucky in that the first people I met in the theatre world were all exceptional: they were men and women of the theatre rather than mere "show folk."

I never met Eugene O'Neill though he was officially one of my employers in the production of *The Saint* and I later directed four of his plays. I saw him once at the Greenwich Village Theatre in Sheridan Square, at a meeting Robert Edmond Jones called to inspire the members of the acting company engaged by Kenneth MacGowan, a former theatre critic and the most active partner of the MacGowan, Jones, O'Neill trio. During the rehearsal period of *Mourning Becomes Electra* in 1931, I caught a glimpse of O'Neill in the Guild Theatre lobby—well dressed, handsome, all fiercely concentrated. His gaze bordered on the hypnotic. But apart from a letter he wrote me in 1932 answering my appeal for a play to be done by the Group Theatre, to which he had contributed a thousand dollars (he said that from then on he intended to spend at least two years writing each play), I never had direct contact with him.

Jones, though a hard worker, was a delicate creature. There was something ineffable about him. One hesitated to confront him with any crudity. Once, when he was working on the set for the Group Theatre's production of Maxwell Anderson's *Night Over Taos,* in irritation over a stagehand's dilatoriness, I used the word "masturbate." Jones blanched. I was more astonished at his reaction than sorry for having caused it. His personal delicacy—I had heard that he had been psychoanalyzed by Jung—was like his art, so exquisite in its lovely quietude and sense of balance that it seemed to be apologizing for itself. It was difficult and perhaps impossible to get close to Jones: one always felt like an intruder on his privacy.

Stark Young too was very special. He tried to stage his play *The Saint* himself, because he imagined, mistakenly, that he could do better than most of the duffers who directed the plays he was called upon to review. He was an aesthete, something of a Platonist in his thought and manner of expression; he was also something of an academic, when the term connoted wide learning and noble aspiration. He was perhaps the least suitable person to be a drama critic for the New York *Times*. For one thing, he could not bear musical comedies, and much of what was best on the American stage in the twenties was musical comedy.

He had the breeding of the old-time Southern gentry. He once wrote of a Group Theatre play that it wasn't a true picture of the middle class because none of its characters were in the least degree *soigné*. The photographer Ralph Steiner, a Group Theatre devotee, submitted a letter to the *New Republic,* in which Young's review had appeared, suggesting that Young, a native of Mississippi, belonged "Way Down upon the *Soigné* River."

Stark Young was an authentic theatre critic, one of the first, and one of the very few, that America has produced. His only rival in the twenties was George Jean Nathan, who, for all his disdain of Broadway, was very much part of it. You read either one or the other of them; hardly anybody read both.

Young was variously talented. He could, for instance, paint. His painting, though not nearly as valuable as his critical writing, was more immediately revealing of his personality. Nature was rendered as in a reverie, the color mellowed by tints of a golden sunset. A youth was often seen in the landscape—yearning. Young loved Debussy's music and leaned toward the melting, the temperate. Asked after his first Martha Graham recital why he refused to attend a second, he was capable of replying, "I'm so afraid she's going to give birth to a cube." He later came to admire the dancer.

As for Nathan, he performed his most telling service to our theatre between 1915 and 1925. He was vociferous in his denunciation of the sleazy values of the preceding era, when someone like William Winter, the author of a long biography of David Belasco that was hardly more than a venal puff, could rule the theatrical world, and when Shaw's *Mrs. Warren's Profession* could be prosecuted as immoral. Nathan championed O'Neill, O'Casey, and the early work of Saroyan.

There was a certain gallantry about him. In a review I wrote for the *New Republic* of his book *Art of the Night* in 1928, I indicated that though he had contributed a great deal, he was no longer the critic our theatre needed because he was more college-boy iconoclast than perceptive aesthete or intellectual. Despite this, Nathan recommended that his publishers give me a contract for a book I planned to write on the aesthetics of the theatre.

Lillian Gish, who knew Nathan well, said that he was above all an actor. (In my review I had called him an incorrigible show-off.) He was dark and Latin-looking, very handsome. He dressed impeccably and was said to possess an enormous wardrobe of expensive suits, coats, shoes, and shirts. He had, of course, independent means. His politics, his colleague Richard Watts said, were slightly to the right of Marie Antoinette's.

At Cornell Nathan had been a flashy undergraduate, a foppish playboy with pretentions to continental sophistication, which he never quite abandoned. He was capable of writing that he did not care how many people were starving in Arkansas, and that a person who did not enjoy fox hunting could not be truly cultivated. Yet he was an admirer of Shaw. All this was an evasion, a mask to hide something in his background that might cast doubt on the validity of his snobbishness and his aristocratic stance. One day, acting on a hunch, I asked Sinclair Lewis whether Nathan was Jewish. "Only a hundred per cent," Lewis answered. Nathan, he went on to explain, had broken with Lillian Gish, his intimate friend, because she went ahead and visited his mother in Indiana after he had asked her never to do so and thus discovered that Nathan was Jewish. Though in his youth he had declared himself unyieldingly atheistic, his funeral was conducted as a High Mass at St. Patrick's.

He used to boast of his hedonism. This at least was genuine; even his attachment to the theatre was in a way carnal. At a meeting of the New York Drama Critics Circle at the Algonquin I noticed that he would not eat his dinner; I remembered his once telling me that he could not possibly eat any meat served in Hollywood restaurants. He was proud of his taste for *cordon bleu* cuisine and expensive liquors.

He paid a price for all this. When I visited him in his apartment at the Royalton Hotel on West Forty-fourth Street, it was positively stifling, and no wonder: all the windows were closed, though it was a warm spring day. I learned that he always kept the windows closed to keep his room as hot as possible—perhaps his doctors had told him to. I could see that he was suffering from liver trouble; at least he kept his hand pressed against it while we talked.

He was shamelessly conceited—once I heard him say, discussing a Russian play with other critics, "I can't say anything about that because I know only French, German, and Italian." Brooks Atkinson, always friendly to Nathan but also always the soul of honesty, whispered to me at one of the critics' gatherings, "He went to the University of Baloney"—a reference to Nathan's year as a graduate student in Bologna.

With it all, there was in Nathan a love of the raffish, the heteroclite, the noisy braggadocio, the vulgar sensuality of Broadway before the black-out of the thirties. These qualities are reflected in his literary style. What was best in him was his respect for originality: his realization that Gordon Craig was a great figure, though he did not fully understand Craig's significance, his admiration of Max Reinhardt, though he could not wholly define his talent.

George Jean Nathan at his best was more effective than Stark Young, who, however, now makes for more profitable reading. Today Nathan is hardly known at all, as he would be if the history of our theatre, in the development of which he played a creditable part, were more meticulously studied. But how much of any history is known in our country, except among specialists?

In 1925, when I first met Lorenz Hart, I did not know enough about the popular arts to appreciate his talent. A brilliantly witty and often touching versifier, he could produce, within a matter of minutes, a wonderful lyric to Dick Rodgers's musical specifications.

As stage manager of Rodgers and Hart's earliest Broadway success, the first *Garrick Gaieties,* I had ample opportunity to see Larry at work. There was a sketch in the *Gaieties* ridiculing William Jennings Bryan's role in the famous Tennessee "monkey trial." Bryan died during the play's run and the sketch had to be dropped. At the Sunday conference called to discuss a replacement for it, Dick Rodgers produced a hitherto unused melody. Larry Hart scanned the notes Rodgers hummed and disappeared into an adjoining room. In less than half an hour he was back with a lyric about the flapper morals of the twenties—scribbled in pencil on a piece of scrap paper. The song was introduced to the audience the following night and became the hit of the show.

Larry's idol was Heine, whom it was his dream to emulate. Heine's combination of tenderness, mischievous humor, and virtuosity was something Larry realized he could never achieve, though on the narrower scale of Broadway entertainment these qualities were certainly his. He saw himself as a failure. He longed to be attractive, and he was swarthy, short, and square.

He became increasingly neurotic until he could hardly sit still for even a few minutes. He paced and paced and paced, a large, thick cigar always in his mouth. He drank heavily, despairing all the while of his drinking. He was horrified by his homosexuality; he had been brought up in a stereotypical Jewish family where such things were "unheard of." He felt thoroughly disgraced and acted as if he were determined to punish himself for his anomaly. He began to grow remiss in his responsibilities to his collaborators and lived in an agony of fear that they would cut off their association with him. One day in 1943 he just gave up, and died from an attack of pneumonia.

Perhaps if Larry Hart had been composing lyrics at a time when such shame as he felt was alleviated by deeper understanding and more general permissiveness, he might have gone on to even greater achievements. He was without doubt one of the three or four best (some might say the best) lyric writers in the history of the American musical theatre.

Alfred Lunt, as all but the very young know, was, after John Barrymore defected from Broadway, the finest actor of our stage. I saw Lunt in his earliest success, Booth Tarkington's *Clarence,* in 1919, a few months before women acquired the right to vote. Helen Hayes was also in the cast, and actors whose names only old-time theatre buffs would recognize. . . . On my return from Europe in 1924, one of the first plays I saw was Molnar's *Guardsman,* which starred Alfred Lunt and his wife, Lynn Fontanne. I had first seen her in 1917, in a propaganda play for America's entry into the war called *Out There* starring Laurette Taylor; Lynn, who had only recently arrived in America, played a Cockney shopgirl with unforgettable comic acuity. Little did I dream that I would one day get to know and even on occasion to act— if what I did could be called acting—with Lunt and Fontanne.

This was in the Theatre Guild production of Franz Werfel's *Goat Song,* which included, besides the Lunts, Edward G. Robinson and my good friends Philip Loeb and Lee Strasberg. Loeb, as a peasant elder, took pleasure in tormenting me by blowing smoke from his pipe into my face as I began to speak my lines as the village scribe. Strasberg found this hilarious—none of it was called for by either the script or the direction!

During the rehearsals, I cued Miss Fontanne in her part. When this was jokingly pointed out as a "warning" to Lunt, he said, "It's perfectly all right." . . . I also played with him in Werfel's *Juarez and Maximilian*. Eddie Robinson and I were both generals. And I was also a Mexican peon in a later scene.

I came to know the Lunts best when Jacques Copeau, my first teacher in the theatre, directed them in his version of *The Brothers Karamazov* in 1927.

Copeau spoke English passably well, but he welcomed my suggestion that I translate his more subtle comments for him at rehearsals. In addition to having attended his lectures in Paris, I had written a newspaper piece explaining his capital role in the development of the contemporary French theatre. New York's playgoing public did not know that Copeau, before having become an actor and then a director, had been a splendid theatre critic, the first editor of the *Nouvelle Revue Française,* and a close associate of such men as Gide and Jules Romains.

One of the things I learned at the *Karamazov* rehearsals was that a first-rate foreign director, who is also the author of the play, working with such incomparable actors as Lunt and Fontanne, does not inevitably produce a satisfying theatre event (I was later to see the same thing happen with Max Reinhardt). This is not from any lack of mutual respect or from temperamental conflicts between the American actors and the foreign director; it is just that the company and the director do not speak the same artistic language—their stage traditions differ, often hopelessly.

The Lunts—except in the case of *The Visit,* staged by Peter Brook—were rarely happy with serious foreign plays and even more rarely happy with European directors. When in 1938 they appeared in *The Sea Gull* (directed by a man whose only qualification for the assignment was that he happened to be the son of a famous Russian actor), Lunt himself, aware that something was amiss, confessed over-generously, "I don't think we're good enough for this play!" The failure, however, was due not to any insufficiency of talent but to the lack of a common cultural background between the actors and the playwright and to a director unable to bridge the gap.

It was characteristically sweet of Lunt to say what he did, to take the blame. "Not good enough for this play!" Why, he is a superb actor. His acting is based more on instinct than external or conscious technique. It is Lynn who is the technician. They are both extremely scrupulous and hard workers, arriving at their results each in his and her particular way. The European director tends to set his own pattern, to which the actor must then adapt himself. The American actor needs greater freedom. This is especially true of the Lunts, who direct themselves, so that the "outside" director is only nominally in charge.

Copeau thought Lunt *un gosse,* "a little boy." He did not mean this at all unkindly; there is in fact something tender, vulnerable, and invincibly boyish in Lunt, which is the source of his acting. Lynn is the tougher of the two. Copeau could not altogether understand the fluidity of Lunt's inspiration, the spontaneous emotionalism that makes him so poignant an actor, even in comedy. Copeau enjoyed the veteran Dudley Digges, of whom he said, "The more Russian he tries to be, the more Irish he becomes." It was Digges whom Copeau called *an actor, the actor* (that emphasis bespeaking the highest professional regard). And Digges for his part appreciated Copeau's direction because, he said, he liked a director "who could show what he wants by doing it himself," by demonstrating his intention through his own acting. Which is precisely what Lunt didn't need and didn't want.

There were no real clashes between Copeau and Lunt. However, Copeau, when he insisted on some point and Lunt demurred, could barely contain his impatience and would cry out, *"But I know the play; I've seen it performed for hundreds of audiences,"* which Lunt, in an undertone, would counter with, "But not *American* audiences."

Art is not as international as we ordinarily suppose. What Lunt said reminded me of an incident at the International Modern Music Festival I had attended the previous summer, 1926, in Zurich. An ordinarily sympathetic French critic had called a piece by Copland "sentimental." Copland was not at all nettled by this criticism—he receives all criticism with remarkable equanimity—but he did point out that there is something typical in the art of every country which is often described pejoratively in other countries. Thus, the French speak of German "heaviness" (for instance, in regard to Brahms), the Germans complain of lack of substance in French music (even in Debussy), and American candor is often called "sentimental."

Lunt was surely on as solid ground in his personal and American vein as Copeau was in his. While it may have been true that Lunt lacked something of the extremely masculine tempestuousness of Dostoevski's Dmitri Karamazov, he is a much greater actor than the highly intelligent Copeau was and a much greater actor, besides, than anyone Copeau had ever directed in the part.

Copeau realized that the "machine" was not working, but he could not quite comprehend why and where he had failed to inspire the actors. "Go out front and learn from my mistakes," he said to me one day, creeping quietly into the seat beside me in the back of the auditorium so that he was invisible to the company. He was, in effect, withdrawing temporarily from the production. When Lynn Fontanne as Grushenka, troubled during a dress rehearsal by the arrangement of the bed sheets and the uncomfortable mattress she had to lie on, called out, "Aren't you going to do something about this?" Copeau, hidden in the dark of the house, did not answer. "Monsieur Copeau, Monsieur Copeau," she entreated, "have someone fix this; I can't play the scene on this bed." But Copeau was "absent." This maneuver went on a little while longer. If anyone besides myself knew that Copeau was in fact there, he or she said nothing. Finally Fontanne undertook to do the scene as if nothing were wrong. This is a trick that directors find themselves resorting to at times: they refuse to stop over details that momentarily seem all-important, refuse to be drawn into a discussion over matters which agitated actors complain about but which the directors know will ultimately be taken care of in one way or another.

Copeau made incisive remarks *sotto voce* to me, which I wish he had addressed in less blunt fashion to the actors. Of one who had a beautifully resonant voice he whispered: "He will never act—he's always listening to himself." Of an actor playing a monk: "That is how one walks in trousers, not in a cassock." The Theatre Guild company, in training and spirit, was alien to him and he must have felt that he could never exercise any real influence on it.

The Lunts, especially Alfred (Lynn was the impresario and *grande dame*), were very considerate of all the actors with whom they ever played, particularly of those who had the small parts.

Years later, I was auditioning actors for Sam Behrman's *The Cold Wind and the Warm* at the Morosco Theatre, where Lunt was then appearing. As he approached his dressing room, Lunt noticed a group of actors gathered in the wings, waiting their turn to be heard. "What's going on?" he asked the stage manager. "We're casting a play," he answered. "Oh, they're *reading*," he whispered, adding, in genuine commiseration, "poor bastards."

The Great Russians and Gordon Craig

The Group Theatre's first box-office success, *Men in White,* enabled me to visit Moscow in the spring of 1934 to see what the Russians were doing in the theatre. I had been dazzled by the performance of the Moscow Art Theatre during its 1922 run in Paris, especially by its production of *The Cherry Orchard,* in which Stanislavski, as Gaev, did the unforgettable by restraining himself from bursting into tears in the famous farewell scene.

Stella Adler and Lee Strasberg, who had preceded me to Russia, came with me to Meyerhold's production of *La Dame aux Camélias,* which they had already seen. What struck me most on my first night out in the Moscow theatre was the rapt and excited attention of the audience, its freshness and paricipation. Later I learned that certain authorities did not approve of Meyerhold's producing so bourgeois (and probably "decadent") a play, but that night I saw many in the audience crying shamelessly at the plight of poor, doomed Marguerite Gautier.

The ten productions I attended in two weeks left me with more impressions than I could possibly assimilate, and I resolved to return the next year for a longer visit. On our way back to New York, Stella and I stopped off in Warsaw, where Goebbels, with a Nazi delegation, was ensconced at our hotel. We attended a performance of *The Merchant of Venice,* at which a helpful Polish gentleman sitting beside us explained that the play was by Shakespeare. Then off to Paris for a few days (we thought).

I called on Copeau, who was now a theatre critic for *Les Nouvelles Littéraires.* The first thing he did was apologize for the mildness of his reviews. When one saw so many plays, he explained, and was writing for a public that might be counted on to attend the better ones, one ought not to be overly severe. I tried to convey my enthusiasm for what I had seen of the Russian theatre: the great number and variety of performances, the diversity in the styles of production, the lavishness and inventiveness of the staging, the universal passion for the theatre. Copeau lost no time in suggesting that I see Stanislavski, who happened to be in Paris at the time.

I dropped Stanislavski a note and received an answer by return mail. Stella was shy about accompanying me, but I insisted. When we came upon Stanislavski in his flat, he was ransacking his dictionary for the French equivalent of a Russian theatrical term he might wish to use in explaining his method.

When he looked up and saw Stella with me, he rose to his great height—he must have been six foot four—and addressed himself first to her, saying that he had heard that her father had been a wonderful actor. Then he invited us to the Bois de Boulogne, where his doctor had advised him to sit for several hours every day. He had suffered a heart attack in Moscow the year before and had been ordered to spend a year abroad under a doctor's constant care. The Soviet government had underwritten all expenses. He had passed most of his time in Italy and the South of France and now, before returning to Moscow, he had chosen to stay a few weeks in Paris. The only place he found congenial in all of Europe was Italy; everywhere else, he felt, had been spoiled.

I was touched and amused to see how shy he was as we all went down from his apartment in the lift, one of those tiny cubicles that could hold no more than three. As we entered it, he contrived to keep from being close enough to Stella to touch her.

He was regally handsome, with beautiful white hair and must have had a decided appeal for Stella: her father had also been majestically tall, with snow-white hair. But Stanislavski, despite his imposing figure held erect in perfect relaxation, was somehow reticent, whereas Jacob Adler had never been at all shy with women.

In the park, Stanislavski's doctor sat in attendance nearby, reading a book. Stella said at once to Stanislavski that she didn't like his "system," that in fact ever since the system had been imposed on her she had taken no pleasure in acting.

Stanislavski's reply is by now well known: "Perhaps you don't understand the system. But if it really worries you, forget it."

He offered to rehearse a scene with her so that she might better understand his technique. "I'll take it for granted that you are an accomplished actress," he said. He urged her to choose a scene she had played before, in public, and had been dissatisfied with. As Stanislavski had no English, she chose a scene from a play by John Howard Lawson that she had translated into French. In rehearsing the scene with Stella, Stanislavski outlined, illustrated, and explained the chief elements of his method. To fix the matter in her memory, he drew a chart that Robert Lewis reproduced years later in his book on acting, *Method—or Madness?*

I was not present at these sessions—I had to return to my professional duties in New York—but Stella's account of them was to alter the Group Theatre's rehearsal methods and to a considerable degree help propagate the Stanislavski system in America.

From various books we had read about Stanislavski and from those he himself had written, we had the impression that in his theatre he was something of a tyrant, a feared "boss"; indeed, an actor told me that Stanislavski had greeted his every effort with a cold "I don't believe you." But with Stella and me in 1934, and with Cheryl Crawford and me the following year, he was always simple, direct, easy, and at moments even "cute." I was to discover that nearly all Russian artists are more concrete, straightforward, and unaffected than French, German, and English artists and intellectuals. This was certainly true of Stravinsky, who never in his life expressed himself in the manner Robert Craft ascribes to him.

One afternoon Stanislavski, Stella, and I were joined by Chekhov's widow, the actress Olga Knipper-Chekhova. Stanislavski proceeded to tell us how lazy actors were about perfecting themselves in the externals of their craft. "They will work as much as you please if you speak to them of interpretation, characterization, and the soulful side of their task, but they are neglectful and undisciplined when you ask them to improve their speech or voice," he said, playfully shaking his finger at Knipper-Chekhova, who ducked her head like a contrite schoolgirl. Both she and Stanislavski were then past sixty.

I knew that Stanislavski had always kept aloof from politics. He talked with great respect and affection of Vakhtangov, whom he pronounced his most outstanding pupil, but added in sorrowful disapproval that he had turned "political"; whenever he spoke of artists who had turned "political," he grew sad. As for the new Soviet plays, he stated flatly that they were all false because they were politically motivated.

It was probably tactless of me to question him about his relationship with Stalin. His only comment was, "He's not stupid." To illustrate what he meant, he told me how Stalin had asked his cultural advisers what director or theatre had trained or produced the largest number of fine actors, and how, when he was informed that it was Stanislavski and his Moscow Art Theatre who had done so, he ordered "every actor to study his method." Thus Stanislavski became *persona grata* with Stalin. The great director never had trouble with commissars or other party intermediaries, who realized that he could always call on Stalin and discuss his problems with him.

Still, when any question directly relating to the regime came up, Stanislavski glanced about to see if some stranger might be listening. Once he murmured, "There are things going on . . ." but stopped himself from saying any more.

Stanislavski was unequivocally aware of his upper-middle-class origins as the son of a rich Moscow businessman. Most of the actors of the original Moscow Art Theatre were children of the old middle-class intelligentsia—"Chekhov people"—and thus, according to Stanislavski, not capable of playing Communist roles convincingly. I nodded in agreement and he added, "Still, some of them do." He spoke of the difficulty men of his background had playing peasants. The company had to employ "specialists" for peasant parts. A peasant, he said, is someone who can stand still for hours, gazing off into the distance with such an empty look that no one could ever guess what he was thinking or whether he was thinking at all. Then, looking like a lordly giant, he got up and illustrated the peasant posture in a way I couldn't imagine anyone had ever done better.

I asked him about some of the legendary people he had directed, known, or seen on the stage. Did Gordon Craig, who in 1910 staged *Hamlet* for the Moscow Art Theatre, understand acting? Stanislavski answered that he did. (Craig, when I met him later, was not at all complimentary about Stanislavski.) What did he think of Michael Chekhov, an actor all of us in the Group admired enormously? Chekhov, Stanislavski answered, was an actor of extraordinary talent, especially when he played the weak or nearly feeble-minded; he was an actor, Stanislavski emphasized, not a director, not a teacher . . . an *actor*. "And Chaliapin?" I asked. "Ah," he said, "what a student *he* was! When he was at the dramatic academy, he simply swallowed the teachers and all their instruction! Swallowed them!" Stanislavski imitated the extreme concentration of the young Chaliapin. I have since read that he considered Chaliapin the complete embodiment of what he demanded from an actor, though Chaliapin never studied the Stanislavski method.

French actors, in general highly regarded for their speech and vocal excellence, did not measure up to Stanislavski's standards. "They speak on a five-note range only," he complained. He himself, like Chaliapin, had learned to recite Pushkin satisfactorily, but he admitted that neither he nor Chaliapin had the range for the proper delivery of Shakespeare. He went on to describe the vocal capacity he maintained one needed to do Shakespeare. I was appalled; it seemed impossible of achievement, especially as the great

range and color he specified had also to be emotionally justified.

Our conversations, all in French, extended over several
days. I simply couldn't stop asking questions. At one point
Stella whispered to me, "Why don't you *say something* yourself? You're behaving like a student." "I haven't come to tell
him anything," I said, "I've come only to listen and to learn."

Finally I asked him if my questions were tiring him.
"Not at all," he answered: he often was obliged to talk for
hours at a time. When he felt threatened by loss of voice from
acting and from long sessions of teaching or rehearsal, he did
exercises to fortify and restore the vocal cords. In this way
too he had rid himself of a slight lisp, which recurred whenever he failed to do the exercises.

A question he asked me about Boleslavsky, once a member of the Moscow Art Theatre, with whom I had studied
direction in New York in 1927 and who had gone on to become a Hollywood film director, prompted me to ask why
he himself had never engaged in film work. "I've devoted
my life to the theatre," he said. "How could I begin to study
another art?" Yet he had established an opera studio. Yes,
he admitted, he had done so when he returned from abroad
to discover that his codirector, Nemirovich-Danchenko, had
independently opened an opera studio because, and here he
hesitated, he, Danchenko, had become "interested" in a
beautiful opera star, Olga Baclanova. It was clear that
Stanislavski didn't altogether approve of Nemirovich-Danchenko's opera studio, which in 1925 had played a successful season in New York; it was too "operatic" for him in that
the acting was insufficiently informed with dramatic truth-
fulness.

The last thing Stanislavski said to me on my 1934 visit
impressed me the most: "After all my years of study and
work in the theatre, I have come to the conclusion that I
know nothing about it." This I took to mean that however
much one attempts to seize the essence of an art it always

remains mysterious. The very glamour of the theatre—and of life itself—consists in the fact that neither can ever be fully understood, nor even, for that matter, defined.

To this record of my first contact with Stanislavski I feel impelled to add two anecdotes related to me, one by Theresa Helburn, managing director of the Theatre Guild, the other by Joseph Schildkraut.

During the New York engagement of the Moscow Art Theatre in 1923, Stanislavski went to see the Theatre Guild production of *Peer Gynt* in which the young Schildkraut played the title role. After the performance, he was invited backstage to meet the company. The actors lined up tremulously like a group of children before their headmaster. Stanislavski had a kind word to say to each of them. When he reached Schildkraut he hesitated for a moment, smiled, extended his hand and said, "Ah, your *father* was a great actor."

Miss Helburn, in awe of the perfection in ensemble and the excellence of the individual performances in the Moscow Art Theatre, determined to engage Stanislavski to direct a Guild production. "Do you think," she asked him, "that you could achieve similar results with American actors?"

Stanislavski said, "Yes."

"How long would you need to rehearse?" she asked.

"Two years," he said.

"Two years!" she expostulated. "But that's out of the question!"

"In that case," Stanislavski reassured her, "two weeks."

As a visitor concerned chiefly with the Russian theatre, which was then pre-eminent in Europe, I could not know all that was brewing in the Soviet Union. I saw vitality everywhere, hopefulness in the countenances, an exhilarating and contagious enthusiasm. One day I complained about the unconscionable amount of time it took a waiter to serve a plate of soup at the Hotel Metropole; my dinner companion,

Jay Leyda, an American studying film making in Moscow, patiently explained that the waiters were not interested in my soup. And when I asked, "What are they interested in?" and he replied, "In building Socialism," I did not laugh. The heroic attitude that knows no humor was still impressive in those days. Yet I could not help seeing that the workers were learning their jobs *on* their jobs.

Harold Denny, the chief Moscow correspondent for the New York *Times,* assured me that he was being spied on, that everyone was, but I was not convinced; he hated the regime and everything about it—except its theatre. The truth was that the repression after the assassination of Kirov, the party chief in Leningrad, had already begun, a repression that would soon affect everyone, in every walk of life.

I should have realized that something peculiar and deleterious was going on when, during my second visit, in 1935, a Russian theatre student told me that the "experimental" productions of Meyerhold, Okhlopkov, and other adventurous directors he admired were now being frowned upon as "formalist," which connoted something much worse than an aesthetic misdemeanor. But there were as yet no overt signs of change; these did not become marked till about 1937. To my innocent eyes the theatre and the aspect of the streets were even more joyous than they had been the year before.

The Russians' favorite playwright was Shakespeare. The tenth-year jubilee of the Theatre of the Revolution, a new theatre devoted to plays about the revolution, was celebrated by a production of *Romeo and Juliet,* the most elaborate and exciting mounting of a Shakespearean play I had ever seen. And Gordon Craig, who was in Moscow at the time, told me that the Jewish Chamber Theatre production of *King Lear* was the best Shakespearean production *he* had ever seen. I went to the theatre thirty-five times during my five weeks in Moscow, and still I did not see half the plays there were. It would have taken six months to see everything, since all the theatres offered their plays in repertory on alternate nights and there were at least three productions in each theatre's schedule.

With Cheryl Crawford, the third of the "triumvirate" that oversaw the affairs of the Group Theatre, I interviewed all the leading figures of the Soviet theatre.

I had persuaded Paul Strand to join us in Moscow; he accompanied Cheryl and me to the theatre and enjoyed what he saw, but I was eager for the Russians to get to know *his* work. I arranged for him to meet the Russian theatre critic Boris Alpers, whose admirable essays on Russian stage directors and actors Lee Strasberg had had translated for us in the early Group Theatre days, and, more important, Sergei Eisenstein, whose *Potemkin* had exercised so signal an influence on film making the world over.

The photographs Strand showed at Boris Alpers's apartment were luminous both in their delicate sensibility and in their gravely contained power. Alpers studied them with penetrating attention. "He makes tragic landscapes," he said, which was true enough. "He ought to include people," he added, implying that the photographs lacked a social dimension.

When I returned to Moscow in 1963, Alpers was a professor at the official state school of the theatre. I was glad to see him again; he was a critic of acute perception. But when I addressed him in French he answered in Russian, claiming that he did not understand French. I reminded him that we had spoken only in French on the night of Strand's visit and on the few other occasions when we had met. Then he said, "I've forgotten my French." I think that he insisted on his ignorance of the language for two reasons. If we had spoken French, the two colleagues who were with him and the Russian interpreter who was with me would all have been excluded from the conversation. Also, the propaganda against "cosmopolitanism" instituted in the latter years of Stalin's rule, though it had to some extent abated, made it inadvisable for Russians in the Soviet Union to use any language other than their own when speaking to foreigners.

Strand's visit to Eisenstein was more promising. I was surprised to find that whereas Alpers lived in a relatively comfortable and pleasant apartment, Eisenstein occupied one room of a flat shared by a number of families. I wondered if this meant that Eisenstein was out of favor at the moment, or if it was just that Alpers was a married man and Eisenstein a bachelor. In 1935 there was still a shortage of living space in Moscow, and the breaking up of apartments into single rooms for the various tenants was almost as common then as it had been just after the advent of Soviet power. Presently Eisenstein explained that he was soon to be moved to more adequate quarters. But he seemed perfectly satisfied with his single room. Books were piled high along the walls and even in the middle of the room. Roaches crawled on the floor, and Eisenstein, amused, pointed them all out to us. He was sturdy, stocky, square, with something of the aesthete and the intellectual about his face, with its broad forehead and great shock of disheveled hair.

He seemed preoccupied with the subject of pathos. "What is pathos?" he asked several times. We could give him no quick and easy answer—and what answers we eventually and tentatively did offer failed to satisfy him. "I have been studying the matter for some time now," he said. "All these books deal with it." I noticed that the volumes crowding the small room were in several languages—mostly French.

Eisenstein examined Strand's photos with a sobriety that bespoke both caution and respect, or caution occasioned by respect. Opinions of all kinds in the Soviet Union were advanced with utmost reserve. This, I believe, was due not solely to the political significance attached to all artistic manifestation. Throughout Russian history, art has never been viewed as simply a source of pleasure or entertainment;

it has been judged in terms of content beneficial or deleterious to living or being.

Eisenstein said even less about Strand's photographs than
Alpers had. This might have been considered an affront, but
I later heard that Eisenstein invited Strand to remain in
Russia to work with him. At the end of his brief stay in
Russia, though he maintained a receptive attitude, Strand
was dissatisfied, almost suspicious of its too narrow, socially
mechanistic approach to all phenomena, an approach inim-
ical to the more idealistic and aesthetic atmosphere of the
Stieglitz circle in which he had been reared.

In later years, however, Strand became so attracted to
the rigorous logic and monolithic completeness of the then
prevailing Soviet-minded ideology that he cooled not only
toward the Stieglitz circle, but also toward the Group Theatre,
which he had championed. He saw Stieglitz's world and the
Group as suffering from various sorts of middle-class taint.
Strand's nature craved a strictly binding faith in an organized form such as a church or a special order, and in the
Soviet doctrine he found it.

That spring of 1935, at the Maryinsky Theatre in Leningrad, at a performance of Tchaikovsky's *Pique Dame,* I
stopped to speak for a moment to Edmund Wilson, at whose
New York apartment I had met a good many American
writers who were toying with Communism. In 1932, in the
foyer of the Guild Theatre, during the intermission of a
performance of Denis Johnston's *Moon in the Yellow River,*
a play about the conflict between industrial materialism and
Irish mysticism, Wilson had shouted out to me, "Don't you
think that Communism is the only solution?" (I shall never
forget—as a sign of the times—the evening not long before
this when Wilson attended the Group Theatre performance
of John Howard Lawson's *Success Story:* on the line "There's
nothing in the world so rotten as business," he applauded;
someone else hissed.) But now in Leningrad, just three years
later, it was evident that his enthusiasm for Communism

was waning, for reasons that appeared to be less political than literary: he was put off by the tendency in the Soviet theatre to revise texts to suit the momentary party line.

Cheryl Crawford and I were granted an interview with Meyerhold; we had seen ten or more of his productions. His career as a director went back as far as 1902, the year he left the Moscow Art Theatre, where he had played Treplev in the original production of *The Sea Gull* and Tuzenbach in *The Three Sisters*. In my experience of the theatre, Meyerhold was the greatest of all stage directors. His productions both before and after the revolution anticipated almost everything we consider avant-garde in the theatre today. There was a technical mastery and artistic inventiveness in his work that no one since has equaled.

At the time we met him, criticism of Meyerhold had already begun; in 1938 it would lead to the closing of his theatre and finally to his imprisonment. A party bigot took me aside to denounce Meyerhold's bourgeois ("stylized," "mystical") tendencies; he was particularly outraged by Meyerhold's choice of *La Dame aux Camélias* for production in his theatre. Meyerhold was well aware of these attacks and defended himself by explaining in German to Cheryl and me, as he had already explained publicly, that while the form of the play was old, its content, particularly as he produced it, was still relevant to Soviet audiences.

The point of the Dumas *fils* play, Meyerhold maintained, was the wretched and contemptible bourgeois attitude toward women: when Armand believes himself betrayed by Marguerite he flings money in her face, and so on. But, Meyerhold went on to say, there was a further social intention in his production. In the early years of the Bolshevik regime, the relation between the sexes had become too crudely, too functionally, physical. He called this attitude "biologic." It had its positive side, he allowed, but it had finally resulted in shabby promiscuity. His production was intended to convey the mutual regard that ought to obtain between the sexes. To explain what he meant, he called our attention to a charming little gallantry: Armand, helping Marguerite into her coat, carefully buttons it for her! It was unthinkable in the Soviet Union to sound the slightest note in any artistic event without making some didactic emphasis.

Meyerhold was far more erudite and formally cultivated than Stanislavski. (When I asked Alpers about Stanislavski's education, he said: "He has probably read no more than two hundred books in all his life, but he has studied those books more closely than anyone else.") Meyerhold had devoted himself to a free reinterpretation of the great classics of the theatre. I should add that his transformations of such works as *The Inspector General* and Ostrovski's *Forest,* though vilified by conservative and academic critics, were true to the spirit and character of the original plays. Meyerhold told us that, although all he would need to do an interesting production of an ordinary contemporary play was six or eight weeks of rehearsal, he had spent years thinking about *The Inspector General.* He was then involved with a production of *Othello,* which had preoccupied him for a decade, but he was never able to fulfill his dream of mounting the play or even of seeing the completion of the new theatre building he had designed.

Meyerhold's rebellion against the cultural authorities and his ridicule of "Socialist realism" at a time when he was expected to humble himself in apology for his "deviations" led to his arrest. Only after the Twentieth Congress, in 1956, wherein Khrushchev exposed the malefactions and crimes of the Stalinist era, was Meyerhold "rehabilitated." But by then he was dead; it is more than likely that he had been shot in a Siberian prison camp about 1940.

Others were luckier than Meyerhold, or less courageous. The director Okhlopkov, who in 1934 was head of the Realistic Theatre, which was anything but traditionally "realistic," had been rehearsing an "unorthodox" *Othello* for nearly a year; it was about to open when an injunction against it was issued. In a matter of days Okhlopkov tried to adjust the production so that it might escape the accusation of being "formalist"; the effort caused him to suffer a nervous breakdown.

When I met Okhlopkov in Moscow, in 1963, he was running his own company in what was known as the Mayakovsky Theatre. He immediately proclaimed himself a disciple of Meyerhold, but the next day he took pains to correct himself: he was, he said, a disciple of Meyerhold *and* Stanislavski. Both men, he explained, were pursuing the same goal, but each began at a different starting point. I gathered that this equivocation on Okhlopkov's part was required for ideological "correctness."

Cheryl Crawford's and my last interview with Stanislavski took place in his home, now the Stanislavski Museum. He was one of the few artists allowed to have a whole house to himself. There was a special room designed for rehearsals, from which, because of the precarious state of his health, he ran his theatre; his doctors feared that a visit to the theatre itself might prove too exciting and bring on another heart attack.

Stanislavski asked eagerly after Stella, and inquired about the Group's progress. I told him that I had just mounted *Awake and Sing!*, my first professional production, by Clifford Odets, who had been a member of our acting company since its beginning in 1931. "And is he still acting?" Stanislavski wanted to know. Before I could answer, he went on, "He should. It will help his playwriting."

He asked what I thought of the productions I had seen in Moscow. I spoke of the remarkable *Romeo and Juliet* at the Theatre of the Revolution, particularly of the splendid settings and costumes. "Yes," he said, "the scenic arrangements are ever more magnificent in proportion to the mediocrity of the acting. Whenever in our theatre, for example in our production of *Pickwick Papers,* we use our younger, less experienced actors, we take care to construct elaborate, eye-catching scenery." Though Stanislavski knew everything about the mechanics of the theatre, his main interest was the actor. He told Herbert Biberman, a young American who in 1928 had come to study the Soviet theatre, "If you came to learn directing, watch Meyerhold. If you're interested in acting, stay with me."

He claimed that the rehearsals he enjoyed the most— the ones he considered the most fruitful—were those he held in the intimacy of his home. When there was trouble at the theatre, he was notified at once by phone. If the difficulty concerned an actor or any other member of the artistic staff, the person was required to report to him—always a scary moment for the troublemaker. Stanislavski was reputed to be far more severe than his debonair associate, Nemirovich-Danchenko. (Something of Stanislavski's imperiousness has been amusingly caught, and caricatured, in *Black Snow,* a novella by the playwright and novelist Mikhail Bulgakov.)

Cheryl and I met Danchenko at the twenty-fifth preview of *Romeo and Juliet,* a production that had been in rehearsal for nine months. Poetry readings had been held to perfect the actors in the speaking of verse; every one of Shakespeare's plays had been perused; professors had been brought in to lecture on Shakespeare's England and his theatre as well as on the modes and manners of Renaissance Italy. The superb production, which was supported by state funds, made Cheryl sick with envy; neither of us had seen anything remotely like it before—or since, for that matter.

After each act the distinguished guests were invited to a reception room off the main lobby and theatre restaurant, and here Cheryl and I met Nemirovich-Danchenko. He was trim and elegant with a finely cut old-time aristocratic beard; he was in fact a descendant of Russian nobility. He asked questions of the director—for instance, in the scene of the masked ball, why does Romeo appear as a bear and Tybalt as a bat? We could not understand everything the two men said to each other, but their postures made the relationship between them entirely clear. Danchenko sat cross-legged with a taken-for-granted superiority, asking his questions with a smile and offering his suggestions with unruffled calm. The director, who was half Danchenko's age, leaned forward with a reverence approximating anxiety, rather like a student being quizzed by a kindly but formidable professor.

Danchenko had overheard some of my conversation with Cheryl and now turned to ask us, in English, what we thought of the production. Influenced by the relaxed atmosphere in Russian theatre circles, we answered simply that we liked it, whereas in New York we might well have exclaimed, "It's great!" and gone on to elaborate. "Yes," said the Russian master, "it's nice. Only," he added, "I wish some of the text were better spoken. I missed some of the lines." This brought to mind Stanislavski's complaint to me the year before about the young actors' poor diction, which he "forgave" on the grounds that "they were not of a generation brought up by governesses and well-trained or meticulous teachers."

Danchenko said something about having seen Duse as Juliet. "How was she?" I asked.

"Her partner—the Romeo—was very bad," he answered.

"Yes," I urged, "but how was *she?*"

"Her partner was bad," he repeated.

It then occurred to me that what Danchenko meant was that no actor could be good by himself; he or she could be good only as part of a team, an *ensemble.*

We heard that Gordon Craig was also staying at the Hotel Metropole and asked to see him. He sent a note saying that he would be glad to meet us in the restaurant. When he arrived I noticed that he had a little card with our names scribbled on it: Clurman, director; Crawford, producer.

He was tall, with long silvery hair and a head of classic

beauty. At sixty-three he could still arouse admired attention anywhere. He looked a sage, a romantic figure, an artist in a way very few artists really do. One day, seeing him rage at the desk clerk of our hotel that a car he had ordered was late, I thought the very heavens would thunder; the clerk at any rate quaked.

Craig was positive and unequivocal in all his opinions. Politicians, he declared with an illustrative gesture, were pygmies compared with artists. When Aaron Copland said to me years before that art was my religion, I had objected, but it could be truly said of Craig that art was his religion. He dismissed Stanislavski as a mere "businessman"—this not only contradicted what he had written about Stanislavski in his book *The Theatre Advancing,* but was the very opposite of the respectful way Stanislavski spoke of him. The modern playwright Craig admired most was Synge. The Moscow production that had excited him the most was the Jewish Chamber Theatre's *King Lear* with Solomon Mikhoels as Lear. "Jews," he said, confidentially, "understand emotion."

I saw *Lear* as soon as I could and went back afterward to meet Mikhoels in his dressing room. He was fervid about what the Soviet Union had done in establishing the Jewish Chamber Theatre. The Jews in czarist times, with a few exceptions, had been restricted to performing in their own Yiddish-language theatres, and lived in small restricted towns. Now, not only did they have their own theatre in Moscow, frequented in large part by non-Jews, but as actors they were privileged persons, employed fifty-two weeks a year and given such benefits as paid vacations and free medical care. In the thirties, actors and theatre folk generally—along with engineers—constituted the elite of Soviet society. Stanislavski, Meyerhold, and Tairov were among the few private citizens allotted limousines. It is not much of an exaggeration to say that Mikhoels was in seventh heaven.

Seven years later, during the war, when Mikhoels was sent to America to speak to American Jews about the Soviet

Union's benefactions to Soviet Jews, there were facts to bear witness to his words. Was it not true that, as Odets had proclaimed in *Waiting for Lefty,* in the Soviet Union "anti-Semitism was a crime against the state"? After the war, Stalin began his savage purge of Jews, whose persistent nationalism, or consciousness of their Jewishness, he was determined to wipe out. The Jewish Chamber Theatre was closed, and Mikhoels, like many other Jewish artists, was exiled and then, I suppose, killed.

King Lear was as extraordinary as Craig had led me to believe. We do not recognize many truly great works of art at our first contact with them. Mikhoels's Lear was not like anything I could have imagined. He himself was no more than five foot two, and bald and ugly to boot. His Lear was beardless, and looked and acted more like a mad clown than a foolish king; from the very first, he was a wild man. In the hurricane, he became a wisp blown in all directions; there was strength only in his inner frenzy, which matched the storm of nature.

What did all this mean, I wondered. When I saw Craig again a few days later, I admitted to him that *Lear* had put me off. He made a contemptuous gesture: I was a Philistine! Well, he was right to dismiss my superficial reaction. I had not yet fathomed Mikhoels's interpretation.

It was Boris Alpers who helped me to understand it. Mikhoels's Lear was puny and insignificant, a primitive who thought himself all-powerful and deserving of worshipful love because he was a king. In the scene in which Lear divides his kingdom among his daughters, Mikhoels raised an enormous sword of gold—so heavy he could hardly lift it —and split a crown in several parts as a symbol of his omnipotence. But once he gave the royal emblem away, he was subject to the humiliations that follow when one is dispossessed of ego. Now he was nothing, a rag and tatter of humanity, "a poor forked animal." Only when he was healed by Cordelia's love was his ego restored and his manhood regained.

Alpers's elucidation of the production made me realize anew the true function of the critic: it is not to criticize, that is, to find fault, to deliver opinion of praise or blame, but first of all to illuminate, to offer insight into the object of attention.

Craig could not forgo asking me what sort of person the imaginative designer Lee Simonson was. In his book *The Stage Is Set,* Simonson had attacked Craig as a thoroughly impractical visionary whose drawings for projected settings could not possibly be realized on any existing stage. Though Craig smiled as he asked about Simonson, one could see that he deeply resented Simonson's misunderstanding of his aims. The impracticality of Craig's designs for specific use in production was quite beside the point; the designs indicated a new direction and a new aesthetic without which the work of such artists as Robert Edmond Jones or Simonson himself could never have evolved. Men like Craig or Artaud are not great for what they did as much as for what they portended. Though I admired Simonson, I was tempted to cite for Craig what a Hungarian director had said to me when Simonson's book appeared: "I prefer what Craig did not do to what Simonson does."

Face to face with Craig, I understood more than ever his giant contradictions—his lofty idealism, his prophetic role as an artist, his devotion to a concept of the theatre without which all playmaking becomes trivial, and also his enormous egotism, his self-protectiveness, the canny common sense underneath the posture (and the *reality*) of his grandeur. To neglect the essence of Craig's teachings—which go far beyond the limits of scene design—is to condemn oneself forever to a basic ignorance of the nature of the theatre.

I also met Sergei Prokofiev. On his arrival in the United

States, where he was hailed as one of the "wild men" of music, he had seen and become enamored of Stella Adler and arranged to give her piano lessons; she never failed to remind me that whenever she struck a false note, he would kiss her hand. When Stella and I were in Moscow, she looked him up.

I remembered my young man's wonder at the first Paris performance under Koussevitzky of Prokofiev's *Scythian Suite*. I also remembered how eager Koussevitzky had been to introduce Prokofiev to the young American composer Aaron Copland, whom he had "discovered": Prokofiev looked through a Copland score and said only that he had found one passage he particularly liked. (Copland remarked later on that this was the section of the score that most resembled Prokofiev's own music.) I had seen a note Prokofiev had written to Paul Bowles, who in 1930 had sent him a minuet in which five measures were repeated over and over again. "I have never been able to judge a composition on the basis of five measures," Prokofiev's note began, "and never has a composer sent me five measures as a basis for the judgment of his music."

Prokofiev invited Stella to a play at the Moscow Art Theatre, but he had not taken the trouble to reserve tickets. When he arrived at the box office, he was told that the house was completely sold out; the Moscow Art Theatre, and most of the other theatres in Moscow in those days, were nearly always sold out by performance time. Prokofiev said, "I am Prokofiev!" With this, he turned to Stella and confessed, "I feel very nervous about this—like stage fright. I am anxious to know if my name counts here." Without further ado, the box-office lady gave him tickets for the two best seats in the house.

After the performance I joined Stella and Prokofiev for supper in the Metropole dining room. He refuted me when I made some slightly adverse remarks about Shostakovich's *Lady Macbeth of Mtsensk*. Tasting his champagne, he remarked, "As champagne it is not very good; as wine it isn't bad." When Stella asked, "Where exactly is White Russia?" he answered, "In Paris." Stella said that he had made a wise decision in returning to the Soviet Union. "I made two wise decisions," he corrected her. "The first was to leave for France."

Group Theatre
Marginalia

Though the Group Theatre had its unofficial beginnings in 1928 with Lee Strasberg, Sanford Meisner, Morris Carnovsky, and Franchot Tone and came to an official end in 1941, its inner life spills over to the present day. In a personal way, the Group Theatre has never ceased being. With its feuds, its celebrations, its cult, its derelicts, its legends, and its binding love, it is like a close-knit family.

I realized how like a family we are when, a few years ago, one of the very few Group Theatre actors who had never "made it" called me in desperation: he was broke, he was ill, he had been abandoned. I gave him my time, money enough for clothes and a good doctor, and my patience. A young man who witnessed these transactions wrote a play about them, called *The Sponsor*.

When the actor, astounded by what to him seemed inexplicable generosity on my part—for we had not been close since the period of our professional association and I had more or less lost track of him in the years that followed—asked me why I was doing so much for him, I answered, "Because I'm crazy." He burst into laughter; he had hoped I would reply, "Because I love you!" The tie that bound us all together in the Group Theatre days was more binding than any of us had supposed and not unlike the spiritual unity that was central to our conception of the theatre. The Group Theatre was a home. The house collapsed, but the feeling for the home—in which there was also, and necessarily, anger and frustration—never vanished altogether.

In *The Fervent Years* I described, in the kind of detail appropriate to a history, the Group as a theatre organization and as part of the cultural aspect of the thirties. Here I shall set down some brief sketches of people in and around the Group at the height of its activities, though it would be years before I knew some of them intimately.

I am always amused when I hear Leonard Bernstein speak of his first contact with the Group. He was then either a senior at Harvard or a recent graduate. Copland had described Bernstein to me as an extremely talented student conductor under Koussevitzky at the Tanglewood school of music in the Berkshire Mountains of Massachusetts, where Copland had been teaching composition. He asked me to permit Bernstein to attend one of the rehearsals of Odets's *Rocket to the Moon,* which were then being held in Boston.

As Lenny tells it, with some degree of exaggeration, he expected to find the Group Theatre atmosphere one of supreme intellectual exaltation. But as he waited to hear me explain a scene in which Luther Adler was involved, he heard Luther complain, "But Harold, I don't know what my action ["action" is a Stanislavski term indicating a character's immediate will] in this scene is supposed to be," and then me answer, "Dammit, Luther, it should be perfectly clear: you want to *fuck* the girl." Luther, satisfied with the interpretation, responded with "Ah, now I understand."

In those far-off days when profanity in public places was little heard, I was constantly shocking my actors by my enthusiastic or exasperated recourse to four-letter words. Carnovsky told me one day that I simply had to give this up or he would leave the company. But when Elia Kazan took up the unseemly practice, and then, or so it seemed, the whole world did, I became much more chaste in speech.

I began to see Lenny more and more often at various musical events; this was, of course, before he had started playing a central role in them. Copland asked me what I thought of him. "He is doomed to success," I replied. Copland wanted to know why I thought so. "He has a lush personality." When these observations were reported to Lenny, he was not at all displeased.

I have always been astonished at Lenny's vulnerability to the slightest bit of adverse criticism—for instance, my captious notice of *West Side Story.* I alone among reviewers had reservations about it. Lenny said he'd never speak to me again. Indeed, the next time I saw him, he gave me what is known as a dirty look. A long time later, all was forgotten or forgiven and he resumed his fond relation to me, embracing me—as he does all his good friends—every time we meet. A playwright is rarely reviewed more than once a season; a conductor is reviewed almost every week of the year. And Lenny reads his reviews after each concert or operatic performance—never failing to writhe with displeasure at any demur. I know that this is common among artists, yet I never cease to wonder at it. For surely Lenny's concerts or compositions will last longer than any reviews of them. But the artist is forever young and never learns that he who does not experience a setback will always remain an amateur. After each review he should be made to repeat to himself, along with Tristan Bernard: "A critic is a virgin who wants to teach a Don Juan how to make love." Beethoven insisted that he never paid the slightest attention to anything a critic ever said about him. I don't believe it, but it is a state of mind an artist should do everything in his power to cultivate.

Edmund Wilson, who had published some of my early book reviews when he was literary editor of the *New Republic,* lived below me on West Fifty-eighth Street in 1932. I had admired his play *The Crime in the Whistler Room*, in which his first wife, Mary Blair, had acted, and I knew he was eager to become involved with the theatre again. I decided to commission him to write a play for the Group Theatre.

As luck had it, he had just finished *Beth and Bess,* a bitter comedy about the transition from the boom of the twenties to the bust of the thirties—symbolized by a two-room apartment, rented by a cartoonist much in vogue, of which one room was sumptuously furnished and the other almost bare. The model for the cartoonist was commonly thought to be Ralph Barton (once married to Carlotta Monterey, who subsequently became Mrs. Eugene O'Neill), who committed suicide just after Wilson's play was finished. Some of the play's scenes—especially the one in which a character described the fraudulent manner by which large real-estate enterprises were floated in the twenties—were not only socially telling but also hilarious.

I rather liked the play, though it was technically unfinished. But my associates Crawford and Strasberg didn't. Strasberg went so far as to call it "disgusting." With an honesty bordering on stupidity, I reported this to Wilson with my apology for rejecting the play. He listened in silence, but as I was about to leave his apartment he burst forth in an outraged harangue beginning with "Who the hell does Strasberg think he is, calling my play disgusting?"

What I learned from this was that one must never be utterly frank with any writer if one is not laudatory about his work. Wilson's prose was always balanced, always cool and calm, but his temperament was frequently the polar opposite. He was a tormented man, capable of hysterical fits of anger, even of violence.

There were the savage and sometimes drunken quarrels I overheard from my bedroom window, directly above his—quarrels that ended with his tearing the curtains from their rods and with the frightened cries of his wife, Margaret, who was later to die from the effects of a fall on the stone steps of the apartment house. Both she and Wilson drank nonstop; once he came upstairs to visit Stella and me, spoke a few hurried words, and fell down drunk in front of us.

When I visited him ten years later at his summer house in Wellfleet, on Cape Cod, I saw that he had learned to keep his temper. By now he had taken on the gravity of a recognized authority. He murmured, half to me, half to himself, "Things are getting to the point where life is unbearable." He was speaking, I felt, not so much of his own life as of the burden of the times; he took things hard. (There was something of this in his next play, *The Little Blue Light*, which he wanted me to direct.) No matter how turbulent his feelings, how dim his view of things, his writing, especially his critical writing, was dispassionate in tone, intellectually objective, reserved, and clear. In one of his most famous essays, "The Wound and the Bow," he decried the notion that the classic Greek tragedies were majestically "Apollonian"; he found imprecation, awful rage, howling hurt in them. Through Wilson I came to appreciate the gap that exists between an artist's personal self and his art and to wonder where the bridge is. Very little creation takes a direct route. My father used to say that an artist should not make his problems the world's, but, rather, the world's problems his. We may perhaps find in this distinction one difference between the romantic and the classic temperament.

Another person the Group Theatre brought me into contact with during its first days was Frank Lloyd Wright. He had heard of the adventurous new organization and invited its three young directors to see a model for a theatre building he had recently designed.

Galvanizing as the model was, I must confess to having been more impressed by him than by it; he was tall and noble looking, with a collar of special make around which he wore a handsome neckpiece resembling an ascot, but rather more opulent, like the neckerchiefs associated with "bohemians," yet it was neither one nor the other. He might have been described as an American aristocrat of the mid-nineteenth century. He was superbly dressed withal; in short, an august figure. Everything about him was imperious: his self-assurance, his finely modulated voice, his poise.

The model he showed us (not the one for the theatre he later built for Paul Baker in Dallas) was palatial, absolutely Roman in spaciousness, modern in concept. "It's great," I managed to say (Crawford and Strasberg remained silent, in awe of both the man and the edifice), "but where can such a theatre be placed in our city?" "Oh," he said in scornful grandeur, "if you wish to remain in the rubbish, noise, and filth of New York, you are not as advanced a group as I thought you were."

Alas! Alas! We functioned in the rubbish, noise, and filth, not only without a splendid new building but also without subsidy or funds of any kind.

Two other people closer to the Group, good friends in fact, were Gerald Sykes and Dorothy Norman. Sykes, a young man from Covington, Kentucky, and a friend of the Liveright editor Louis Kronenberger, was Copland's and my constant companion. He looked up to us because we had been to Paris and had had an experience of the arts different from his own. There was something Flaubert-like about his commitment to the very *material* of literature: words. I remember his spending hours one day trying to work out how to convey dampness verbally, an exercise I found both admirable and funny.

Hoping he might someday write a play for us, I made Sykes a Group Associate, along with Copland, Stieglitz, Waldo Frank, and others. He did write a few plays, one of them about the French situation in Algeria before the final conflict (he had spent several years in Algeria with the State Department), but none were ever produced. Sykes now lectures at the New School for Social Research on literature and the various theories of psychoanalysis. In addition to novels, he has written several volumes of cultural criticism. His work and conversation are marked by a meticulousness of expression and thought altogether exceptional in literary circles today. He was the first American to hail the special genius of Kafka, in a review of *The Castle* published by the New York *Times.* "I didn't understand the book," he told me, "but I felt greatness in it."

In the Group days, Sykes and I—more than Copland—used to frequent An American Place, where we listened for hours to Stieglitz and learned so much about painting. There we met Dorothy Norman, a Philadelphia girl married to one of the Sears, Roebuck heirs, whom I sometimes think of as a collector of souls. She was magnetized by outstanding personalities and proceeded to cultivate them. She possessed a gift for recognizing them from the first. In the house in the East Seventies that William Lescaze built for her, she has over the years kept a salon for politicians, sociologists, philosophers, educators, and artists. It was at her house that Sykes met the painter Buffie Johnson, who was to become his wife. On one of my recent visits, Indira Gandhi—Dorothy had long been a great friend of her father, Nehru—addressed many of Dorothy's spiritual colleagues—among them Alfred Kazin, Allen Ginsberg, Edward Albee, and Max Lerner—and answered questions about the crises that culminated a few days later in the India-Pakistan war. I was much more impressed with Mrs. Gandhi's terse and lucid answers than with the questions, but it nevertheless occurred to me that the generally apolitical intellectuals present were politically a lot more astute than our government proved to be. . . . I was struck by the fact that while Mrs. Gandhi was proud and confident of her country, we Americans appeared sorrowful and shamefaced about ours. Pride in her land lent her added stature, our attitude toward our own country seemed to diminish us. Mrs. Gandhi ended the colloquy by saying, "You've asked me many things. Now let me ask you something. What is the women's liberation movement?" No one ventured to answer.

Dorothy Norman championed the Group Theatre from its beginnings, and encouraged me always with her warm regard. I laughed at her a lot, because of her endless seriousness. I am not myself perpetually high-minded.

And then of course there were the Adlers! Stella Adler was my "girl" and then for many years my wife. Bobby Lewis, one of the Group's actors and the Group director of Saroyan's first play, *My Heart's in the Highlands,* on hearing that I was writing a book about the Group's doings, suggested that I call it "My Wife in Art," in contrast to Stanislavski's *My Life in Art.*

Of Stella's "grand" style I shall give a single illustration.

The period between the dissolution of the Group in 1941 and the start of my career as a "Broadway director" was particularly arduous, as I was very poor. When Stella complained that it had been a long time since I had given her a gift of any kind—a jewel, for example—I protested, "But Stella, don't you realize that I have debts amounting to twenty thousand dollars?" "A man of your stature," she flashed back, "should be in debt for a hundred thousand."

The Adlers as a clan—the harmonica virtuoso Larry Adler, asked what his connection was to the Adler acting family, replied, "I'm not an 'Adler,' only a sympathizer"— sometimes exasperated me by the powerful hold their very faults had on me, and I compared them to a litter of cats. Despite the family's extreme individualism and even more extreme disputes, they seemed to dwell in a cozy nook, all heaped upon one another. They wriggled, twisted, parried, shoved, scratched, and flayed, which only testified to their consanguinity and their indissoluble unity. They kept warm together and exuded a most captivating heat. They were a race unto themselves; nothing in the world could separate them. They all loved the theatre passionately, down to its minutest details, and were "idealistic" about it withal. They would talk all through the night, reminiscing, telling tall tales, and, above all, laughing. "We shall laugh our lives away," Stella would say.

The focal point of their lives was their father, Jacob Adler, the "king" of the Yiddish stage; over fifty thousand people attended his funeral in 1926. I met Stella a year later. As a boy I had seen him act, unforgettably, in several plays. He had a magnetism that combined devastating charm with strong physical appeal. (I say "physical appeal" rather than "sex appeal" because to use the more facile catchword would be to reduce something warmly endearing, nobly earthy, paternally encompassing, to the accidental and petty.)

Jacob Adler was a celebrated lover. He had many

children by several women. Men as well as women were attracted to him. There was something maternal in his father-liness, an enormous tenderness. His smile was inescapably seductive. He "seduced" not only his audiences, but his servants, his colleagues, his community, and most of all his family. None of them were immune to his effect, whether they succumbed to it or rebelled. Profligate in everything, he was a man of perilous weakness compensated for only by the amplitude of his gift. His children inherited much of both the weakness and the gift—especially a certain inex-pugnable pride—and what they did not inherit, they made up for by unconscious imitation.

My own deepest regard was for Adler's third wife, Sarah, who lived with Stella and me until she died. She was a pioneer in the establishment of the Jewish theatre in Amer-ica, and one of its first genuinely realistic actors. Jacob Adler might also be called a realistic actor, yet there was in his playing a marked propensity to the romantic which was part of his nature. Sarah was a woman of strong constitution, of energy, will, and hard sense. She was tiny, but her voluptuous figure gave her "size."

She taught Jacob Adler much about acting. He was her second husband; her first had been a manager, the first producer of the Yiddish theatre in America. When she saw Jacob on the stage for the first time in New York—he had made his earliest appearances in Russia and Romania, and then in London—she thought him ridiculous: "He dressed badly," she said, "wore yellow shoes!" She immediately de-termined to marry him, however.

Despite his great popularity, he was never entirely confident of himself. He never believed himself "well liked," and lived in fear of some public rejection. Sarah Adler told me that when he undertook a part in a play by Jacob Gordin, in which he was later to become famous, he broke down in hysterical tears, despairing that he could never do it justice.

She slapped his face. "Of course you can play the part; get up and begin. I shall help you with it." "He had to be treated like a woman," she explained.

When Jacob left her for a while and took to living with a servant-mistress, Sarah formed her own company, with Rudolf Schildkraut, a former Reinhardt star, one of the finest actors in my playgoing experience, and the father of Joseph Schildkraut, as her leading man. She chose and directed the plays, she designed and sewed most of her own costumes, she polished and arranged the fruit sold in the theatre during intermissions, and, of course, she acted the main female parts. Audiences said of her, "She acts the way people act in real life"—which was not characteristic of the acting of the day, either on the Jewish stage or on Broadway.

When I saw her act I observed that her realism—meticulous, subdued, though still intense—never failed to convey a largeness of feeling, the kind of grandeur that comes through only when a sense of life's high drama is present.

From Sarah Adler I learned about tenacity in living, the pride it gives which is also its effect. (One had only to hear her say "I like to eat *mashed* potatoes" to understand what appetite—in every sense—means. At the table I imagined her devouring not only the meal but also the plates, the cutlery, the cloth—and the guests!) She once entered a hospital to have a cataract removed, and the surgeon asked her age. "Seventy," she replied. After the operation, he said in reproof, "You told me you were seventy. It isn't true. You're nearly eighty. Why did you lie?" "Because," she answered, "if I had told you the truth, you would not have operated."

A newspaperman came to interview her. "Madame Adler," he began, "I don't mean to embarrass you, but would you mind telling me your age?"

Without blinking she replied, "Sixty-eight."

"But Madame Adler," the man rejoined, "how can that be? I just asked your son Jack his age, and he told me he is sixty."

"Well," she reasoned unhesitatingly, "he lives his life and I live mine."

No one knew her exact age: some said eighty, others ninety. Till her very last illness she went out every night alone to the Café Royal on Second Avenue, the perenially bubbling meeting place of Jewish actors, journalists, and crackpots, returning home after midnight. She took tango lessons when she was well past seventy. I never saw her— no one ever did—when she wasn't entirely presentable. When Marlon Brando came to the house to visit her granddaughter —now Ellen Adler Oppenheim—in the days when he set the style among young actors in shabbiness of dress, Sarah greeted him, in the expressive contralto of her Russian speech, with "My God, Marlon, you look so *ugly!*"

When her health began to fail, her children insisted that she retire from the stage. The family doctor said she was afflicted with a variety of ailments in most of her vital organs. Though I knew that she had had tuberculosis, as had Stella, I could never think of her as anything but a power-house—not even when I saw her back up against the wall of a building on Fifth Avenue to wait for a sudden pain to pass. I never saw her weep.

I was with her one afternoon when she suffered a dangerous attack of acute indigestion. When the worst spasms were over, Stella pleaded with her to take a sleeping pill. "No," her mother screamed, "if I fall asleep, I'll die." It was clear that she had no intention of doing either.

Jack, the family's prodigal son, was the old actress's favorite child. Once, when he was returning from a long stay in Hollywood, she went to the airport to greet him. After the welcoming embrace, she blurted out, "Jack, you got money, give me. If you got no money, I give you."

One summer Stella went abroad and left me alone with her mother in our new Fifth Avenue apartment, still barely furnished. I lay in bed all day, reading Egon Friedell's *Cultural History of the Modern Age*. Came evening, I grew tired of my seclusion. But I felt guilty about leaving the old woman alone in the apartment. I began to apologize for preparing to go out. "Go out," she said, "and have a ball."

She was more than doughty; she was wise. Stella one day said to her, "You think Harold is a good man. You ought to know that he likes women." "If he didn't like women," her mother snapped back, "he wouldn't like you."

But nothing she said—and she spoke brilliantly about acting—impressed me more than what I heard her tell Stella about how, as one grows older, one's senses and one's organs atrophy. "One becomes like stone," she concluded. What truth there may be in this I can't yet say, but the objectivity of her observation revealed a stoicism that struck me as positively heroic. Whenever Stella, so easily hurt, was seized by a fit of sorrow, her mother would say, "Don't let your pain reach your heart."

There were giants in the earth in those days.

The first play I directed for the Group Theatre, *Awake and Sing!*, was designed by Boris Aronson. He was born in Kiev in 1900, and as a youth served in the Soviet Army. After the revolution, he was trained in his craft by the artists of Tairov's Chamber Theatre in Moscow.

Russian theatre design in those days was extremely stylized and, in the Tairov school, more painterly than architectural. Boris is a painter who in his apprentice days was most attracted to French painting. After leaving Russia, he lived for a while in Berlin and wrote a book about Chagall. When I met him, the painter he preferred was Rouault. Yet the first settings he designed were not at all somber or hectic, but, rather, joyous, often humorous. He was playful, witty, and could freeze a person or event with his tersely articulated insights.

He is an artist always in quest of new modes of expression: paradoxical and imaginative, he has his keen eye and his ever-inquiring mind fixed on the astonishing spectacle of contemporary life. From the first—though his *Awake and Sing!* and other of his early designs for the Group Theatre were more or less traditional—I thought him the most adventurous and interesting of our scene designers. But very few people agreed with me.

His settings were not "jobs," but attempts to seize upon something more than the outward attributes of a play, responses to something more than its specific geographical or technical demands. He wished to penetrate to some essence of which even the playwright himself might not be aware. Think of the huge mirror, both concave and convex, in which the audience saw itself as it entered the theatre in *Cabaret*. He rarely worked from illustrations or historical models. When I asked him to make the setting for William Inge's *Bus Stop* look like an Edward Hopper, he smiled and asked, "Why not like an Aronson?" But "an Aronson" cannot readily be categorized; it always assumes a new look. When one remembers the settings for MacLeish's *J.B.*, or for *Company, Follies,* the opera of *Mourning Becomes Electra,* and *Fidelio,* one understands at once why so many producers and directors both here and abroad (he designed the Peter Hall–Laurence Olivier *Coriolanus* at Stratford-on-Avon) have competed for his services and why so many theatre folk have come to share my estimate of him.

It is the composition of his personality as much as of his art that has always interested and arrested me. But how can I convey its quality, which is a compound of an idealistic quest for meaning in existence and a carefully constructed mask that conceals this quest? Perhaps by quoting him.

"I didn't like Stalin," he once said to me, "because I don't like buttons!" The buttons on Stalin's jacket were the image for him of harsh Soviet conformity. But then he would also say, "What I like about democracy is that it doesn't work."

"*Time* magazine," he once declared, "gives you too much for fifty cents."

He despairs of the theatre not because its professionals condemn its hazards in dismay and disgust, but because the world has become too madly, chaotically complex to be confined by the theatre's frame. "All artists," I once remarked, "have only one basic thing to say." "All I have to say," Aronson mused, "is that everything has become too big."

"The only experimental thing about most experimental theatres today," he has said, "is that they don't pay." When a reporter asked him, "In which of your productions this season did you take the greatest pride?" he answered, "In the plays I refused to design." Also: "I have been accused of being a limited artist. But an artist's limitations are a definition of his strength." On hearing me harangue the Group Theatre acting company, he quipped, "If Harold were not a theatre director, he would have become a Father Diwine." . . . "I used to quarrel with my father [the chief rabbi of Jerusalem], but now that I am older I see that we are exactly alike, except that we belong to different unions."

He is adaptable, but he works best when he is permitted to take his time. To rush him is only to impede him. He is so careful about the smallest details of his settings that he drives the builders and painters who execute his designs quite crazy. But his meticulousness finally wins their respect. "That's the most important ting"—he has never mastered the pronunciation of English—"that's *the* most important ting," he will say over and over about a nuance of decor which no one but he perceives. When objection is taken to his fussiness, he says, "But you don't understand the *w*alues." He examines everything with the same uncompromising visual rigor. Seeing Elia Kazan one day in a bathing suit, he remarked, "You see, from the waist up it is a masterpiece, but from the waist down it is a disaster!"

When Harold Prince, the producer, saw the elaborate and costly mirror being set up for the first time on the *Cabaret* set and asked Boris, "Do you really think it will be worth the trouble and the expense?" Boris replied, "Only if the show is a hit." The Broadway theatre today is a trial to him, an exasperation, and more than that, an agony. Yet he smiles and says, "The theatre is no place for anyone who can't accustom himself to crises."

I think of Boris with special pleasure because he is one of the few artists in America—particularly in the theatre— who have reached the pinnacle of their achievement and ac- claim at the age of seventy. Most of our artists, alas, grow dim in the public eye by the time they are fifty. Shortly after the rush to his telephone and his door on the morning after the opening of *Fiddler on the Roof*—a day of wide recogni- tion for him—he said to me, "Harold, I'm a success and I like it." I remembered how, years before, when I called to ask him to design *Bus Stop,* he had said, "I'm so glad you want me. I haven't had a call all year—not even a wrong number."

Like many artists, Boris is fantastically self-centered, complains endlessly, and is under the impression that others imitate or plagiarize his work. He doesn't realize that if this is so, it is the greatest compliment of all.

CHAPTER 7

The Golden West

"The greatest men," Juvenal said, "who set the great examples, can rise in stupid towns, in Meat Head Land." Hollywood is reputed to be such a place. A loneliness seeps through the thresholds of its gimcrack mansions like fog. Built up as it was, Hollywood often struck me as just so much empty space. The desert underneath affects the atmosphere. Nevertheless, for me it was the fairground of magical encounters and even of worthy action.

I will not speak of *Deadline at Dawn,* a run-of-the-mill RKO movie I directed in 1945, for which Clifford Odets as a favor to me wrote the screenplay. What I remember best about the enterprise is the appearance of someone from the Johnson (censor's) office to protest that Susan Hayward, the film's leading lady, was showing too much cleavage; both Miss Hayward and I insisted that this was one of the more pleasing features of the picture. Miss Hayward has now retired from screen display, but meeting me in the late sixties she took care to assure me that she had become rich and was about to make her first stage appearance, in a road tour of *Auntie Mame.*

Hollywood! When I think of the abstract Hollywood of the New York myth, I think of a story Budd Schulberg told me about his childhood. Son of the man who ran Paramount Pictures in its height and glory, he had become accustomed to receiving expensive Christmas gifts from the studio's stars. Accompanying the gifts were cards inscribed "from Uncle Cary" or simply "Cary," "from Aunt Ginger," or just "Marlene." . . . But the holiday season following Schulberg *père*'s fall from power, though there was the usual Christmas party, Budd received presents from no one except his parents. He wondered why all his nice uncles and aunts had forgotten him. On Christmas holidays thereafter, his parents took to buying lots of presents and signing the cards that accompanied them with the names of the Carys, the Marlenes, and others of the tribe.

When I think of the abstract Hollywood of the New

York myth, I think also of this: in 1941, when I was engaged as an associate producer by Columbia Pictures, I lunched almost every day with Harry Cohn and some of his aides in the studio's commissary for the "brass." One day one of the aides asked me where I had bought the tie I was wearing and what it had cost. I mentioned a shop and the price—eight dollars. "Oh," he admonished me, "a person in your position should buy his ties at ———." He mentioned a more fashionable place, and added, "Ties there will cost you fifteen to twenty-five." Several days later another aide asked me where I had bought the suit I was wearing and what it had cost. I said it had cost a hundred twenty-five. This was frowned upon. "A Columbia Pictures man should have his clothes made at ———." Again, a particular tailor was mentioned. "A suit there will cost you from two to four hundred dollars." And so on, till at the end of two weeks I had received advice on my entire wardrobe.

Even Odets suggested that I take my meals in less modest restaurants. "The scale of life is different out here," he said.

That Hollywood never touched me. I wrote *The Fervent Years* there and had time to read *War and Peace*! I was also at last able to repay many of the debts I had accumulated on behalf of the Group Theatre in those not so far-off days that seemed, however, as distant as the moon.

In Hollywood I came to know Thomas and Heinrich Mann, Lion Feuchtwanger, Max Reinhardt, and Bertolt Brecht, all brilliant men whom the ill wind of Nazism had blown our way.

The two places we met most frequently were Clifford Odets's apartment and Berthold and Salka Viertel's home. Berthold Viertel, Austrian poet, stage and film director as well as critic, had come to America just before Hitler's rise to power, which he had been prescient enough to anticipate (as we may read in Christopher Isherwood's *Prater Violet*, of which Viertel is the pseudonymous hero). He was a man of refined thought, passionate temperament, and generous nature, with a head so noble that a Russian soldier seeing him in Vienna during the Soviet occupation exclaimed, "Mozart!" He was married to the indomitably womanly Salka, who became the hostess nonpareil to Hollywood's most select. The French playwright Marcel Achard told me after the war that it was Salka's Saturday-night gatherings that had made his life in the film capital bearable.

Salka Viertel, whose father had been the only Jew ever elected mayor of a Polish town before the war, left Poland to become an actress on the Austrian and German stages. Eventually she made her way to Hollywood, where for some time she supported her husband and three sons by working as a screenwriter and as a special consultant on most of her great friend Greta Garbo's pictures. An intrepid woman of unquenchable vitality, she was "the mother of us all," the catalyst for the extraordinary assemblage—American, German, French, British—that collected under the Viertel roof: actors, writers, directors, painters, composers—all men and women of both talent and good will, all given to convivially heated argument.

The birthday party Salka organized for Heinrich Mann afforded us a view of ante-bellum German patrician social behavior. First, Thomas Mann rose and, extracting a paper from his dinner jacket, read a high-minded tribute to his older brother: it was Heinrich, he declared, who had been right about the evil genius of Nazism (long ago diagnosed by such men as Heine and Engels); he, Thomas, had been too unpolitical, too optimistic, not sufficiently aware of the poison within the much-vaunted *Kultur*. To this Heinrich, as tall as he was bulky, rose and read out, affectionately, almost reverently, a written encomium about Thomas. Thanks both to the vicious Corporal Hitler and to Salka, the rift between the two brothers was healed in Hollywood.

Sundays at the sumptuous villa in Santa Monica which Franchot Tone and his wife Joan Crawford had just bought contrasted sharply with the Viertels' Saturday nights. Franchot had not forgotten his former Group comrades. Shortly after noon every Sunday, an ample brunch was served, followed by nostalgic theatre talk and reminiscences of the Group's past struggles and pleasures. In the evenings we were shown some recent film. At one of these Sunday afternoons, Stella, who was working in a film for the first time, remarked to Joan that it seemed peculiar, not to say unspeakably strenuous, to get up at six in the morning to go to work *acting*. Joan countered with, "For what they pay us, it's more than worth it," and Stella retorted, "For what they pay *you*."

One afternoon I suggested that Franchot return to the Group. Joan was offended because I had not also invited her to join us. She was so wrought up over this that for some weeks afterward she refused to appear at her own lunches.

Franchot suffered all his life from ambivalence of conscience. He thought of his defection from the stage—particularly the Group stage—as a fall from grace. But he was split in other ways as well. Immediately after he had contributed a thousand dollars for an ambulance for the Spanish Loyalist forces, he rapped out a flip "Foolish, wasn't it?"

Joan was an iron rod of ambition. She was forever "improving" herself. I came upon her one day when she was standing on her head. She was trying to strengthen her neck muscles and to preserve her perfectly trim, steely figure. She also took voice lessons. When I sent Franchot a copy of Stanislavski's *An Actor Prepares,* she grabbed it and read it first; her bold markings covered its pages. Franchot always liked to educate his women, none of whom had had much formal schooling. He was shy of women whose minds might already be as good as or better than his.

I predicted that Joan would one day run MGM. I was wrong: she became one of the heads of the Pepsi-Cola Company instead. She always made me think of a Léger painting in which people are depicted as machines. Yet many years later she came up to me in Sardi's and, thinking I had forgotten who she was, introduced herself: "I'm Joan Crawford," she said.

Franchot confessed to me that the strain of life at home with Joan had impaired his virility. Joan later told me that he used to boast—to prove it was all her fault—that he laid a girl extra in his dressing room on the set every night before going home to her.

Different from both the Viertel and the Tone-Crawford get-togethers were those at Clifford Odets's place. (Odets at that time was married to the actress Betty Grayson, whom I had introduced him to and whom he had made his mistress at their first meeting.) His walls were covered with a large collection of paintings, many of them Klees; I called them the Odets "stamp collection." Later he did collect stamps, and later still, tropical fish.

Though there were few writers at the Odetses', the atmosphere was refreshingly civilized. Hanns Eisler, Boris Aronson, and Charles Laughton were often there, and that delightful actor from Dublin's Abbey Theatre, Barry Fitzgerald, who told me that he thought the Atlantic a much more "interesting" ocean than the Pacific, and, in a tone of profound affection and acute regret, that the Irish loved to "philosophize." That's what we were all doing at the Odetses'— wonderful people, dissatisfied with our lives, much addicted to philosophy—as in Chekhov's plays.

Another frequent visitor to the Odetses' was Charlie Chaplin. I had seen him only once before, at the Plymouth Theatre in 1918, on the opening night of the Arthur Hopkins production of *A Doll's House,* with Nazimova as Nora. He was attracting so much attention that the management begged him to leave. On his way out he stopped to speak to someone in the rear of the house, and I overheard him say he didn't like seeing children on the stage. A year later he made *The Kid.* I was arrested by his princely good looks: his brilliant eyes, jet-black hair, lithe, well-knit body, and perfect profile.

When I saw him again at the Odetses', he was fifty, yet he still looked as handsome and vital as he had more than twenty years earlier.

Chaplin was the life of every party. He could tell stories for hours, holding forth with relentless conviction on his opinions—and they were many. He acted everything out, imitating the manner of every person he mentioned. He did scenes from the old music hall turns he had performed in his youth. One of them was a parody of a French bedroom farce in which he played husband, wife, and lover, all in a Gallic gibberish. Odets and I introduced Laughton to Chaplin one night at Chasen's restaurant in Beverly Hills, and Charlie did his stuff. When he left, Laughton sighed, close to ecstasy, "What an actor!" Chaplin's every conversation was a complete performance.

It was clear that doing a role only once was never enough for him. If you mentioned a picture he had made, he would play most of his part in it all over again for you. "Do you remember the dance with the globe I did as Hitler in *The Great Dictator?*" he asked me, and then and there went through it all again for me. I asked him about *Monsieur Verdoux,* which he had just finished shooting. He began by describing it and then enacted all of it, sequence by sequence. He did not do just his part, but all the parts, including, he made me feel, the very props. When he finished his demonstration—all of it, by the way, at the dinner table—I said, "Charlie, you don't ever have to run the picture for me; I've seen it."

He was always "on," always the star. Odets and I invited him to a friend's place where most of the guests were unknown to him. From the entrance door there was a step down to the slightly sunken living room. He tripped and fell. He immediately got up and performed a jig ending with a sort of arabesque—by way of a "bow"—as if the fall had been part of a prepared number. Irrepressibly he reigned over every gathering, and his audiences, who were the lucky guests, were always spellbound.

Throughout these various antics, his wife, Oona, sat silently by his side, smiling a small benevolent smile. She loved him, she understood him, she knew that nothing could stop him, that nothing should. There is an irony in the fact that of all Eugene O'Neill's children, Oona, whom her father disowned as a reprobate when she married Chaplin, who was three times her age, is perhaps the only one whose life has done him any honor. (Eugene O'Neill, Jr., a brilliant classical scholar, committed suicide; and Shane, the youngest O'Neill son, led a wretchedly drugged existence.)

When I first met Oona, Chaplin was somewhat defensive about the disparity in their ages. He whispered to me, "When I die, she'll be very rich." She was and is a blessed woman. I was infatuated by her sheer beauty. "Her flesh is like soft marble," I said to Chaplin, and the compliment almost brought tears to his eyes. When I visited the Chaplins in their estate in Vevey, Switzerland, a few years ago, I commented on how lovely the very streak of gray in her hair was. "Yes," he agreed, "but it hurts me to see it."

Charlie's opinions were often peculiar and sometimes downright wrongheaded. He had instinct rather than intellect. The political bouts that caused him so much trouble were emotional impulses rather than considered thoughts. In the main, they arose from laudable impulses. He went around delivering muddled speeches in favor of opening a second front some time before America did so. Like many artists, he was fundamentally a benevolent anarchist. He was subversive only of sham and deceit.

After *The Great Dictator*, William Randolph Hearst, who had been friendly to Chaplin, turned on him, causing him all manner of difficulties. Before the war Hearst had been well disposed toward the Fascists. "What have you got against Hitler?" Hearst had asked Chaplin; then, before Chaplin could answer, Hearst broke off with "Oh, I understand: you're a Jew." Charlie had fired back, "That has nothing to do with it." "But are you a Jew?" I interrupted. Charlie paused for a moment and looked at me, surprised, almost baffled, then continued, "Hearst was a monster and a great man."

The interest world figures took in him was a source of great satisfaction to Charlie. He told me that Churchill had once faulted him for failing to answer a letter he had written him. "Think of it," Chaplin said to me, *"Churchill* wanting to hear from *me!"* At that moment he was the poor wide-eyed boy he had once been.

I was not surprised to discover that Charlie didn't like Shakespeare: too many words, he said—they get in the way of the acting. I also understood his reaction to an idea Odets had suggested to me as a subject for a Chaplin film. "Odets thinks you ought to make a picture," I said to him, "about the 'little man' of *The Gold Rush* after he strikes it rich, about what he would then suffer." "It's not true," Charlie snapped. "I like being rich." The point was that Chaplin had fulfilled himself through money and Odets hadn't.

Chaplin's shrewd financial sense has never failed him. I asked him why he hadn't become an American citizen. "The reasons," he answered, "were mostly financial." Passing a school in Lausanne, he remarked to me that all his children had gone there. "An American school?" I asked. "No, no. A French school, because when I die they'll have enough money to paper the walls with. The American school is too easy. They must learn discipline."

Chaplin, who had hoped for a great deal from the Soviet Union, as had many of us when we knew too little, was shocked to learn from me, one afternoon at the Odetses', that prostitution was punishable there. "Girls who choose to be prostitutes," he insisted, "should be permitted to be prostitutes. They like it!"

"There's nothing wrong," I argued, "with a woman accepting money or other gifts from a man she cares for, but a prostitute gives herself only for the money. Her likes or dislikes don't enter into the matter."

"Prostitution is a social necessity," he countered. "We are attractive men," he said, pointing around the room, "and don't require a prostitute's services, but what about the ugly fellow or the poor little lonesome clerk without a friend?" I thought it more funny than flattering that Chaplin should include unprepossessing fellows like Boris Aronson, Hanns Eisler, and me among the "attractive."

I suspected, mostly from the evidence of Chaplin's movies, that though he had always been drawn to women, he had a deep-seated distrust of them. The only women treated sympathetically in them are helpless waifs: the blind, the poor, and the deprived. Monsieur Verdoux murders many women, but not the mother of his children. And he reprieves the woman he has planned to kill when he learns that she is an orphan!

Chaplin used to rail at Roosevelt for taking so long to get us into World War II. "Charlie," I argued, "a statesman can't do everything he feels like doing or believes is the right thing to do any time he wants to. He must be convinced of the country's support." But he would not be appeased. No, he wasn't a politician or a thinker. Merely a great artist.

Kurt Weill was also part of the German emigration. With his usual shrewdness, he had anticipated the rise of Hitler and left Berlin with the first rush of Nazism in 1933. When I met him shortly afterward, the music of his *Three-penny Opera* was already familiar to me through its original recording, which I played over and over in 1932–33. I asked him to compose the music for the Group's 1936 production of Paul Green's *Johnny Johnson*. This was to be Weill's first American score.

Despite this early association and many meetings with him later in New York and Hollywood, Weill never stamped himself on my consciousness as much as Hanns Eisler. They had been rival composers in Germany—both had been associated with Brecht—and each claimed, not surprisingly, that he had influenced the musical idiom of the other. My impression is that Brecht was the master of them both. But it is even more likely that the twenties in Berlin produced a common tone—a "sweet pain" that affected them all. Be that as it may, each went his own route: the more versatile Weill (who could adjust to any situation) to great American success, and Eisler, fiercely individualistic, back to Germany after the war, where he continued his collaboration with Brecht and presently was appointed director of the Berlin Conservatory of Music; he died in 1962 and is now a culture hero in both West and East Germany.

If their destinies were glaringly different, so also were their personalities. Weill—short, thin, almost mousy, with a mouth pursed as if he were withholding some special secret— might easily have passed unnoticed at a large gathering. He never wanted attention. Eisler, on the other hand, could never be overlooked. Whereas Weill spoke in a small, almost piping voice, Eisler always rasped or boomed. Copland remarked that the enormously gifted Weill always reminded him of "the smartest boy in the class," the inconspicuous runt who receives the highest grades. Apparently simple, he was sufficiently deceptive in demeanor to have made an efficient spy; he was someone, one guessed, who could extricate himself from any scrape.

When I asked Weill whom he wanted to direct *Johnny Johnson,* he answered without hesitation, *"You,* of course," though it was common knowledge that he preferred Lee Strasberg, who did eventually direct it. Weill knew how to take advantage of every circumstance. His powers of assimilation were extraordinary: he could write music in any country so that it would seem as if he were a native. He did in fact write some good "French" and "English" music after short stays in Paris and London. If he had landed among the Hottentots, he would have become the outstanding Hottentot composer of the Hottentot theatre. Weill was all theatre— and all "mask."

Eisler lacked Weill's sense of diplomacy. In German and in English, he growled. His tone was often one of mocking exasperation. He was short and tended to fat. He voiced his opinions with violence. He too was sly, but with a much less cagey sense of humor than Weill's. He was crushingly erudite; he remembered everything he had read, and he had read everything. I never saw Weill angry, but Eisler could be ferocious. They had one great gift in common, the gift for survival, although Eisler sometimes drank dangerously.

Eisler was formidably tactless. He could hardly conceal his scorn when a woman I know expressed admiration for Rachmaninoff's compositions. He exploded when Charles Laughton spoke in highest praise of Chekhov, whom he refused to admit into the company of the great dramatists: he preferred Molière! One evening at the Laughtons', I was witness to the worst, the most laughable, of Eisler's outbursts Laughton was the proud owner of a Renoir, which Odets and I had just expressed our genuinely warm response to, much to our host's delight. Suddenly, Eisler lashed out: "It's terrible, it's just terrible. Disgusting!" Amid the general consternation, I asked quietly, "But why, Hanns?" "It's not a landscape, it's a butcher shop," he cried, as if mortally offended. The fleshiness of Renoir's art was repellent to him.

I found his comment instructive: he saw what was in the picture—sexuality in the palette. The difference was that Odets and I admired this quality. Eisler loathed it. He was a sound critic; as I have said, it is not the critic's *opinion* that matters so much as his ability to see the salient ingredient in what he judges.

In 1936 Weill predicted an inevitable struggle between Fascism and Communism. It was clear that he would always remain in the center. Eisler was a Marxist who spoke of the German Communists in terms of "we" and "us." But when questioned by the House Un-American Activities Committee as to whether he had been a member of the German Communist party, he replied, "I'm so undisciplined I could not even be a member of the Boy Scouts." In a radio interview shortly before he died, he said, "The Marxists' attitude toward art is often barbaric." Still, Eisler wrote some inspiring songs on behalf of the international left, marching songs particularly, that I associate with the Spanish Loyalists. He wrote the scores for several of Brecht's didactic plays, most memorably for *The Measures Taken*. If he had written these songs to less risky verses, they would be as universally acceptable as anything by Weill. But they are stronger, more stirring. His knowledge of music and his criticism of it were broad and deep.

Eisler was a devoted pupil of Arnold Schönberg, who was also living in Los Angeles during my time there. He was neglected by nearly everyone except a few sympathetic Americans, Oscar Levant among them, and some German and Austrian refugees, most of whom were quite unable to help him. For a while Schönberg taught at UCLA. Apart from the company of such men as Eisler, who introduced me to Schönberg and asked me to send him a birthday greeting when the old master had reached seventy, Schönberg's lot in the golden West was not a happy one.

One day I asked Eisler if it were possible to understand Schönberg's music and still not like it and was astonished to hear him reply, "That is my case." Eisler appreciated the purely musical advances Schönberg had made in the "grammar" of composition—advances that have become a permanent part of musical speech; he also understood Schönberg's essential content. He said that Schönberg's music conveyed the fear and trembling inspired by the atom bomb before the atom bomb had even been invented. In retrospect, it is easy to comprehend the gap between the two men. Schönberg, the initiator, was an artist who was first of all concerned with being appreciated by an elite; Eisler wished to move the masses. They respected each other, but Schönberg teased Eisler about his leftism. "Joseph II [Emperor of Austria 1765–90] did much more for culture," Schönberg declared, "than Stalin ever will."

One afternoon Copland, Odets, and I accompanied Eisler to Schönberg's living quarters (I rarely thought of any residence in Hollywood as a "home"). Schönberg asked me why theatre didn't occupy the same eminent position in our culture as it did in Europe. I tried to make him understand the suspicion in which the theatre was held by most of the early settlers in the States and how the theatre had developed into show business, that is, entertainment for profit. Schönberg remained indifferent to this explanation; viewing everything in terms of his own career, he believed that with great determination one could accomplish whatever one wished. In Vienna, he said, he had organized modest concerts of his and his pupils' music and slowly, arduously persuaded an important, though still limited, public to value their works. He was convinced that progress in all the arts could be made through the fanatic devotion of a small band committed to a sound ideal. After the ten years of the Group Theatre's struggles, I had become weary of such discussions. So, fresh guy that I was, I suggested we talk about what we all really knew something about—music.

This part of our conversation was very brief: Schönberg had no more inclination to speak about his "field" than I had had to speak about mine. He did say that he considered Arthur Nikisch, Gustav Mahler, and Richard Strauss the greatest conductors, that he admired Toscanini only when he played Verdi, and had greater respect for Furtwängler and Klemperer, especially when they played Beethoven.

While this rather desultory conversation was going on, a tall thin man of perhaps forty hurried through the room. "My son," Schönberg explained, not bothering to introduce us. A few minutes later a child of three or four came running in, howling. Schönberg paused for a moment and said, "Also my son." The kid's noisiness didn't bother him a bit.

As we took leave of Schönberg I couldn't help recalling with a smile the first time I had seen him, at Town Hall in New York, shortly after his arrival in America. An all-Schönberg program had been arranged. One Schönberg piece would have been an excruciating experience for most of the audience, but a whole program of his later works must surely have been torture. After the concert, there was a little party (cake, coffee, drinks) in the upper foyer, and Schönberg, then rather stout and slightly sweaty, went about accepting the congratulations and good wishes of the concert's organizing committee, especially of the women. Extending her hand to the composer, one of the women gushed, "Oh, thank you, Herr Schönberg, for the darling music you have given us."

When Odets recommended Eisler to do the music for *Deadline at Dawn*, which I was directing, he encountered resistance from the head of RKO. Odets insisted that Eisler was first-rate. "If he's so good," the big shot interposed, "why hasn't he any picture credits?" "Because," Odets heatedly shot back, "you haven't used the two greatest composers of our time, Stravinsky and Schönberg, who both live in Hollywood, in any of your films either."

Eisler and his wife, Lou, a Hungarian of immense vitality and humor (somewhat bored with the heroes of the twelve-tone school of music, she later married the Austrian Marxist critic Ernest Fischer, expelled from the Communist party of Austria some years ago for his refusal to constrict art within the boundaries of "Socialist realism"), were practically driven from America by the first assaults of the House Un-American Activities Committee. The Eislers admitted to me on the evening before their departure that they did not want to leave the country. I assured them that returning to Europe was the best thing they could do and that Eisler would find his rightful place there.

I had offered something of the same advice to Fritz Kortner, an actor of great power and broad intelligence, who had come to me in 1946 to ask if I could find a role for him in a Broadway play. I urged him to return to Germany and resume the distinguished career he had interrupted to come to Hollywood. In Berlin, he achieved further eminence not only as an actor but as a director and, to some extent, even as a writer. My advice to such men as René Clair, Julien Duvivier, and Jean Renoir (published in *Tomorrow* magazine) was, "If you *like* America, go back where you came from." Artists—especially theatre artists, who work with other people—create best when close to their roots, not individually or "privately."

When the committee questioned Aaron Copland (yes, Copland too, though he was less "political" than most of the other artists of the period), McCarthy kept drilling him about his association with that notorious Communist party leader Eisler. Copland corrected the Senator—surely he must be referring to Gerhardt Eisler, for whose brother, the composer Hanns Eisler, he, Copland, had merely sponsored a concert once. But the rabid interrogator persisted in demanding what Copland knew about this Eisler fellow who had jumped bail, gone to East Berlin, and become a minister of information. Copland repeated that he was acquainted only with Eisler the composer. The cross-examination went on in this vein for some minutes: a good example of the employment of the Big Lie. But on this occasion it didn't work.

I asked Eisler why Ruth Fischer, his prewar-Trotskyite sister, had denounced both him and their brother Gerhardt to the American authorities as dangerous subversives. I expected his reply to be a long account of their ideological differences. Instead he said, "Perhaps we weren't kind to her when we were children."

After he sailed for Europe, I didn't see Eisler again till some years later in Paris (though born in Leipzig, he had become an Austrian citizen and so could travel freely). I asked him how the Communists in East Berlin had reacted to Khrushchev's exposure of Stalin at the Twentieth Congress in Moscow in 1956. "They *discuss*," he said, with a wry smile.

The last time I saw Eisler was at the Café Royal in London, where I also met his son, a painter, who I believe had become an English subject. Hanns invited me to a rehearsal of a BBC broadcast of one of his early works, *German Symphony*, which had a text by Brecht. Halfway through the performance he suddenly rose and left the room. I supposed that something about the orchestra's playing had displeased him. When he returned to his seat beside me I asked him what had been the matter. "It brings back too many painful memories," he said, with tears in his eyes.

Only once before his death, which went largely unnoticed in America, did I have word of him again. A mutual friend told me that he was now sometimes picked up drunk in West Berlin. He was an amazing character, a man of exceptional and varied gifts. Generally unrecognized in our country, he was one of those whose careers make me doubt that the great of any period will be remembered or that we can ever be certain who among the living will endure in future repute. But posterity is a long time, and only recently I was encouraged to read a tribute to Eisler by Peter Hayworth, the astute music critic of the London *Observer*.

I first met Bertolt Brecht in New York in 1935, and if I saw very little of him then, I knew even less about him. *The Threepenny Opera,* directed by one of Brecht's assistants, had opened at the Empire Theatre in 1933 with a good cast that included Burgess Meredith, but it closed after twelve performances. The original German film of it, which I had seen, meant nothing to me beyond its special atmosphere and the wonderful Weill score. Stella, always curious about new modes in theatre practice, asked Brecht, just as the year before she had asked Stanislavski, to expound his theories of acting to her. He did so by rehearsing a scene from his *Saint Joan of the Stockyards* with her.

Brecht was eager to have this opportunity to work with an American actress and all the more eager to work with Stella, since he had given her half sister Celia Adler a difficult time when the Theatre Union down on Fourteenth Street had produced his version of Gorki's *Mother*. No one had known what he was talking about, what he wanted. I did not sit in on Brecht's sessions with Stella. All I understood of his ideas was that he rejected emotion, in acting and in the theatre generally—which is, of course, a distorted view of his "doctrine."

I heard a little more about him from Weill during the *Johnny Johnson* rehearsals—nothing much, chiefly anecdotes. (Weill told me that on a visit to Marseilles Brecht visited a brothel and came out vomiting, and continued to vomit for an inordinate amount of time. When asked what was the matter, he ascribed his sorry condition to ptomaine poisoning.) But I did gather that neither he nor Brecht was interested in having their songs done by singers. They wanted *actors*, who would make the words as important as the tunes.

Orson Welles, whom I introduced at a theatre discussion during the run of his Mercury Theatre's outstanding production of *Julius Caesar* in 1937, referred disparagingly to Brecht's theatrical ideology; this was an oblique way of slighting the Group Theatre, since Welles was under the impression that we were committed to Brecht's theories. Amusingly, Brecht himself thought the Group disastrously in thrall to Stanislavski.

In Hollywood, from 1943 to 1945, I saw and visited Brecht frequently. He wrote some ironic poems about his stay there, set to music by Eisler, and some of his best plays. He had also written the original story for *Hangmen Also Die*, directed by Fritz Lang, but he had disowned the finished screenplay. Though our contacts were all intimate and in the main cordial, I understood him as an artist no better than

I had before. I only recognized him as an endlessly fascinating man.

He might have been thought unprepossessing. He looked, I used to say, like an El Greco in mufti. His frequently unshaven face was lean and rather long, with one eyebrow raised haughtily. He dressed shabbily, a mannerism he had adopted early and never abandoned: it was "proletarian." He smoked five-cent cigars. For all that, as I later discovered, he was attractive to many women. Most of those I saw him with had at one time or another been his mistress. A Danish woman came clear across the ocean to be near him. His wife, the actress Helene Weigel, who resembled a Käthe Kollwitz drawing, knew all about his other women. After he died, in 1956, she became the artistic director of Brecht's theatre, the world-famous Berliner Ensemble, and carried on in that capacity till her death, in 1971.

Brecht was witty, shrewd, sly. At his hearing before the House Un-American Activities Committee, he outsmarted its members every step of the way. When challenged as to the subversiveness of one of his songs in *Mother* which instructs workers to educate themselves beginning with A B C and ends with "You must learn to take over," he denied that he had ever written it. How could that be so? he was asked. "It's a translation," he declared. The committee was glad to dismiss him.

There was always something wily—self-protective, if you like, or just realistic—about him. After the war, he offered his theatrical resources to the West German government. They refused them. The East Berlin government accepted, offering him every facility, every advantage the head of a theatre might desire. The Berliner Ensemble became one of the chief attractions of the region. He assumed Austrian citizenship, which gave him the mobility he would not otherwise have had, and he banked his money in Switzerland.

He loved discussion and dispute. He devoted himself

to books on science. He predicted that the theatre of the
future would be largely electronic. However, he wrote,
"Today every invention is received with a cry of triumph,
which soon turns into a cry of fear." He was fascinated by
the technique of Hollywood's gangster films. One could learn
much from them, he maintained; in their own way they
revealed the mechanism of capitalist enterprise.

Because none of the movie studios would employ him
and because none of his plays except *Galileo,* translated and
acted by Charles Laughton in Hollywood and New York,
were produced during this period, Brecht was supported by
the more affluent German *émigrés:* Lion Feuchtwanger, the
director William Dieterlie, Ernst Lubitsch, and a few others.
Though the author of poems and plays directed against the
Third Reich, Brecht as a German citizen was not permitted
to leave his Hollywood living quarters after sundown. "How
long do you think this exile in paradise will last?" he asked
me.

He greatly admired Charles Laughton, and the admiration was mutual. Brecht said that he had never heard anyone
read the Bible so beautifully as Laughton. He coached
Laughton in the role of Galileo. He also admired Spencer
Tracy, especially in *The Seventh Cross.* I didn't share his
enthusiasm for Tracy then, and I told him so. "You lack
sufficient understanding," he commented coolly. "That," I
am ashamed to confess I retorted, "is typical German arrogance," and I walked away.

Organized left-wingers in the theatre attacked him. They
thought his ideas "aristocratic," which in a way they were,
and even anti-Marxist, which was foolish. In 1963 in Moscow,
I asked Alexei Arbuzov, a leading Soviet playwright, if he
liked Brecht's plays. "Yes," he said cautiously, "but we Russians prefer more heart." Except for *The Threepenny Opera,*
Brecht has never been popular in the Soviet Union.

In 1953 I set out for Berlin to seen the Berliner Ensemble in action. Its productions turned out to be among the very few truly great ones I have ever seen. Brecht liked acting to be "cool," uninflated, and his productions were relatively simple. He was one of the world's outstanding directors (I use the word advisedly: there have been precious few in theatre history, though reviewers seem to discover several every season).

Inspired by the theatrical offerings, I began to read Brecht's essays and poems. The essays, doctrinaire in the beginning, end with Brecht's saying, "To hell with my writing." Unlike his productions, they are somewhat opaque and are read with difficulty. His poems, on the other hand, are among the most beautiful in the German language; they made it clear to me that Brecht was first and foremost a poet.

On my second visit to Berlin, in 1956, on which I was joined by Alan Schneider, I saw Brecht for the first time since Hollywood ten years before. I had not been able to see him in 1953, as he was ill. Now, three years later, he appeared to be recuperating from the heart ailment he had suffered, but it was to kill him a few months later. When Helene Weigel, Alan Schneider, and I sat with him on the rear veranda of his large house on the Friedrichstrasse, there was a doctor in attendance, who brought to mind another doctor at another time and place, the one who had accompanied Stanislavski when Stella and I had met with him in the Bois de Boulogne. And Brecht kept smoking his rotten cigar.

He seemed genuinely pleased to see me. I have reason now to be surprised by this, because three years ago a college professor working on a book about him showed me a letter Brecht had written home from Hollywood in which he spoke of me unflatteringly as one wholly enslaved by Stanislavski and, what is worse, as a person with no conception at all of collaboration in the theatre. The professor explained that when Brecht was in Hollywood he believed that nearly all American theatre folk were enemies, but that after he achieved world renown he became friendlier and more generous.

I should not have wondered at the antagonism of Brecht's letter. In 1946, when Elia Kazan and I formed a partnership to produce plays—we produced only two, Maxwell Anderson's *Truckline Café* and Arthur Miller's *All My Sons*—I proposed that we continue with a "revival" of Brecht's *Galileo,* which had originally been presented "experimentally" by ANTA at the Maxine Elliott Theatre on West Thirty-ninth Street, with Joseph Losey as director and Charles Laughton in the title role. I learned through the play's agent, Audrey Wood, that Brecht was agreeable to my serving as the producer but that he wanted Kazan and not me to stage it. I was prepared to accept this arrangement. But Kazan, worried, I suppose, that Brecht's reputation as a Communist might render him similarly suspect, told me he didn't want to direct the play. Perhaps too he didn't admire it as much as I did. At any rate, I was determined to do it and I proposed that Kazan help me persuade Brecht to entrust the direction to me while Kazan would serve as coproducer.

Brecht received us at the Chelsea Hotel on West Twenty-third Street, where he was then staying; Laughton was also there. I assured Brecht of my enthusiasm for the play and fortified what was to be my plea by saying that whatever I failed to understand about its staging I would be happy to learn from him.

Brecht's response was a categorical "No!"

"I'd rather a circus director do it," he went on. "You are a Stanislavski man and cannot possibly understand how to approach my play."

At this I roared, "My name is Clurman!"

But he roared back, if possible even louder, "You don't understand, no one understands, even Piscator doesn't understand. . . . You will try to get 'atmosphere'; I don't want atmosphere. You will establish a 'mood'; I don't want a mood."

I began to scream at the top of my voice—my fortissimos, I have been assured, are quite impressive—"Tell me what you're after and I will follow your instruction."

At this point poor Laughton, as touchy as he was fat, pleaded, "But why do you both have to shout so?" and very nearly crawled under a table. Kazan never uttered a word. I think Brecht and I had a good time. But the Kazan-Clurman combine never acquired the play.

On my 1956 visit to Brecht in Berlin, he was charming to me. Of course, I had written a number of laudatory articles about him by then. We talked theatre the whole time. There were some stray remarks about Goethe and Clifford Odets. He denied that Goethe had been a political reactionary. He said he was shocked by Odets's testimony at the hearings of the House Un-American Activities Committee. "Tell Odets to write a play about it," he said. "A defense, if he likes. Anything. He doesn't have to have the play produced. Let him write it for himself. It'll do him good, it will help him."

Alan Schneider asked Brecht what he thought of theatre in the round, of which Schneider was a champion. Brecht didn't favor the proscenium stage any more than he did the box set, but he was positively opposed to theatre in the round. Brecht's Berlin theatre, close to the Friedrichstrasse station, is an old-fashioned house with a very large stage. To Helene Weigel, theatre in the round was a blasphemy. "The actors," she declared, "would always be obliged to face one another!" With Brecht, the actors are usually placed so that the audience is included in the relation between one and the other, and they often speak directly to the house.

I asked Brecht if he believed all plays ought to be done in this manner. "Certainly not," he answered. Then I asked if *his* plays could be satisfactorily staged in a style other than his own. "Of course," he replied. I was inclined to contradict him.

On my way home, I stopped over in France to review

some Brecht productions unfamiliar to me that were being given at the International Festival in Paris to great acclaim. . . . A few months later, Brecht died in his sleep in the house on the Friedrichstrasse. No matter what else may be said of him, he has undeniably influenced theatre practice—in writing and staging—everywhere.

Max Reinhardt, Brecht, Meyerhold, and Vakhtangov, were, in my view, the four great directors of our time. (Grotowski too is of enormous importance, but he is still only at an early stage of his career; Stanislavski's greatness consisted in his contribution to the study of the technique of acting and the formation of the spirit and special product of the Moscow Art Theatre.) Brecht served his apprenticeship under Reinhardt. He could not have chosen a better master, though they were vastly different in both aim and temperament.

Brecht had spoken contemptuously of a "culinary" theatre that the well-situated bourgeoisie might consume as a kind of goody or dessert. He also said, "Nothing needs less justification than pleasure." But in a sense Reinhardt's theatre was "culinary." Culinary despite magnificent productions—with some of the finest actors of the day—of *Oedipus Rex,* most of Shakespeare, Goethe, Lessing, Pirandello, Büchner, *Everyman,* Tolstoi, Wedekind, Gorki, and others. He was quick to recognize genius wherever he encountered it. When he saw a Moscow Art Theatre production for the first time, he was heard to murmur to a colleague beside him, "This is something we aren't capable of."

The hallmark of Reinhardt's art was sensuousness. He was a master of the Viennese baroque. No matter how tragic or painful the play itself, the effect of his production was ingratiating. He had abundant humor and a vaulting imagination. He loved the stage with carnal ardor. He wrapped his audiences in soft dreams of warm delight. No wonder, then, that he was the toast of Wilhelmenian Germany, Franz

Josef's Austria, and most of Europe. "Imagine," said Heinrich Mann at the Hollywood memorial tribute to him, "making Goethe popular."

Reinhardt spoke of only two of his contemporaries with the glowing enthusiasm one accords genius: the archbishop of Austria, and Toscanini. His favorite theatre building was the eighteenth-century Fenice in Venice, after which he modeled his own theatre, the Theater in der Josefstadt in Vienna, though he often said that small theatres were insufficiently theatrical, that they lacked splendor.

He projected gigantic ritual celebrations, and most American theatre critics—except George Jean Nathan, who admired him extravagantly—thought of Reinhardt solely as a producer of grandiose spectacles. This was largely due to his 1923 New York production of *The Miracle,* with sets by Norman Bel Geddes, and to his 1936 production, spectacularly eye-filling, of Werfel's *Eternal Road,* also with sets by Bel Geddes. In both instances the theatres had to be reconstructed to house the shows. The back wall of the stage had to be broken through to accommodate the bulky, elaborate setting for *The Eternal Road.* But most of us did not know that Reinhardt's repertoire also embraced the intimate and frolicsome enchantment of such productions as that of Goldoni's *Servant of Two Masters.*

I had learned all this about Reinhardt before meeting him in Hollywood, where his sons—Gottfried, a producer at Metro-Goldwyn-Mayer (who said, "I never was a success out here till I gave up caring about the artistic value of my work"), and Wolfgang, a producer at Warner Brothers—had provided him with a palatial residence. Nothing less befitted him. Special cigars were ordered for him; in all such matters the best was none too good. Before the war, he had bought Leopoldskron, an eighteenth-century archbishop's castle in Salzburg, which he had remodeled to include a beautiful library and a garden theatre. Hundreds of distinguished personalities from all over the world were invited to the fabulous castle. The Nazis seized it during the occupation, and when they were disposed of the Austrian government gave it back to Reinhardt's widow, the actress Helene Thimig, who promptly sold it to Harvard. Today, several incarnations later, it houses the Salzburg Seminar for American Studies.

Reinhardt boasted that he took pleasure in practically everything, including brushing his teeth in the morning. At Chasen's restaurant in Hollywood, he ate only the choicest dishes. Very few people, he said, knew how to savor a meal. I insisted that I did, but he denied this; he had watched me at his table, and I ate too rapidly to appreciate the food properly. His clothes too were of the finest materials, cut to rare yet unostentatious elegance. He was a prince.

How he loved to laugh! He laughed not only at funny stories but at people's idiosyncrasies. He told me how Joseph Schildkraut, who had acted for him in Vienna, came to ask why he would not employ him in Hollywood. Reinhardt indicated that he considered Schildkraut troublesome. "Oh," Schildkraut assured him, "I go to an analyst now to improve my character," at which Reinhardt exploded with laughter. I noticed too that when Reinhardt watched his production of *Die Fledermaus* in New York, with Kitty Carlisle and Oscar Karlweis in the cast, he laughed heartily at every funny piece of business, even though he had staged the play himself in almost every country in Europe and had rehearsed it over many weeks on this occasion as well.

I told Reinhardt that I was lazy. "You're not lazy," he said, "you just don't like working in the movies." He proposed a theatrical association with me in New York. I was somewhat skeptical about this, though I held him in the highest esteem. I suspected that old Vienna and contemporary New York would not mix, but I told him I would consider the proposal.

Either to involve me further or to give his European friends a chance to hear about the Group Theatre, he invited me to address a house party he was giving. I spoke generally about my continued faith in the theatre as a cultural instrument even at a time when films had become the most popular medium of entertainment. I went so far as to say something like: "If the values inherited from our common cultural past are to disappear, let the bomb fall!" The audience seemed pleased, and Thomas Mann, who was present, said, "I approof of that young man!"

Thornton Wilder, a devoted Reinhardt fan, asked the producer Herman Shumlin to engage Reinhardt to direct his play *The Merchant of Yonkers,* an adaptation of an old Austrian play which Wilder was later to rewrite as *The Matchmaker* and which still later would become the source for *Hello, Dolly!* Kermit Bloomgarden, then both the Group Theatre's and Shumlin's business manager, had told me that Shumlin couldn't understand why Reinhardt would rehearse for no more than five hours a day when he was permitted seven. When I reported this to Reinhardt, he said, with his characteristic poise, "Four or five hours a day of good work are sufficient. Longer than that it becomes labor."

Stella Adler acted in Reinhardt's New York production of Irwin Shaw's *Sons and Soldiers,* starring Gregory Peck and Geraldine Fitzgerald. A boy of ten who could play the piano well had to be cast. There were the usual auditions, with hundreds of applicants for the role. Reinhardt listened to each one of them play a piece. Some of the selections were rather long, and some of the kids played badly. But Reinhardt never interrupted any of them with the usual "Thank you, that's enough. Next, please!" He listened with respect; he would not hurt the children's or their mother's feelings.

At one of the rehearsals Stella took Reinhardt aside and said, "Professor [important German directors were always called " Professor"—especially Reinhardt], the characterization you have suggested to me is first-rate. I shall be glad to fulfill it. But I have something else in mind." Reinhardt said, "Show me!" When she had done the scene her way, he said, "Much better. You should play the part your way."

I had watched Reinhardt several times at rehearsals of

The Eternal Road. I knew that he prepared his production by setting down, in voluminous books, elaborate descriptions of the characters along with the actors' moment-by-moment behavior, readings, positions. He began rehearsing in the afternoons because he preferred to work alone most of the night. A remarkably versatile and effective actor himself, he would act out every part for every member of the company. While this method did not disturb his German-speaking companies, it upset the Americans, unaccustomed as they were to such detailed coaching.

Reinhardt was incredibly generous, as in the matter of *The Russian People,* a Soviet play by Konstantin Simonov, the direction of which he had been all but promised. An agent, having heard that I was available, asked if I would be interested in the project; when I said yes he proceeded to "sell" me to the producer. My stepdaughter Ellen, as fond of Reinhardt as was her mother, pleaded with me to defer to Reinhardt. But I was broke, and I took the job. My production was not all it should have been: it was, in fact, quite bad. But Reinhardt not only displayed no resentment, he even said some kind things about the show. He understood how, after the Group's collapse and my unprosperous adventures in the Hollywood studios, I had to pick up my New York career.

Everyone of note seemed to gravitate toward our golden West. I would not have believed it possible to encounter Thornton Wilder there, but I did. When in the early Group days we announced a play by Jules Romains called *Donogoo-Tonka* and commissioned Gilbert Seldes to translate it for us, Wilder, who had never met me, sent me a handwritten note cautioning me against producing the play. Now, hearing that he was in Hollywood and that he had a new play about a department store, which I hoped he might permit me to read and perhaps direct, I asked to meet him. Louis Calhern, an actor I liked and the best Lövberg in *Hedda Gabler* I had ever seen, told me that Wilder's play had greatly impressed him.

We had a meal in a delicatessen near the Hollywood-Roosevelt Hotel, where I was then staying and where I had just begun writing *The Fervent Years*. I was so bitter about the state of the American theatre—the Group had just folded—and so distressed about American life in general that I couldn't have pleased Wilder very much. He is an irrepressible optimist, an enthusiast. When I left him that evening he said, "You worry me."

Since then I have had many pleasing conversations with him. He is always buoyant. His stream of anecdotes, literary allusions, references to historic occasions and faraway places, personal reminiscences couched in French, German, and Italian, make for marvelous listening. His verbal energy is unique in being astonishing without being fatiguing. He is all good will and delight. He says nice things whenever possible; without ever appearing didactic he is always teaching, setting an example. If he leaves you standing in the lobby of a theatre during a dance recital, he explains politely with a slight instructional innuendo that he is returning to his seat for a moment of *recueillement*. He loves to travel and stays for weeks at a time at the Red Lion Inn in Stockbridge, Massachusetts. He makes his home with his sister Isabel just outside New Haven. He never revised his play about the department store, and so far as I know never showed it to anyone.

I went to see John Steinbeck at his house in Los Gatos, near Salinas, the scene of several of his novels; I wanted to extract a new play from him. A large man of conspicuous muscularity, Steinbeck struck me as one who was suffering intense internal pressure; it was not easy to determine whether this was anatomical or spiritual. He spoke with marked affection of the folk in the surrounding country, about whom he wrote *Tortilla Flat* and other picaresque novels.

When I broached the subject of his writing a play, he

spoke instead of a wonderfully comic novel he was writing. He read some of it to me, chuckling over every page. But as he went on I could detect that he was beginning to doubt the book was as funny as he had first conceived it to be. He never finished the novel. His wife was at his side most of the time, but he seemed to me very lonely. He seemed disappointed when I left before the weekend was over.

I met Steinbeck again, in Paris, where he had rented a magnificent house off the Champs-Elysées. He had remarried now, a woman who had been the assistant stage manager of *The Russian People*. He spent a year in Paris, writing *The Short Reign of Pippin I,* which the city had inspired.

Of Paris, Steinbeck said, "These stones speak to me." My own response was "I suppose I love Paris because I'm in love with my youth." The last thing he said to me in Paris was, "Come on and have a drink with me"—at eleven in the morning!

He took me to the studio of a Czech painter, and remained silent, breathing heavily, while the painter presented one canvas after another. It was left to me to make all the polite comments. Not even after we left the studio would Steinbeck discuss what we had been shown. A week later Steinbeck told me he had bought one of the paintings.

Alice Toklas came to tea at the Steinbecks' one afternoon when I was there; Lemuel Ayers, the designer of *Oklahoma!*, and his wife were also there. Slightly mustached, with a somewhat gravelly voice, Toklas spoke gustily and incessantly of food and Gertrude Stein. Gertrude, she said, had believed in Picasso; her brother, Leo, in Matisse. . . .

I was more interested in Lemuel Ayers. I had repeatedly been told by his wife that he was dying of leukemia. Her mentioning this so often was perhaps a way of making the eventuality less terrible to her. Ayers, with a pallor which terrified me now that I knew the cause of it, was quiet, relaxed, resigned. There was not a trace of self-pity in his manner. He was aware of his condition, and he and his wife had resolved to accept it as a decree of fate which brooked no complaint. Only once before had I witnessed such fortitude.

(I would meet with it again in my own father's house, immediately after his funeral. A physician friend of the family whispered to my brother Moe, "In two years I shall die of heart failure." He died on schedule. . . . And my brother Will, riddled with cancer, asked his son, Dick, to find out from the specialist attending him how long he had to live. "Several months," Dick reported back. "Let's never mention it again," Will said. I saw him a few weeks before his death, at a party at Clare Luce's. As always, he was dressed with meticulous care. In a voice made hoarse by his illness, he talked to Oscar Hammerstein about how proud he was of me. He never mentioned dying, except once, at the table, when he said to Moe, "When the angel of death summons, one must answer the call.")

There was tragedy too, though I didn't realize it at the time, in my meeting with Ernst Toller, one of the German *émigrés* who did not succeed in triumphing over the trials of exile. He had been one of the first and most persuasive of the German expressionist dramatists. He had been active in the short-lived Workers Republic of Munich, which was established after the Social Democratic government had crushed an attempted left-wing take-over in Berlin. The revolution in Munich was also doomed, and Toller was imprisoned. In jail he wrote *Masse Mensch* ("Man and the Masses"), produced by the Theatre Guild in 1924, directed and designed by Lee Simonson. Toller also wrote a play about the inflation years in Germany, which Erwin Piscator produced in Berlin to great acclaim. But by the time Toller arrived in Hollywood, his day had passed.

He was handsome and beautifully groomed, his steel-gray hair always trimly cut; he was a romantic figure. "My Jewish mother conceived me," he used to say, "Germany nurtured me, Europe formed me, the earth is my native country, and the world is my fatherland."

I told him of my struggles on behalf of the Group. His reaction was very different from Thornton Wilder's. "Clurman is a fanatic," he told Stella. "But the world needs fanatics."

I met him again in New York in the autumn of 1939. He sat erect, spoke with self-assurance and a sovereign pride. But his words were foreboding. "The twelfth hour has passed," he declared, with a haughty smile that said: Hitler will win and the ensuing holocaust will envelop you all. There was also accusation in his sibylline remarks: the democracies were responsible for the doom that lay ahead; they had trafficked too long with the devil.

Soon afterward, Toller hanged himself in his New York apartment. Stefan Zweig had been too thin-skinned to await the outcome of the war, Toller too desperate. His suicide was a sort of malediction.

I attended a memorial service for him arranged by some of his literary compatriots. The main speaker was a man, well known in Germany, of clearly Communist orientation. He said, in German, that while he did not share Toller's utopian humanitarianism, he respected it. Leaving the service with Sinclair Lewis, I was appalled to hear a successful American writer of lightweight plays say that he could not approve of Toller because suicide betrayed weakness.

Lewis and I lingered on a street corner to talk about Toller. I had met Lewis in California, when he had just begun to write plays and was acting a bit in stock—he once played the Stage Manager in *Our Town*. I had a plan to contact every respectable writer who had evinced any interest in the theatre as well as all those able playwrights like George Kelly, author of *The Show-Off*, and *Craig's Wife*, who had not been heard from in years. (Kelly, who had made a fortune through wise investments during the Depression, lived in a mean-looking apartment in which there wasn't a semblance of decoration or a comfortable appointment. His pale face and his immaculate black suit and generally formal attire gave him the look of a clergyman forever turned to an ascetic existence. He had perhaps decided that he had no more to say.)

When I knocked on the door of Sinclair Lewis's house in Beverly Hills, a somewhat chubby young woman who looked all of seventeen greeted me. Lewis rushed toward the entrance, introducing her to me as his niece and secretary. I would meet them both again in the large penthouse apartment on Central Park West in which they later lived in New York. Eventually she married the head warden of a prison.

I lost no time in asking Lewis why he had taken to writing plays. He explained that he found writing novels lonesome work; he didn't enjoy the solitude any more. He wanted company, and this, as I well knew, the theatre could provide.

Another German writer I happened on in Hollywood was the Prague-born Franz Werfel. When he was trapped in France on his flight from Hitler's army, he needed the testimony of noted American writers like Lewis as to his character, politics, and literary position in order to obtain a visa for entry into the United States. In the early twenties, I had played bit parts in two of Werfel's plays, *Goat Song* and *Juarez and Maximilian,* in both of which Alfred Lunt had appeared for the Theatre Guild. I assured Lewis that Werfel, though inclined to Catholicism, was kosher.

I arrived at Werfel's home to find his wife, the oft-married Austrian noblewoman Alma Mahler, playing the piano while he croaked a German *lied.* He had a large round head with a high, wide brow and wildly tousled hair. Also, he was obese and had bad teeth. We talked about his play *Jacobowsky and the Colonel*—best known through S. N. Behrman's adaptation—which I described enthusiastically to Kazan, who later directed it for the Theatre Guild as a ballet of ideas. Werfel was pleased to hear me describe it as a humorous parable dramatizing the vital energy of a Polish colonel in contrast to the age-old wisdom of the Jew Jacobowsky.

Werfel was something of a mystic and was suspicious of purely rational and materialistic attitudes—he spoke disapprovingly of Arthur Schnitzler on these grounds—and he ascribed all latter-day moral lesions to the work of such men of the "Enlightenment" as Diderot and Voltaire. It was just their gnawing away at the pillars of faith, he maintained, that had resulted in the cursed French revolution. One day at the Viertels' he was holding forth on this topic at particularly great length, to the hearty, big-busted approval of Alma, who didn't like Jews although she had married several. Finally, brave, beloved Salka Viertel spoke out. "Really," she said, laughing with abandon, "I've heard people inveighing against the *Russian* revolution, but to get so wrought up over the French—ha, ha, ha!" It was too funny, she couldn't go on.

At Max Reinhardt's, Stella Adler was seated beside Werfel at a dinner party. I asked him from across the table what he thought of Alfred Kerr, the most influential theatre reviewer in Berlin before Hitler. "A bad critic!" he replied. Evidently Kerr, a "rationalist" too, had not been kind to Werfel's plays. I said no more, but Werfel was wound up and, having finished off Kerr, proceeded to discourse on a number of somewhat abstract matters. Finally Stella could stand it no more. "Please, Mr. Werfel," she interrupted, "I am a woman sitting by your side. If you can't speak to me in recognition of that fact and are going to continue as you have been doing, I must tell you, I can go out to a bookstore and buy your ideas for five dollars!"

In the delicatessen where I had first spoken with Thornton Wilder, I met another man—a strange one. His strikingly Russian Jewish face could hardly be said to have clashed with the environment we were in. For a while he said very little. To draw him out, I asked him what he thought of Cézanne.

(The mutual friend who introduced us told me that he was a painter, but I hadn't caught his name.) "Cézanne bores me," he replied. "Picasso?" Picasso bored him too. "Matisse?" Matisse too. And on and on like that till I gave up. I had heard similar absolutes of negation in the heyday of Dadaism in Paris. But I felt very strongly that this intense young man was not a joker as many of the Dadaists had been

"What sort of painting do you do?" I tried again. "Mythical painting—painting which makes myths," he answered, not bothering to explain.

Some years later I discovered that the painter I had met in that Hollywood delicatessen was Mark Rothko, unknown then, but soon to become fashionable—perhaps too fashionable.

When I met him next at one of Max Lerner's New Year's Day parties, I reminded him of our meeting in Hollywood. "Are you still as objectionable as ever?" I asked, to Lerner's astonishment. Rothko was about to flare up—he no longer had to tolerate such treatment—but he saw by my smile that I was merely twitting him.

I saw him again at Gerald Sykes and Buffie Johnson's, where I asked him whether he thought as highly of the recent retrospective show of American painting at the Whitney Museum as had M, one of his most prominent colleagues. "M is full of shit," he said. No, he had not changed: he was as absolute as ever. He asked why I didn't visit his studio to see *his* paintings. In the intervening years I had, of course, seen a great many. I wondered why he gave the impression that he was still somehow unrecognized. Perhaps he felt that no one was quite convinced of the analogy he had once made between his work and Dostoevski's!

Before I could visit his studio, he took his life. Whatever else he may have been, he was a generative artist. He spawned many minor Rothkos. The Chinese say every genius gives rise to a hospital.

I have said little of my experience of working in Hollywood, except that I did make a film—*Deadline at Dawn*—of no importance. My almost casual attitude toward the job met with resentment, perhaps because I finished the film on time and it proved moderately profitable. I spent most of my Hollywood nights writing *The Fervent Years*.

At the studio one day, in a collection of new American writing, I read a play, called *The Man Who Had All the Luck,* that interested me. It had opened in New York and closed in a week. I sat right down at a table in my office and wrote the playwright, Arthur Miller, offering to produce his next play. I did: it was *All My Sons*.

If nothing else, Hollywood was fun. I watched Leo McCarey make one of his clerical films, *Going My Way,* with Bing Crosby. Someone asked Crosby to speak his lines while playing the piano, and Crosby said, with quiet conviction, "If you want someone to do that, you'll have to get an *actor*."

One of my favorite Hollywood stories of the time was told me by Irwin Shaw. A producer asked Irwin to make a film of a French comedy; Irwin read the script and warned the producer that it was unproducible—this was the early forties—because its central point and situation was a joyously consummated adulterous affair. "But there's no adultery in the play," the producer protested.

"But look at the curtain of the second act," Shaw insisted. "The lover lifts the lady, a married woman, into his arms, goes to the bedroom door, and says, 'I shall have my will of you!' "

"No, no, you're wrong," the producer raged, "there's no adultery."

"What makes you so sure?" Shaw challenged.

"The author told me so," the producer declared, implacably.

CHAPTER

8

The Doldrums

The fifties were a time of massacre in Hollywood. I say Hollywood, but the phenomenon was nationwide. McCarthyism was rampant. Why then do I speak of Hollywood as a focal point of the wretched situation? It hasn't been sufficiently stressed that McCarthy and his hounds rarely pursued the inconspicuous; they were after stars, "names." What they hunted was not Communists but publicity. And a politically gullible people and the movie moguls who always ran scared succumbed to the blackmail.

The story of some of the victims goes back a long way. Political awareness in our epoch began in the thirties. In the early twenties, five Socialists elected to the New York State Assembly were unseated because they were Socialists—"reds" —and hardly anyone gave a damn. The oil scandals of the Harding administration were a joke to most of the citizenry. "Everyone" was making money. During the Palmer pogrom of the late Wilson era, suspected foreign "agitators" were deported to their native countries. The offices of the *Call,* a mild Socialist paper, were raided by the police and a few heads were broken. None of this was taken too seriously by the general public. The Sacco-Vanzetti case was more notorious in Europe than here: after all, it centered on two obscure Italians. James Walker's peculations also had their comic side; political scandal was nothing people got excited about. Judge Samuel Seabury, who prosecuted the mayor, was resented rather than admired. I *liked* Walker: he went to the theatre a lot and had a very fetching girl friend in the chorus of one of the best musicals. Anyhow, he resigned.

No one paid much attention to the Soviet Union; local Communists were thought petty troublemakers. In the thirties there was no hue and cry when so-called leftist plays were produced. The leftist characters in plays were not depicted as particularly unsympathetic; they were wrong, but they were tolerable. The Depression made them topically interesting, lent them a degree of plausibility among respectable people. When a character in Odets's *Waiting for Lefty* shouted, "Strike! Strike! Strike!" and inveighed against the bosses, a wealthy oilman sitting beside me in the audience asked peaceably, "Do they mean it?" Odets, who was thought a "red," was invited to posh parties. People were curious rather than alarmed about Communism.

There was ignorance aplenty on all sides. When Odets arrived in Hollywood as the white-haired boy of the radical writers, he re-encountered his old acquaintance Walter Winchell, who insisted they have lunch. Winchell wanted to learn what Communism was all about. Odets, in an almost pedantic mode, began to explain. But Winchell quickly grew bored or could not follow the explanation. "Oh, never mind!" he interrupted. "I'll find out what I want to know from the top man—Stalin."

I had lunch with Sam Behrman at the Ritz in Boston in 1934, in the hope that he would write a play for the Group. (It was in Boston just then that Odets was writing *Waiting for Lefty*.) The hotel dining room was pleasant and the lunch a good one. I was somewhat taken aback—but finally much amused—when Behrman asked if I had ever before had a meal in such a place. It took me some minutes to realize that he thought that because I was one of the directors of the Group, which was thought to be a "radical" organization, I must have been born in a cellar where revolutions were hatched. This was typical of the innocence of those days.

Another example, barely credible, of America's political and even geographical innocence was provided me in 1939 on my first meeting with Tallulah Bankhead, then starring in *The Little Foxes*. After the show, loath, like most actors, to turn in after the stimulus of the night's performance, she asked the Group's business manager, Kermit Bloomgarden, if he had any plans. Bloomgarden said he was going to Irwin Shaw's place on East Ninth Street, where several of the Group people had been invited. Tallulah seemed interested, and she asked to accompany him. She was always teasing and chaffing Herman Shumlin, the producer-director of *The Little*

Foxes, for his supposed radicalism, and she had heard that the Group was even more radical. "You won't be able to best Clurman," Bloomgarden told her, smiling. "He's sharp."

At Shaw's place she sat down quietly by my side on the sofa and spoke first about Shumlin. He was so honest, she said, that she would trust him with her last dollar, but, she added, he lacked grace of manner. Then, quite casually, she asked me where I had been born. "In the Kremlin," I answered, without inflection. She turned to talk to others in the room. In a little while, she switched back to me and asked, "Were you really born in the Kremlin?" To which I replied, simply, "Yes."

She repeated the conversation to her husband, the actor John Emery, who laughed and explained that she had been spoofed.

I began to anticipate trouble but was not particularly concerned when I heard, while the Group was playing *Golden Boy* in Chicago, that several of the stagehands were sniffing around asking, "Are there any reds in the company?" Later it was rumored that one of the Group's actors was an FBI informer. I gave this little credence until one day in the fifties when the actor called me in Hollywood, where I had gone to cast a part in a play I planned to direct. "What are you doing in Hollywood?" he asked. "I'm casting a new production," I replied. "Are you interested in a part?" "No," he said, "I just want to know what you're doing out here now."

This was in 1953. The Group had died a natural death in 1941, and in the meantime I had written *The Fervent Years,* which explained in some detail the Group's relation to politics. I had also embarked on a career as a "Broadway director" (how I abhor the designation!) with *The Member of the Wedding.* I could not imagine that any of my friends or associates might be considered "subversives," dangerous, or anti-American. If anything, they seemed to me all too American!

When an FBI agent questioned me directly in 1954 about John Garfield's political leanings, I replied that I doubted he had any to speak of. A girl in Hollywood, the agent advised me, had said that Garfield had urged her to join the Communist party. "Was she in bed with him at the time?" was, I was surprised to discover, all I could say in response. After a pause, I added, "Garfield is naïve." "Politically naïve?" was the next question. "Naïve in every respect. Why else would he be on the stage? We're all naïve in the theatre." This was certainly not a considered statement on my part, but I believe there is a measure of truth in it. Theatre folk are generally innocents: unpretentious, sentimental, credulous, enthusiastic, and, where their immediate professional interests are not threatened, generous and kindhearted. They are usually glad to help the unfortunate, as the record of wartime charities, and of contributions in time and money to those caught in natural or social disasters, amply testifies.

This was especially true of Garfield, who was a thoroughly sweet boy. Orphaned young, he became a problem child. A wise educator, Angelo Patri, the principal of a Bronx high school, took him in hand—so successfully that Jules Garfinkel (the John Garfield of stage and film fame) endeared himself to everyone in the theatre: first to Eva Le Gallienne and later to all of us in the Group.

The total absence of malice in him, his love of laughter and his capacity for friendship won him the confidence of all sorts of people everywhere. Even his constant malapropisms charmed everyone. But he was poorly educated and unable to think through to any firmly held conviction, so that when he was not playing and enjoying life, he went around looking utterly bewildered. He acted from instinct, and most of his instincts were generous.

He came to me for guidance as to whether to remain with the Group or to accept a long-term film contract. He was unable to come to a decision—the film offer was tempting, but he was genuinely attached to his Group colleagues and to the goals they had set themselves. "I cannot decide for you," I said. "What do you want in life? What are you after?" I asked him. "That's the trouble," he answered. "I don't know."

Life buffeted him as if he had little will of his own, fully as much when Hollywood's soft life bemused him as when his little daughter suddenly died of a rare form of pneumonia. Outwardly of rugged physique, he had a bad heart, worried about it, yet still played a taxing game of tennis. He was helpless in all matters that demanded rational self-awareness.

I did not follow his appearance before the House Un-American Activities Committee. I couldn't take seriously any of the "cases" involving my friends and acquaintances. I knew the truth: Communist party members or not, they were sentimentalists with little practical understanding of any political issue. For each of them, being a Communist was like belonging to a club in aid of the poor, the downtrodden. They were all on the side of the good. The committee made being a Communist seem a heinous sin, something to be ashamed of—and the "kids" were frightened: frightened that they would have great difficulty finding jobs, frightened that they would be ostracized. That is why nearly all of them behaved as if they were indeed guilty: "If I were not guilty," they felt, "would I be up here being investigated?"

Garfield stood his ground. He would not admit to any guilt. He told the truth and he refused to implicate anybody else, which must have been especially galling to his "judges," who were bent on breaking him: he looked so "easy."

While Garfield was playing in a revival of Odets's *Golden Boy*, he was still under investigation. But since no damning evidence against him could be turned up, the pressure on him had diminished; it looked as if he might be cleared so that he could resume his film career—the studios were eager to have him back.

The last act of the Garfield story was short and shocking. In the offices of the committee members in charge of the

Garfield case, Garfield's attorney argued persuasively that since no evidence to disprove his client's testimony had been adduced, he should now at last be given the official bill of health required by the studios for reinstatement in the film industry. The attorney was confident that the committee would clear his client. Then the telephone rang. The man in charge picked up the phone, listened for a moment, hung up, and said, "The Garfield case is now closed. He just died of a heart attack. . . ." He then added, "Easy come, easy go." The attorney struck him.

Others co-operated with the committee: they named names, causing themselves a certain distress but causing others incalculable hardship. The informers were not motivated by any sense of guilt—after all, their political "errors" had been committed five, ten, or fifteen years before; they simply wanted to be allowed to go on working in Hollywood. The more prominent and talented among them were rich and could certainly have made a living working in the theatre. They named names because they could not bear the black mark against *their* names. The fact that betrayal of friends was considered by many to be far more reprehensible than any past association with the Communist party did not weigh as heavily on the informers as the anathema of their unimpeachably respectable associates.

Men who are bent on getting ahead will stop at nothing, even when they happen to be, in most other respects, altogether decent—like gangsters who love their families, their neighbors, and the lowly. "Brigands are convinced of what?" Baudelaire once asked, and answered himself, "That they must succeed."

There were those who, through strength of mind and spirit, would not yield to the wicked madness to which they were being subjected. Others left the country before the committee could summon them and, after a time of desperate struggle, established themselves in Europe. Doomed to obscurity or neglect in California, they achieved fame and wealth in England, France, Spain, though for a while some were persecuted in those lands too, through the pressure of American film distributors.

The situation was so muddled and hypocritical that some of those who were black-listed, or even jailed, for their inimical attitude toward the committee—Dalton Trumbo, for example—contributed screenplays under pseudonyms, without injury to anyone. It has not been sufficiently stressed that among those accused of being "un-American" were many who had written, directed, or produced ultrapatriotic pictures during the war years. Some of these pictures should have invited censure on other grounds: they were awful!

All this is ancient history. While the terror was on, I declared at a party at the home of Hume Cronyn and Jessica Tandy that even if Stalin and his henchmen were permitted to speak in every American city, even if the Soviet government were to drop several million leaflets of Communist propaganda, the political effect on the United States would be practically nil. Revolutions don't spread, they grow. And they grow only when the ruling power is too weak to govern.

We realize all this now, but we were then, and probably still are, a politically immature people. The reason "intellectuals"—and one may be an intellectual without having much of a mind—so often collapsed in panic during the doldrums of the fifties is that whereas the European activist knows that there may be some extremely unpleasant experiences in store for him, the American intellectual, because of the success of the democratic tradition, thinks of politics chiefly as a matter of debate that at worst may make him unpopular, and not as a struggle for power that may lead to something more than inconvenience. The thought of going to jail for *an opinion* is totally alien to our intellectuals, who never suspected that the unpopular might one day be equated with the illegal. When they discovered this, very few of them were ready to speak out clearly and boldly on behalf of what —mistakenly or not—they believed or deeply felt.

Odets, in his testimony before the House Un-American Activities Committee in May, 1952, had taken several different tacks in his defense. He admitted that he had been a member of the Communist party for about six months, but maintained that he had resigned when he felt he was being used by it. The Communists, he said, weren't even enthusiastic about his plays: they were simply exploiting his name. When the *Daily Worker* severely criticized his *Waiting for Lefty*, this proved to Odets that from the outset there had been marked ideological differences between him and the Communists.

On the other hand, Odets asserted, veering to a position that would show his former comrades that he was no turncoat, there were still good arguments (or, as he put it, "good tunes") for Socialism. But none of this hairsplitting counted in the view of his left-oriented or politically neutral colleagues, who blamed him for listing the names of the members of his party "cell." The irony was that in doing this he did not even satisfy the committee, since he had not declared an emphatic opposition to his early radicalism, and the committee did not thank him for his testimony, as it did in all cases when the witness was clearly "friendly."

The intellectuals' retreat after they had reached safe ground damaged them more profoundly than they realized. They lost self-confidence, became homeless within themselves. This had little to do with their quasi- or pseudopolitical ideas. Odets told me once that he was going to join the Communist party because he wanted to be called "Comrade." When he left it in short order, as I told him he would, he became increasingly troubled, not from any political indecision but from sheer loss—of a base, an element of firm faith, something he could identify with and cling to. There are people who are able to maintain an inner equilibrium within insecurity, but Odets was not one of them; he was constantly torn by the conflicting tensions of his own nature. In many artists, such a state can often be the source of special insight and creative power; to a degree, this was also true of Odets, but he could not live with it for very long. It killed him.

In a diary he kept for a while, he wrote that he feared psychoanalysis, not because it would disturb his "angels" but because it might suppress his devils. But those devils were gnawing at his innards.

He was generous to the point of improvidence with his torrential earnings. When I chided him for his incessant purchase of paintings, he assured me that they were a good investment; although he genuinely appreciated painting, his passion for the acquisition of paintings was a jag. He was trying to inebriate himself or to exalt his soul, hungry as always for some ideal. There was also an element of self-aggrandizement in the building of his collection. He sold most of the paintings later at a loss.

He was eager to help young artists, just as he was eager to prove to those more renowned than he that he was their equal and perhaps their superior. The desire to "reign" (his word), to be "first," took many guises, some of them almost comic. To show Theodore Dreiser, whose acquaintanceship he cultivated for a while, that he understood his work better than anyone else, he wrote a paper on *Sister Carrie* and read it to the towering old novelist. And he tried to convince Jascha Heifetz, who also "collected," that his own collection was in every respect more valuable and that Heifetz really had a limited understanding of the graphic arts.

When Odets bought a car it had to be the best, the most expensive; first it was a Cadillac, then a Lincoln Mercury. It tormented him that playwrights he believed decidedly inferior to himself (he was often right about this) should be more successful, more "in demand." I pointed out that there had been similar discrepancies in all fields at all times, and though he nodded his recognition of the fact, he could not bear it.

I felt him slipping away from the theatre—not just the Group but all theatre—not because he had a special regard for films but because he coveted the huge incomes of the successful screenwriters. "If you write ten plays in the next ten years," I reasoned with him, "let's say only three will succeed. They may not even be as good as the plays that flop. But still your yearly earnings will easily amount to twenty thousand dollars—and surely you can live on that." He agreed that he could. Then, a few minutes later, he "bargained" with me—"Only twenty thousand a year?"—as if I had offered him a contract.

A coolness developed between us, mostly over his play *The Big Knife.* I urged him to return from Hollywood with a new play. He outlined several ideas to me. He always had a supply of notes, scenes, scenarios; enough, he said, to furnish twenty plays. Some of his outlines—completely plotted—were ample in themselves. One of them, which he called *The Quartet,* dramatized the gradual decay of a tightly unified group of dedicated artists. Its intention was to show how various forces in our society conspire to destroy harmony and understanding among people who could realize themselves fully only through preserving their collaboration. But Odets decided to write a "Hollywood play" instead. The others, he explained, were too personal.

Arriving in New York, he spoke as if the play were nearly finished. Soon enough I learned from his wife, Betty Grayson, that he had not even begun writing it. "If I had admitted this," he told me a few months later, when he came round to my place to deliver the completed script, "I would never have written it."

The play had several admirable scenes and a beautifully drawn minor character, but its argument was not convincing. It purported to demonstrate how a good actor with aspirations to serious acting was blackmailed by his studio into fulfilling his contract. "First you must show," I said, "how anxious the actor is to leave Hollywood, how and why he hates it so much. . . ." Odets suddenly blurted out, "He loves it." I said, "That's another play . . . an interesting one at that . . . but it's not what you've written." He indicated that he might revise it.

It never occurred to me that he had no intention of revising it, that he had perhaps resented my objections. There was a long delay in his delivery of the final script. I told him that in the meantime I would have to direct another play and that it would therefore be five or six weeks before I could take on his. A few days later, he dropped me a note saying he couldn't wait for me, that Lee Strasberg would direct *The Big Knife,* which didn't go into rehearsal till six or seven weeks after mine.

I wrote two reviews of *The Big Knife* in which I was forced to repeat my original criticisms. This angered him, though many felt that my reviews had been, if anything, "too kind." In his diary I found the line: "Between my love and hate [for Harold] I don't know what to do." He once said of me to Stella, "Harold is like a dog: he attacks a bone, eats the meat, and having consumed it, turns away from it. . . . He uses only what feeds him." But I can say with Talleyrand: I don't turn away from a person until that person has turned away from himself.

Odets admitted that I had been important to him, but felt that I did not altogether understand his problems as a writer or as a man. He thought I blamed him for not continuing with his career as a playwright. I just wished he would go on writing plays—not for the Group or for me, but for his own sake.

We didn't see each other for some time, but we corresponded, on the whole amicably.

After the comparatively short run of *The Flowering Peach,* produced by Robert Whitehead—which I reviewed favorably—he had yet another offer from Hollywood. One day as I entered Whitehead's office, he said, "Odets is on the phone. He tells me he's had an offer to do a film for a lot of money." Then, turning back to Odets, he said, "Harold has just come in," breaking off to say to me, "Cliff wants to know if *you* think he ought to accept." "Of course he should," I answered. Whitehead repeated this to Odets, put down the receiver, and said to me, "He'll never write another play."

Yet he kept promising to write one. He had many ideas, but his fiber had slackened. Occasionally he would say things like "I can only write plays when I have a *company* to write for, friends who need me to write for them—as in the Group." When Kazan asked him if he really intended to write more plays, Odets answered, "I can't! I really can't."

John Garfield told me that during a visit to Odets in Hollywood, he fell on his knees and burst into heart-rending tears, crying out, "I've lost my talent." I heard that he had gone weeping to Garfield's widow, Robbie Cohen, to confess that he had not testified as he ought to have before the House Un-American Activities Committee.

It pained me most to hear him rationalize writing the screenplay for an Elvis Presley picture by declaring that Presley was something more than what he seemed. He also found excuses for accepting a job as supervisor and writer for a TV series.

The last time I saw Odets while he was capable of functioning, he was unemployed. I called him up from Santa Barbara, where I had gone to lecture at the university, to ask if I could come and see him. "Good," he said. "You'll be interested to know, Harold, that I've just signed to do the book for a musical based on *Golden Boy*."

When I arrived at his place in Beverly Hills, he was rather gingerly, though I could see he was trying very hard. The woman screenwriter who accompanied me had taken the Fifth Amendment when she was questioned by a state Un-American Activities Committee—perhaps Odets was worried by her possible attitude toward him? I had seen him before greet people warily whose good opinion he desired and who he feared would no longer wish to know him. Something was certainly troubling him. There was an air of neglect

about the house, though it was the usual expensively furnished Beverly Hills "villa."

I invited him to dinner at Chasen's. He suggested instead that we extract a full meal from the cans he had stored
in the kitchen. I said I'd like to eat properly—not, at any rate
from cans. He then recommended a modest restaurant
nearby. "But Cliff," I insisted, "I'm offering to buy you
dinner at Chasen's."

When we got there, he walked to the corner farthest
from the entrance. I preferred a more prominent table.
Reluctantly, he sat down at the location I designated, and
we had our dinner in leisurely fashion. Then Billy Wilder
came over to greet us, and Odets stiffened. Too late I understood the difficulty I had had in persuading him to dine at
Chasen's. He was no longer the theatre's golden boy, he was
no longer a Hollywood success, he didn't even have a job. In
the eyes of the Hollywood "court" he was a has-been; he
couldn't bear to face the big shots.

We did not see each other or correspond for a long time
after that. One summer day in 1964 Lee Strasberg called to
tell me that Odets was at Cedars of Lebanon Hospital in
Los Angeles, suffering from terminal cancer, and that he had
expressed a wish to see me and Kazan. We both flew west at
once. We arrived just after Odets's operation; he could consume nothing but orange juice, and he could not retain even
that. He was emaciated, which made his nose grotesquely
prominent.

I wondered if he could have saved himself from this
extremity. He had waited a long time to consult a doctor.
When he began to feel pain in his stomach he treated it as
indigestion. When the pain became too acute to put off
seeking help, he went to a doctor saying that he believed it
was all due to excessive sexual indulgence!

He was entirely lucid on his deathbed. But he fought
off the thought of death. "I may live," he said, shortly after
greeting Kazan and me. "A man who has such friends as

Clurman, Kazan, and Strasberg," he said, "has had a good life." He assured me that my abiding loyalty to Stella, which he had deplored, had also had its good side. Above all, he wanted to assure me that the misunderstandings that had estranged us were "all nonsense." I told him I knew that. . . . Gently I recalled how in the first fond days of our friendship he had said, "Harold, you are my favorite character outside of fiction."

He turned away and after a few minutes thrust his pathetic arm out, as if addressing the world in a sort of stabbingly affirmative gesture, and said, with all the force he could muster, "Clifford Odets, there is so much more work to be done." As with all romantics, fact and fiction were very nearly the same thing for him.

During Kazan's and my visit, a few relatives and some of Odets's other friends appeared, Shirley MacLaine and Cary Grant among them (Grant, Odets once told me, had sent him a check for four thousand dollars when he learned that he needed money); Jack Adler, Stella and Luther's older brother, to whom Odets had said, "If I didn't love you so much, how I'd hate you," was at his bedside saying funny things to cheer him. And so was Danny Kaye, also a devoted friend. But laughing only increased the pain in Odets's stomach. We had all been told by the nurse in attendance that his days were numbered.

Jean Renoir and his wife entered. Renoir stayed only a moment, and uttered no word. He looked at Odets with tears in his eyes. "I may live," Odets repeated. Renoir barely nodded. He leaned over Odets and kissed his forehead. There was compassion in the kiss, but also the most profound humility in the face of suffering and death that I had ever seen. Saying nothing, Renoir left.

Odets's son stood, silent and impassive, beside his father's bed. Odets said little to him, then suddenly thought of something the boy ought to know. "I'm going to marry ——," and here he mentioned a psychoanalyst whom I knew he had consulted when Betty Grayson left him. He had originally chosen Erich Fromm as his analyst, partly, he said, because I had been so impressed by *Escape from Freedom* that I had written a congratulatory letter to Fromm. But his sessions with Fromm had not been fruitful; he had wished more to impress Fromm with his own psychological acumen than to be treated by him, and finally Fromm suggested that a woman analyst might better suit Odets.

Odets's son nodded as his father announced his intention of marrying the psychoanalyst, as if to say, "It's okay with me." Kazan and I promised to come back in the late afternoon, after he had rested. When we returned we found the woman Odets said he was going to marry sitting by his side. Odets said, "Go away now, fellows, I want to be alone with ——." That night we flew back to New York without seeing our friend again.

Two days later Odets's sister Florence called to tell me that her brother was in a coma and not expected to live more than a few hours. Speaking for his family, she asked me to write a eulogy. I did, and it was read at the funeral service by Danny Kaye. Lee Strasberg and his wife, Paula, had arrived in time for Odets's last hours. Strasberg, weeping, spoke at the memorial. Only a few friends from the theatre and film world had showed up; it was not considered a "big" Hollywood event.

I am convinced that the cancer Odets died of was brought on by the torment of his later years, the severance from his base in his beliefs and close companionships, and his inability to find a new base—something to fortify his heart, mind, and body.

CHAPTER 9

Europe Again
and Again

After my first sojourn in Paris, in the early twenties, I went
back to Europe many times, and since 1947 I have spent
between one and three months abroad every year. Among
the recollections I savor most are those of prewar London,
particularly of the strong impression made by the Group
Theatre production of *Golden Boy* at the St. James Theatre,
a meeting with Michel Saint-Denis, and a sudden outburst of
political passion on my part.

Michel Saint-Denis was Jacques Copeau's nephew. He
continued Copeau's work by organizing the Compagnie des
Quinze in 1930, which produced two plays by André Obey,
Noah and *Lucrèce*. Pierre Fresnay appeared in *Noah* in New
York some years later, as Katharine Cornell did in *Lucrèce*.
Saint-Denis was pointed out to me at a lecture on Lorca
given by Stephen Spender, but I did not actually meet him
till *Golden Boy* and the Group had become the theatrical
sensation of London. Our dedication to the establishment
of a theatre with a permanent company spoke kindly to both
Copeau's and Saint-Denis's own efforts, and he invited Stella
and me to dine with him at the Ivy restaurant.

He was somewhat skeptical of the "Russian" approach
to theatre (by which he meant Stanislavski's) because it was
too "theoretical." As a matter of fact, he did not know very
much about Stanislavski then, nor perhaps were his own
ideas thoroughly formulated.

The meeting was important to me only as it laid a
foundation for our future friendship. By 1968, when Saint-
Denis became, with John Houseman, one of the founding
directors of the Drama Division of the Juilliard School, at
Lincoln Center, he had successfully established theatre companies in Strasbourg and in Montreal, and had worked with
George Devine and Glen Byam Shaw to set up the Young
Vic, where Joan Plowright was among his many gifted
students.

On a number of occasions before the initiation of the
Juilliard program, we met to discuss in partial but always

cordial disagreement such subjects as stage and theatre architecture and methods for training actors. But none of these
little disagreements weighed as much with me as my feeling
that Saint-Denis was the most cultivated, innately refined,
spiritually pure person I had ever encountered in the theatre.
Though I was never as intimate with him as I had been
either with my Group associates or with several of my producer colleagues, he was my favorite man of the theatre.

Saint-Denis would travel anywhere and everywhere to
learn about a theatre, however obscure, that he was not
familiar with; I remember meeting him once at a theatre
conference somewhere in Greece. There was no "ambition"
in this; he didn't aspire to make a name for himself. It was
an impulse of love; he was eager to meet and know people.
Because of this, perhaps, he didn't achieve the success that
some less worthy people in the theatre have. But as a man
and as a teacher, he exercised considerable influence. He
could make exceedingly harsh comments to aspiring begin-
ners, but he took care that these criticisms never did permanent injury. That is why I was not troubled by our "theoretical" differences: better a good doctor with the wrong theories
than a bad doctor with the right ones.

That fine spring of 1938 in London everyone I met
seemed very nearly unconscious of the coming war. Only a
barber at the Dorchester Hotel spoke of Hitler as the "prime
bahstard of Europe." In a brief visit to Paris I could see
the seeds sprouting that would blossom rankly into col-
laborationism. Businessmen in cafés gripped their news-
papers, their jaws tight, as if they were prepared for any
iniquity as long as they could maintain their seats of power
and profit. At one of the semipolitical nighttime cabarets
that in Paris are often more truly mirrors of the time than
the ordinary theatres, I heard an entertainer in a supposedly
harmless routine declare that Léon Blum's "Latinity" (acerbi-
cally pronounced) was not to be compared with Mussolini's!
During the intermission I heard a gentleman say of the

entertainer, "He's not really nasty." But in London all was calm and shimmering.

At a grand party on some rich lady's terrace—as the director of a "hit show" in the West End I was constantly being invited to grand parties on rich ladies' terraces—I suddenly blew up at all the complacency around me. Had none of the guests any sense of Hitler's menace? The actress Ursula Jeans turned to me and said, "You're just upset because Hitler is unkind to *your people*" (meaning Jews, of course). After the war, I was most eager to meet her again so I could ask her if Hitler had not also been "unkind" to *her* people.

Despite the satisfaction of success, I didn't feel at home in London until after the war, when, ironically, austerity measures were in full force and food was scarce and of poor quality. The sight of the bombed-out buildings and whole gutted areas of the town angered me and made me sad. But there was a new spirit about, a lessening of the upper-class consciousness that had formerly been so oppressive. Like everyone else, I recognized the stamina of the English, their patience and courage and abiding courtesy.

I came to know Emmanuel Wax, whom I had met years before when he was just down from reading law at Oxford; he was now a solicitor, a play agent, and a producer. His first agency client was Christopher Fry, whose *The Lady's Not for Burning* he had sent directly to me. I read it with pleasure—I was particularly impressed by its delightful wit —and wrote back that it was a play that should be produced in England first. (I later met Fry, in 1954, when I was engaged to direct his translation of Giraudoux's *La Guerre de Troie N'Aura Pas Lieu, Tiger at the Gates,* in London.) Wax's second client was a young man named Harold Pinter.

One day Wax, whom I called Sonny and whom Fry called Jimmy, told me that there was a promising critic recently come down from Oxford who wanted to meet me.

He was a tall, lean, pale-faced, red-haired youth with a bad
stammer. His name was Kenneth Tynan. I soon learned
that, despite his stammer, he had been a prize-winning de-
bater at Oxford! Four years later, when I shared the platform
with him in a crowded hall in Detroit, I noticed that he
spoke smoothly, without the slightest speech impediment.
Eric Bentley later suggested to me that Tynan's stammer
had been a deliberate affectation, but I didn't believe this.

Tynan was especially interested in me because I was
both a director and a theatre critic, at that time for the
New Republic. He had similar ambitions. At our meeting
he advanced very few ideas of his own; he literally sat at my
feet. He ended by asking me if I would read some theatre
essays he had written in various periodicals as well as a book
of criticism he had just had published, *He That Plays the
King*, with a preface by Orson Welles. In those days Tynan
was all for grandeur and panache and more than a little
dubious about Stanislavski's ideas, especially about "emotion" on the stage—prejudices he had perhaps acquired from
his friend Welles.

I wrote him that from the evidence of his book he knew
very little about Stanislavski. He had, for example, asserted
that the finest production he had seen in London in recent
years was *Death of a Salesman*, directed by Kazan, who had
been chiefly trained in the Group and was thus indirectly
of the "school" of Stanislavski, which Tynan appeared to
scorn. I added that I did not think Tynan would ever become a director, but that I was certain he would soon become
London's leading theatre critic—he had that rare quality, a
real theatre sensibility, an innate perception of the theatre
not unlike the gift of "musicality" in those destined to make
their name in music.

A year or two after this he was appointed theatre critic
for Beaverbrook's *Evening Standard*. When I asked him on
one of his visits to New York how his new job affected his

writing, he said that it was causing him to simplify his style, that he could no longer display the full panoply of his mandarin vocabulary. I thought this a gain. So did he.

A few months after our first meeting, in London, I saw him act, as the Player King in Alec Guinness's *Hamlet*. I escorted Elaine Dundee, then Tynan's wife, to the first night. The evening was a fiasco. At the sixth curtain call (how loyal an audience the English make), sharp hisses began to issue from the galleries. It was the first time I had heard an audience hiss an important actor. The next morning one of the reviewers called Guinness "the worst Hamlet ever." After the performance, at a party given by Guinness for the cast and their friends, he made a speech in which he assumed all the blame for the abject failure of the production.

A year or two later, at a party, Tynan called me into another room. He seemed shaken. He said he had just been dismissed by the *Evening Standard*. He had unmercifully panned an old-time favorite, Donald Wolfit. His review provoked a series of letters over a number of weeks, the burden of which was that a man who had proved himself so bad an actor in Guinness's *Hamlet* had no right to condemn an admired veteran like Wolfit.

Tynan had sent a note to the editor saying that he did not mind being attacked as a critic, but if any more letters about his acting were published in the *Standard,* he would be obliged to submit his resignation. It was the policy of the Beaverbrook papers to print all letters sent in by their readers, and Beaverbrook refused to make an exception for Tynan.

I refrained from asking him why he had been so hurt by being called a bad actor, which had nothing at all to do either with his position as a critic or with his right to criticize any other actor (an irrepressible punster, he had, in one of his *Standard* reviews, characterized Gielgud's Richard the Second as Richard the Sickened). I simply told him, "Don't

fret. You will soon be appointed to a more important post."
Indeed, in very little time he was named drama critic for
the *Observer*.

His column in that prestigious weekly had a great deal
of influence in London. Fortunately, after a visit to America,
he modified his views on the "method." He also came to
espouse Brecht, veered to the left, and became much more
conscious of the social connotations of the plays he had to
judge. Above all, he championed John Osborne, Arnold
Wesker, and other young English playwrights. Of *Look Back
in Anger* he had gone so far as to say, "No one is my friend
who doesn't like this play."

He assailed the formidable theatrical Establishment in
England. With all barrels loaded, he fought the Lord Cham-
berlain's censorship of plays. His main action—the "spine"
of his writing, to use Stanislavski's terminology—was, as he
had said himself, to foster or celebrate genius. There is
something of the hero-worshiper in Tynan. His heroes
often change, but there remains a disposition to enthusiasm
for radiant personalities. For all his critical acerbity, he
frequently "raves." A number of other reviewers, lacking
Tynan's wit and acumen, sought vainly to outdo him by performing hatchet jobs. How the mediocre love to see their
superiors mown down!

Tynan is tirelessly ambitious, always aiming to conquer
new territory. He ached to become a critic in New York. His
belief that the theatre was more vital here than in London
irritated many English theatre folk.

I remember one evening in particular when, having
seen a rather poor specimen of Noel Coward's craftsmanship
and wit, we both went back to George Kaufman's house for
a late supper. "That play," I ventured to say to Tynan on
our way to the Kaufmans', "would certainly fail in New
York." It later did.

At the supper party we found Emlyn Williams and
that skillful tease Robert Morley. Hearing that I had for a

time conducted professional acting classes, Morley twitted me with "You know you can't teach acting. You only do it for the money." I immediately conceded the point. Not having succeeded in drawing blood from me, he began to work toward what I correctly assumed was the more challenging target: Tynan.

Morley began by saying slightly disparaging things about the American theatre, with which he knew Tynan was infatuated. I warned Tynan not to snap at the bait, that Morley was merely being naughty. Tynan bridled: yes, the American theatre was more advanced than the English (it would be two years before the English theatre would be "reawakened"). "Why, Clurman just told me that the play we saw tonight would be an immediate failure in New York. Here it will probably run a year." "I'm willing to wager five pounds," Morley countered, "that it won't run more than six months here—if that long." "I'll take you up on that," Tynan snapped back.

I thought the matter would end there. But no, Morley went on to insist that British actors were far superior to American actors. "Name one British actor," Tynan challenged, "who can impersonate a man who earns less than fifteen pounds a week as convincingly as an American actor can." To which Morley's mischievous reply was "Who wants to?"

Finally Morley said, "If you think so well of the American theatre, why don't you become a New York critic?" "I wish someone would ask me to," Tynan replied. Not long afterward, the *New Yorker* did.

As a New York critic, he sometimes praised my direction and he sometimes panned it. Yet we remained good friends. One day, just after he had written that my direction of *The Cold Wind and the Warm* was "stale" (I suspect he was right), we found ourselves at the same party. As I entered the room, I saw him over in the far corner. He ran toward me, almost shouting, "I've just written a rave review of your new book," to which I calmly replied, "You can write whatever you like about me"—which nonplused him for a moment. Perhaps he didn't know what I was referring to. Critics don't always remember the details of their reviews.

Tynan quit the *New Yorker* after two seasons. At a gala farewell party, I asked him why he was going back to England; the *New Yorker* had offered him every inducement to remain. He was, he said, disappointed in the New York theatre. And the English theatre was enjoying a new lease on life.

The intellectual stars of the postwar years were Jean Paul Sartre and all his friends and followers. They were journalists and critics, politicians, philosophers, and musicians, and they gave Paris a new effulgence, as if it might once again lead the world.

Immediately after the war, I heard Sartre speak at a meeting in the small auditorium in Carnegie Hall; on the platform with him was the still little known anthropologist Claude Lévi-Strauss, now a member of the French Academy, who spoke, in English, with astonishing fluency on the new French philosophers. Lévi-Strauss appeared amused, with a twinkle of assured superiority in his eyes. I had the feeling he would have liked to engage Sartre in debate, but nothing Sartre had said lent itself to contention of any kind. Sartre kept looking at Lévi-Strauss as if he were watching a clever juggling feat of which he didn't recognize the necessity or the point.

Sartre's speech dealt with the new drama he and his friends—he mentioned Simone de Beauvoir—were then writing. He spoke of a "poor theatre" (in a different sense from Grotowski's later use of the term), a theatre centered on ideas, not ostentation or scenic opulence. By "ideas" he meant of course those he had just set forth in his pamphlet *Existentialism as Humanism:* there is no God, no metaphysical certainty, no central supportive force; one simply acts and creates a value through the action itself. In times of crisis one had to commit oneself to hazardous choices, although one could not be sure either of their absolute validity or of the chances for their success.

For all its French clarity, there was yet something vague and evasive in Sartre's exposition. The ends with which one was supposed to ally oneself were always progressive and humanitarian—there was surely concern in them for the working class—but one was not altogether convinced of their value. There was, I felt, an unanswered question at the core of Sartre's argument, one which he sedulously avoids. He is a revolutionary dedicated to the overthrow of capitalism, but what we admire most in him are the illuminating, endlessly sparkling fireworks of his brain. The man is courageous, often right, or at least sympathetic, but his existentialism is more a poetics than a philosophy. What I mean is that he plays the kind of stimulating intellectual game in which the French take special pleasure.

Simone de Beauvoir, who had not yet written *The Second Sex,* was in New York with Sartre, and one evening at the Museum of Modern Art I heard her address a large group of French war *émigrés* who were soon to return to their country. When she ended her admirably lucid talk, the chairman of the evening congratulated her; then, as if in special confidence to the audience, he added, "Of course, there are certain things in Mademoiselle de Beauvoir's speech I might dispute, but isn't it remarkable for a woman to be so adroit and intelligent?" I will never forget the look of contempt that De Beauvoir shot at the man: it would have killed him had he noticed it.

At about the same time, Albert Camus appeared at a benefit for some charity at the McMillin Theater of Columbia University and spoke on "The Moral State of Man at the Present Time." As a thinker or reasoner, Sartre was far superior, but Camus was the greater moralist: troubled, hurt, self-accusing, perpetually vulnerable. There was the sound of

litany in his speech, a suppressed sob transformed into something like song. He spoke of the wretched condition of the
world (by which the French nearly always mean France) on
the eve of World War II. "Painting," he said, had "lost
its color and design, novels their narrative interest, music
its melody, philosophy its direction, action its aim." The
war had nevertheless produced civilian heroes. A timid
clerk at the Sorbonne, who had always trembled in the face
of his employers, went out one day during the occupation of
Paris and began shooting down the Nazi occupants from the
apertures of a street *pissoir!* Confronted by evil, men who
had never taken a stand on any issue suddenly rose in revolt
and manifested a bravery of which nobody—least of all themselves—had ever thought them capable. There was an unconsciously religious note in everything Camus said.

Camus's speech was followed by several others. Halfway
through the evening, Justin McCarthy, professor of French
at Columbia University and Camus's American translator,
got up and said, "Ladies and gentlemen, I am sorry to announce that the takes of the evening have just been stolen
from the box office." Camus, with a sort of masochistic delight, slapped his knee in appreciation of the symbolic significance of the episode, as if to say, "There you have an
example of our present moral state." At first the audience
gasped, then laughed, then agreed to pay the evening's modest
price of admission a second time.

In Paris, in 1947, I again heard Sartre speak. It was a
hot summer night and the small room, packed with young
people, was not ventilated. The announced subject of the
talk was "Franz Kafka: Jewish Writer." Sartre spoke for two
hours without halt or fatigue, making point after brilliant
point without arriving at a summation. Hot as it was, he
didn't even have to avail himself of the water in the pitcher
on the table in front of him. When he finished, at about
11:30, he apologized for having divulged so little: he had
merely, he said, sketched an outline. A crowd of listeners,

unconscious of the heat and the late hour, rushed forward to ask Sartre questions. (I was reminded of his apology for being superficial when I heard the Catholic philosopher Jacques Maritain lecture at Hunter College on "The Life of the Soul After Death." He described with considerable logical coherence the soul's travels in the afterlife, as if he were describing a tour. Finally he too asked pardon for having merely broached the subject. One admired the virtuosity of the exercise, but one's mind and heart remained empty.)

Importance accrued to Sartre and his associates not only through their devotees but also through their enemies. The Communists were perhaps even more hostile to them than the Catholics were. They turned radicals away from close collaboration with the Communists just as surely as they attracted disaffected Communists. Sartre's prestige remained so great that, when he provoked the French government by his open allegiance with the rebellious Algerians, and certain authorities were advising his arrest, De Gaulle refused with "One does not arrest Voltaire."

In 1947, before I left for Paris, Waldo Frank gave me notes of introduction to both Camus and André Malraux. Waldo had walked with Malraux through the streets of Madrid during the Spanish civil war and once described to me Malraux's fascinated examination of a puddle of blood they came across.

When I arrived in Paris, I looked up Camus first, as he was the French writer to whom I was most attracted. He received me in his office at Gallimard's, the important publishing house of which he was the chief editor.

I reminded him of the evening at Columbia when the box office had been robbed—he laughed ruefully all over again—and went on to question him about the state of French writing. He pointed to his desk, piled high with manuscripts. "That is French writing," he said. But since this was no answer, he paused for reflection and continued, "We have lost confidence in literature. No one truly believes in writing any more. The *word* has lost its prestige." He thought further and said, "My new book has just come off the press." And he handed me *The Plague*.

I admired it enormously. Whatever its faults, it struck me as one of the most moving narrative statements of the confused courage of a thinking man in contemporary society, a man who undertakes moral action in spite of his uncertainty as to its immediate or ultimate efficacy. It is a pathetic heroism because it sustains itself without God, even without a reified or philosophic substitute for Him.

A few days later, at one of Gallimard's periodic garden parties attended by *"le tout Paris,"* I promised Camus that I would write an enthusiastic review of *The Plague*, which I did sometime before it appeared in English. He seemed very pleased at this prospect—I had heard that he took adverse criticism very badly—but at the Gallimard garden parties everyone assumes a mask of satisfaction: it is considered a great privilege just to be there. Still, I heard invidious whisperings among the guests, evidence of the continuing struggle among the French intellectuals: various mutations of the left in opposition to the new right, which was still being called Fascist. A total stranger hissed into my ear, "There's Raymond Aron: he's a Fascist." But hate at Gallimard's wore the cosmetic of platonic dialogue and lofty lucubrations about belles-lettres.

Malraux came late to our appointment at the Hôtel Pont-Royal, then the Algonquin of Paris. "I detest being unpunctual," he said.

I had met him before, at a party in Hollywood after his speech at the Civic Auditorium of Los Angeles to raise funds for the Spanish Loyalists. He had described, very rapidly and with fiery eloquence, how he had bombed Franco's forces. He has always been a true adventurer.

In those days he had been inclined toward the left,

particularly toward the Soviet Union. But the war had made a Gaullist of him, and by the time of our Paris meeting he was very much out of favor with the left wing. When I mentioned my meeting with Malraux to several film-maker friends, many of whom were then Communists or fellow travelers, they eyed me with suspicion.

Malraux asked if I was more interested in art or in politics. "Art," I said. From that moment he talked almost nothing but politics.

"If you return to the United States and predict that De Gaulle is the 'coming man,' you will establish yourself as a prophet," he began. "Some people accuse De Gaulle of having Fascist tendencies. That is absurd. To begin with, he fought the Nazis. And then, would I, who fought Franco in Spain, become the partisan of a Fascist? What De Gaulle wants is a strong president—ideally to be elected by popular suffrage. There would also be a traditional parliament—in other words, a system very much like yours in the States."

When, within two years of taking office, De Gaulle abandoned power, the disappointed Malraux delivered himself of the famous quip "De Gaulle reached the Rubicon and washed his laundry in it." I was in Paris in 1958 on the night De Gaulle returned to power—the city was bristling with armed police while klaxons were blaring *"Algérie Française"* and automobile windows were being smashed at random. I caught a stone myself, in the leg.

Apart from his writing, I am grateful to Malraux for ordering the façades of the historic Paris buildings cleaned up so that now the city gleams again in its original "gold." He also did well to appoint Jean Louis Barrault director of the Théâtre de France at the Odéon, but then he did the unforgivable by dismissing him for the sympathy he showed the rebellious French youth during the student uprising of May, 1968.

I have read and been impressed by Malraux's several volumes on art, but Henry Kahnweiler, the remarkable man who in 1910 served as dealer for the cubists and made a fortune selling Picasso, Braque, Masson, and others, told me that at a dinner at his home, Malraux and Meyer Schapiro of Columbia University engaged in a prolonged discussion about painting, sculpture, and so on. "Malraux was no match for Schapiro," Kahnweiler said. "Schapiro's knowledge was far more extensive and profound."

I went to see the work of Dubuffet, Balthus, and Fautrier, which Malraux had recommended. I had never before heard of Fautrier. At the Galerie Maeght, then on the Place Vendôme, Maeght himself hauled out a number of Fautrier canvases for me to examine. In semiexpressionist manner, his work reflected the unspeakable horrors of the concentration camp. Malraux maintained that Fautrier and a painter named Wols had preceded our abstract expressionists.

As to Dubuffet, I had written a column about his first show at the Pierre Matisse Gallery in New York. I found his painting in its *art brut* phase much more fascinating than his later work, which has established him as a leading modern painter.

Dubuffet welcomed me to his Left Bank studio and home on the Rue de Vaugirard. He had few admirers then; in fact, he was little known outside a restricted circle of amateurs. Picasso didn't think much of him, but Matisse did and no doubt advised his son Pierre to exhibit him.

Dubuffet was bald, short, stocky, energetic; I thought it curious that this "new" painter should already be over forty. "One shouldn't paint to earn one's living," he said. So he became a wine merchant. This proved a total failure, and he had been "forced" into painting to make money!

Like so many "new" men in the arts, he seemed to have little respect for his immediate elders. Picasso, he said, had had only one good period. I didn't ask him to name it.

Dubuffet's close friend was the poet Henri Michaux, in whose work I recognized a yearning for the void, a flight from reason and reality, and a mood—somewhere between religion and revolution—that was to dominate American writing in the late fifties and the sixties. Dubuffet's own work expressed a hoodlum's derisiveness in a style resembling the graffiti of a Parisian street urchin. Dubuffet agreed with me that his portrait of Michaux made him look mistrustful. "Yes," Dubuffet said, "he is mistrustful." But this may have been truer of Dubuffet in those days than of Michaux. For I remembered a poem by Michaux, which Malcolm Cowley had translated, an ambiguously sad poem that spoke to some of my own lapses into weariness and disaffection during the war years in Hollywood, and which anticipated and foreshadowed so much of what was to come. The poem was called "Clown."

One day
One day soon, perhaps
One day I shall tear loose the anchor
  that holds my ship far from the sea.
With the sort of courage it takes to be nothing but nothing
I shall let go of whatever seems to me incredibly close.
I shall hack it off, overturn and smash it,
  send it tumbling down.
At one stroke emptying myself of my miserable shame, my
  miserable schemes, my slow logical progressions.
Having drained the abscess of being somebody
I shall again drink deeply of nourishing space.
By follies, by failures (what is failure?)
  by explosion, by emptiness, by a total dissipation,
  I shall expel from my being the form that seemed
  so well attached, composed, coordinated, suited to
  my surroundings and to my worthy, so worthy fellows . . .
Clown, groveling in the absurd, in public mockery, in the
  feeling that against
All reason I had formed of my importance
I shall plunge
Penniless into the infinite underlying mind open to all

Myself open to a new and incredible dew.
By dint of being null
And flat
And laughable.

I looked forward to meeting Balthus. His studio was on the Rue de l'Ancienne-Comédie, on the Left Bank, but he lived at a much more fashionable Right Bank address. Tall, slender, pale-faced, fine-featured, he looked like a prince of a moribund race, a man of mystery. I thought I detected a slight limp in his walk. This may have been an illusion, because I fancied him as somehow Byronic. "Balthus" is a pseudonym. He is said to be the scion of a noble Polish family. I have even heard fantastic gossip to the effect that he is the illegitimate son of Rilke!

He spoke in a subdued, melancholy manner. "Paris," he mused, "is no longer the center." He felt isolated, outside the mainstream, because his art was not "abstract." "Everybody nowadays is abstract," he said. The paintings I saw in his studio and later at the Pierre Matisse Gallery in New York were oddly beautiful. His models were nymphets and adolescent boys who looked as wise as serpents, and cats who looked even wiser, who saw through the children, understood their secrets, and seemed to be trying to communicate their knowledge through a "smile." Technically flawless, the paintings glowed in an indeterminate yellow. The figures, immersed in this strange atmosphere, appeared to be separated from the world, to belong to a special realm. Some years later I went to see Balthus's show at the Louvre. Malraux, then minister of culture, had arranged the exhibition and written the critical appreciation for its catalogue.

A couple of years ago in Rome, I was invited to the *vernissage* of paintings by a young Italian artist. As usual at such occasions, hardly anyone looked at the paintings: only the celebrities and the champagne were of interest to the guests. As I made my way to the back room of the gallery, I

saw a tall, gray-haired, slightly corpulent, eminently re-
spectable-looking man, dressed in a suit of rich fabric and
finest weave, whom I would never have recognized as Balthus
had he not been pointed out to me. Seated near him was an
exquisite young Japanese woman in a kimono: his wife.

He said, "I do not paint any more. There's too much
painting." He had for many years now been the director of
the French Academy in Rome (the Villa Medici), where prize-
winners in art and music from the conservatories in Paris are
sent for three years to work at their leisure. There was no
longer any air of mystery about him. He was an aloof member
of the French cultural Establishment, an artist who had
become an academician.

CHAPTER

10

Other Places

On my way to Israel in 1949 to direct *Montserrat* by Emmanuel Roblès for the Habimah Theatre, I stopped off in Rome. I was as surprised to hear the maids at the Ambasciatori Palazzo Hotel speaking German more readily than French as I was to see an invasion of American film folk. The ubiquitous Irwin Shaw was in town, also bound for Israel. The paganism of the Michelangelo ceiling in the Sistine Chapel made a greater impression on me than anything except the lovely Constance Dowling.

I first met Constance when she was seventeen; she was an usher at the Belasco Theatre during the run of *Golden Boy*. Now, she and her equally beautiful sister Doris were living in a sumptuous apartment in the fashionable Parioli quarter. Constance told me with a wicked smile that there was a brothel somewhere in the building. But despite the Dowlings' living quarters, the girls were so broke that Constance had to borrow some money from me.

Constance and Doris were part of a determined band of young American actors who, unable to break resoundingly into movies in Hollywood, looked to Rome as a favorable ground for furthering their careers. The two girls were immediately taken up, Constance by Cesare Pavese and Doris by Raf Vallone.

Through Pavese and Vallone, the Dowlings became ever more intensely involved in Roman life, which they came to love ardently. But the relationships had their difficulties. Raf Vallone, for example, never understood how ambitious an American actress can be. He could not see why Doris wanted to spend an evening at a party with film director Anatole Litvak rather than with him, even after she explained that seeing Litvak might lead to a part in a movie. She was, Vallone insisted, "his" girl.

When Cesare Pavese committed suicide in 1950, the Dowlings' Roman sojourn came to an abrupt end. Pavese's family and friends accused Constance of having distracted him from his critical writings and translations and, more important, from his political commitments. Convinced that her refusal to marry him had precipitated his suicide, the Pavese circle threatened the Dowlings with violence if they did not leave Rome at once. But Constance was wholly blameless. Pavese's letters and short stories reveal in full measure the melancholy hypersensitivity ever present in him —the incapacity to withstand the "slings and arrows."

With Virginia and Robert Whitehead I went to Roberto Rossellini's house in the Parioli district. The atmosphere was warm, cordial, and, between Rossellini and Ingrid Bergman, whom he had recently married, amorous. After the evening's festivity, Whitehead, inspired by the heat the Rossellini-Bergman relation had generated all around, remarked that it was wonderful to witness so much love. "Indeed it is," I said, "but the marriage won't last." He was astonished. "Why do you say that?" he asked. "It is clear that they love each other," I said. "But along with her love there is the star actress's need to be associated with an outstanding director who will cast her in his films and make her shine ever more brightly. Rossellini no doubt intends to do just that. But he doesn't make the kind of film glamorous women can star in."

The next day Whitehead and Bergman and I drove out to an open field near a sheepfold where Rossellini was shooting a film with nonactors about the life of Saint Francis of Assisi. The scene to be filmed that day was a transitional and not very interesting one, and we spent most of our time waiting for the sun to co-operate. During the lull in rehearsal, Rossellini undertook to give us no less than an explanation of Italian Catholicism. "It is not God the Father or Jesus his Son to whom the Italians are devoted as much as to Mary. She is a mother, the Mother who understands and forgives all. The Italian therefore feels 'free': his Mother will always care for him."

We followed Rossellini's Alfa Romeo to a restaurant in the countryside—not an easy feat, for he drove with what at the time I considered maniacal speed. After I had spent a few more holidays in Rome, however, I recognized his driving to be typically Italian.

Rossellini spoke of how the Italians had waited in Rome for the American army to fight its way up the "boot." They were so slow! " 'When will they ever come?' we all thought and said," Rossellini recalled, as if, all these five years later, he was still outraged and impatient.

Later, Whitehead, who had driven an ambulance dur- that campaign, exclaimed, "The Italians were waiting—*we* were *fighting!*"

Four years later, through Richard Basehart, I met Fellini. Basehart, who had acted in my most short-lived production, Maxwell Anderson's dramatization of Brendan Gill's *The Day the Money Stopped,* was now living in Rome with his wife, the actress Valentina Cortesa. He had appeared memorably in one of my favorite Fellini films: *La Strada.* Basehart and Cortesa brought me to Fellini's house, where his wife, Giulietta Masina, prepared the best spaghetti I have ever tasted.

Fellini was easygoing, humorous, playful, even mischievous. He clearly enjoyed teasing Basehart. He spoke frankly of the morals and manners of several stars he had worked with and observed. He faulted Lollobrigida for being too concerned with her appearance before the camera; he preferred Loren, who was much more truly an unabashed woman.

From here, he went on to explain—this was what I had been waiting for—the nourishing inspiration of his films: his boyhood companions in his native Rimini, and their deterioration as they grew older, the theme, in effect, of the endearingly wistful *I Vitelloni.*

When I told him, "If I had done nothing else during my stay in Rome but meet you, it would still have been worth while," he tapped me gratefully on the knee.

By 1965, when he arrived in New York for the first showing of *Juliet of the Spirits,* he had achieved world renown. He was honored at a party at which assorted deep thinkers plied him with questions about the movie's symbolism and its aesthetic, national, social, and sexual implications. Some perversity in me made me remind him of my visit to his house with Basehart and Cortesa and of my abiding appreciation of Masina's spaghetti.

A few days later, I read an interview with Masina in the New York *Times* in which she confessed that she was not as passionate about acting as she was about cooking spaghetti. I had always loved her as an actress, but now I was absolutely wild about her.

In Rome, during the summer of 1971, a former acting student of mine called to tell me that she was covering Fellini's shooting of his latest film, *Roma,* for some magazine and that she hoped I would come one night and watch him direct a scene in the Piazza Navona. I went and reintroduced myself to him. He was friendly, but naturally preoccupied. His work on *Roma* was hazardous and costly and so protracted that it would probably have never ended had not the money and the producer's patience concurrently run out. When Fellini invited me to sit down and follow the sequence he was preparing to shoot—I was not disturbing him at all, he assured me—I left at once, because I did not have all night.

Every day, during the long pauses in the filming while the cameras were being set up and the lights adjusted, Fellini would disappear for long stretches of time—he is a leisurely worker. No one was sure where he went or what he did. One of the things he did, I discovered, was doodle. My ex-student wanted to know what he drew, and she asked if she might have his doodling notebook. He gave it to her, and that is how I came to see the drawings. They were all of penises in fantastic flights of elevation. I mused a bit as to their meaning. . . . Before the young woman left Rome that summer, Fellini asked her to return the book.

In Tokyo in 1965, I was invited to direct *Long Day's Journey into Night* with an all-American cast, of which the late Ruth White was the best Mrs. Tyrone I have ever seen. This was produced as a demonstration for the Kumo ("Cloud") company, which later presented the play in Japanese. We also gave two performances for specially invited audiences composed of many Japanese and some Americans. Three years later, I directed *The Iceman Cometh* in Japanese with the Kumo people. The only thing I loved more than the technical challenges was Tokyo itself.

Tokyo itself . . . "twenty-first"-century in its proliferating industrial lunacy and eighteenth-century in its Nipponese ritualism. Indeed, all is contradiction in Tokyo. There, beauty is found in asymmetry. Morality is not so much a branch of ethics as of aesthetics. The population is at once caught up in the enormous modern energy and embedded in the age-old delight of creature comforts. The atmosphere is deeply sensuous. There is a sexuality in Tokyo far more profound than anything we know in the West. Rigorous, often to us appalling, discipline frequently collapses into its equally frightening opposite, hysteria. Steely strength coexists with an ineffable delicacy. Amid the disarray and the feverish traffic, there is an air of almost atavistic festivity about the streets. The town is full of huge entertainment centers, not the usual tourist traps. The poor don't stay at home in their squalid quarters, they go out to enjoy— and add to!—the general commotion. Tokyo is a mad, fascinating spectacle.

Apart from the actors, I spent most of my time in Tokyo with Tsuneari Fukuda, Koji Numesawa, and Yukio Mishima. Fukuda is the artistic director of the Kumo company, and considered the best literary critic in Japan; he has translated

Shakespeare and written a book on T. S. Eliot. He refrained from speaking English to me, whether from respect for the language or embarrassment lest he speak it incorrectly, I don't know.

I saw Fukuda laugh only once. During an interview on the eve of my departure, I was asked what I thought of an elaborate Japanese production of *Ondine*. "Awful," I said, and Fukuda broke into a quick, loud, unlikely gust of a laugh. The Japanese were not very often as forthright as I was.

He once asked me how long it would be before the Japanese could perform a contemporary European or American play as well as a good Western company. When I answered, "Twenty-five years," he winced. He paid me a great compliment in a short speech he made after the opening night of *The Iceman Cometh*: "I've been directing *shingeku* [the new, "Western" mode] now for several years. Seeing Clurman's production tonight, I realize I'm a lousy director."

Though in establishing the Kumo company Fukuda has provided Japan with a *shingeku* theatre, he is a political conservative. After he wrote an article strongly supporting American intervention in Vietnam, some members of his company reacted to his conservatism by striking out to found a theatre of their own. The political division was so intense that many of the actors of the splinter faction refused to accept the invitation to see *Long Day's Journey* if it was issued by Kumo. But when the American embassy extended the invitation, they accepted.

Lean, erect, always grave and dignified, Fukuda probed me about Vietnam, but I told him that it was my policy never to discuss political matters in a country where I was a guest. On one occasion, though, I did make a few critical allusions to the present American scene. Fukuda, resolutely pro-American, was disturbed by my comments. Perhaps he could not comprehend that a man's patriotism may take the form of dissatisfaction with his country's shortcomings.

"What is the main fault you find with American civilization?" he asked.

"A lack of spirituality," I replied.

"But isn't that true everywhere today?" he countered.

"Yes," I said, "but since we are the champions in everything, we are the champions in this respect as well."

Fukuda was a gentleman, in the best sense of that much-misused word. An actor in my *Iceman* cast (part Korean and therefore, I was told, innately ill-tempered) came in one morning slightly discombobulated by sake; he said he didn't want to stay on stage when he had no lines. When I asked him why he refused to perform his "business," he answerd that it wasn't important. "It's important to me," I told him. (All this through an interpreter.) "That's no reason," he grumbled, and added an insulting epithet, which *wasn't* translated, and stalked out of the rehearsal room.

When the incident was reported to Fukuda, he immediately dismissed the actor. Such infringements of discipline are not tolerated in the Japanese theatre, where the director is an "absolute monarch." The actor's breach of etiquette and professional duty was especially heinous as the director in this case was a guest of the Japanese government. Nevertheless, I asked that the actor be reinstated. Fukuda wanted to know why I was being so lenient. "Because," I explained, "the man is a good actor." "But if he is not punished, he will go on making trouble," Fukuda assured me. I was equally sure that he would not. His behavior from that day on was exemplary, and when I left Tokyo, he helped arrange a cast party for me.

Observing me direct the American actors in *Long Day's Journey*, the Japanese were amazed and enchanted by my gentleness in dealing with actors (I am rarely the martinet). As a director, I was granted every right. I remember how astonished the Japanese actors all were when they saw me embrace Ruth White after she had excelled in rehearsal.

I was fond of Koji Numesawa, the translator of the

O'Neill plays and my chief interpreter at rehearsals, lectures, and interviews. An enthusiast for American literature, he has also translated Hemingway and some of our more avant-garde playwrights such as Sam Shepard—of whom, by the way, Koji told me that beyond the literal meaning of the words, he couldn't make head or tail. I still receive letters from him asking me, in connection with his translations, "What is the Stork Club?" "What does the phrase 'to make a whole production of something' mean?" "What is or are *tzimis?*" But he writes much better English than many of my American friends.

Koji nicknamed me Uncle Fireball, and after a while the name caught on and the entire Kumo company used it in private to refer to me. It was a pleasure to work with these actors. They achieved considerable success with their own performance of *Long Day's Journey* though the Japanese-born American cultural attaché thought the play would be incomprehensible to the audience. *The Iceman Cometh* was the play it found incomprehensible. I suspected that this would be the case, for when I asked the actors at the outset of rehearsals if they liked the play, they could only look at me blankly—Japanese etiquette requires that no question be answered in the negative.

The writer Faubion Bowers, well versed in all things Japanese, had given me a letter of introduction to Yukio Mishima, whose novel *The Temple of the Golden Pavilion* I had read with admiration.

Mishima was one of the most complex and arresting men I ever met. He wrote all through the night, so that when I phoned him for the first time, at noon, his wife answered, in English, that he was still sleeping and suggested I call again at three. When I visited his snug and handsome house, in a neighborhood so remote the taxi driver had great difficulty finding it, I found his workroom strewn with long sheets of writing paper. They were everywhere: on the desk, the shelves, the floor.

He invited me to dinner and after that to a night club. He told me that he had recently testified on behalf of *Lady Chatterley's Lover,* which the authorities had sought to suppress. In view of the long Japanese tradition of erotic literature, this information astonished me. Though he had defended it, Mishima found the Lawrence novel much too "puritanical." He went on to mention that Kurosawa had made a film about a recent kidnaping. "Kidnaping is a new thing in Japan," he said. "We never had it before." A contribution from the West; the Japanese were learning!

He was a short, good-looking man with a powerful, tight-knit body, a long face, and close-cropped hair. He went in for strenuous, even dangerous, sports, especially *kendo,* a kind of fencing with a long stick. He sponsored his own theatrical group, made up of actors who had broken with another company that leaned too far to the left. He had acted in a film version of his *Golden Pavilion.* He had also been photographed in a variety of poses, many of them nude. One of them showed him bent over with a banana stuck in his anus.

He asked my opinion of the translations of some of the many plays he had written. "I trust your judgment," he said. I had favorably reviewed another of his novels, *The Sailor Who Fell from Grace with the Sea,* wherein a group of well-born boys murder a sea captain whom they had at first idolized. They regarded his occupation as romantic, the symbol of a free life. They murder him because he has planned to give up his heroic position and settle down in marriage to the gang leader's mother, who runs a shop selling Western-style women's clothing—a petty, mercenary trade! The boys have trained themselves for whatever act, daring or cruel, may be needed to transform the vulgar world into a nonmaterialistic utopia.

Everything about Mishima was ambivalent. He was strongly drawn to the bygone samurai tradition. It was this chivalric order that he envisioned as inalienably Japanese and therefore lofty and splendid. Yet he lived in a Western-type house, dressed in Western clothes, liked Western cooking, and smoked (not at all customary in Japan) Havana cigars. He was also an avid reader of European literature, Proust in particular.

He invited me to dine with him one evening and to accompany him afterward to the last performance of two of his modern Nō plays. On the way, we stopped off at his house, where his pretty little son was playing just before being put to bed. His wife, a painter, petite and lovely, came in. I eyed her with unconcealed pleasure. "Your wife is very beautiful," I said. "Would you like to go out with her—alone?" he asked. He smiled slightly, with an expression that was curiously challenging, mocking, and mischievous. I remained silent, wondering what would have happened if I had said yes.

After dinner at a restaurant that served the best steak in all Tokyo, his wife joined us and we all went to the theatre to see his plays. At the final curtain, he was called on stage to make a speech. It must have been witty, because it made the acting company and the audience laugh heartily, and the Japanese do not often laugh.

At my last conversation with Mishima, who was soon to leave for India, he told me he had just finished the final volume of a tetralogy. I remarked that Japan was no longer the country it had been, at least as I imagined it to have been from reading its literature. "It has not really changed," he said firmly. "It only appears to have changed. At bottom it is still the same." It was quite clear he did not *want* it to change, he hated the change.

When I read that he had killed himself, under shocking circumstances, I recalled both our meetings and his writings. His early novel *Confessions of a Mask* (1949) was the story of an avowedly homosexual youth. *The Temple of the Golden Pavilion,* written in 1956, when he was thirty-one, was the story of a brilliant student who is badly lame. Mishima himself had been at the top of his class at Japan's most prestigious institution of learning, Tokyo University. The student of the novel is obsessed with love for the temple, which represents the most perfect image of ancient Japanese culture and aesthetic sensibility. Since the image seems to shame or "accuse" his own deformity and all that is equally crippled in the contemporary world, he feels compelled to burn the temple down, to immolate himself in it. In doing this, he is relieved of the burden of its challenging beauty and at the same time becomes part of it.

Mishima's "program" that called for the restoration of Japan's military status is not to be equated with the political ideology of the party said to have precipitated World War II. He was no aggressive militarist, no conscious "Fascist": his ideals were entirely aesthetic. He felt the need to absolve himself from some insidious defect with which he and the Japanese nation were in various ways afflicted. Such redemption could be accomplished, as he saw it, only by the most rigorous discipline, the courage for utmost self-abnegation and sacrifice, a matter of sovereign honor.

I remembered his short story "Patriotism," in which an army officer, commanded to open fire on a rebellious faction among the soldiers, carries out the order and comes home to tell his wife what he has had to do. Because of his act, he must perform the suicide ritual of *seppuka* (or hara-kiri), in which fatal decision she joins without the slightest hesitation or protest. Thus, with exquisite formality and a great letting of blood, they both silently inflict death on themselves.

When the crowd on the street under the window platform where Mishima, in the uniform he had designed himself, made his final plea for the renewal of the military tradition cried out, "You're crazy!" they were right. His commitment to a mystic vision of ineffable *noblesse* was fanatic. The extremes of idealism are always crazy.

Still, I think back to my several Japanese journeys with a smile, which is itself perhaps a reflection of the smile on

200 ALL PEOPLE ARE FAMOUS

the face of the Nobel Prize novelist Yasunari Kawabata, whose countenance was always graced by a twinkling skepticism, a tender melancholy at the enchanting ambiguity of all desire. The sensualist Kawabata was also a suicide. If Mishima's act was a homage to beauty, Kawabata's was a farewell to it.

CHAPTER
11

Return
Engagements

In 1954, Robert Joseph, a gentleman and producer of good taste, asked me to direct Jean Anouilh's *Mademoiselle Colombe*. I had not been enthusiastic about the play when I saw it in Paris. But my enthusiasm for Julie Harris, whom I had directed in both *The Young and Fair* and *The Member of the Wedding* and whom Joseph had secured for the lead role, won me over.

Brooks Atkinson commented favorably in the New York *Times* on the production and the acting, but he called the script "tired." I was nettled. On rereading my own review of the Paris production, though, I discovered that I had said much the same thing.

When, later, on one of my seasonal holidays in London, I went to see the final performance of Anouilh's *Time Remembered (Léocadia)* at the Lyric Theatre, Hammersmith, I found that Anouilh's agent had seated Anouilh and me together. I had never met him, but we had corresponded during the road tryout of *Mademoiselle Colombe*. In the scene in which Julien has learned that his wife, Colombe, has had an affair with his brother Edouard, he cries out to Edouard, "Kiss me!" Believing that this betokens his forgiveness, Edouard embraces his brother in fraternal gratitude. But Julien insists that Edouard kiss him as he kissed Colombe: he wants to know what is so special about Edouard's kisses! The audience howled at this. Louis Kronenberger, who had translated the play and who was also the theatre critic for *Time*, thought the laughter unfortunate. The French, he maintained, might accept the scene, but an American audience never would. Undecided about the issue, I wrote asking Anouilh's opinion. He answered that the French audience also laughed at the scene: it understood the pathos of its absurdity. The scene was retained as written.

Red-headed, wearing gold-rimmed glasses, with a regular but unexceptional physiognomy, Anouilh sat quietly beside me at the theatre watching Paul Scofield and the beautiful young Mary Ure in her first London appearance (she would later marry and divorce John Osborne) and Dame Margaret Rutherford. He made no comment till almost the very end of the performance. "Margaret Rutherford does outrageous things," he murmured, "but I like actors who do outrageous things."

In the taxi with Anouilh, on the way to the party for the cast and author, I mentioned that I was planning a production of Giraudoux's *Tiger at the Gates*. "Giraudoux!" he exclaimed. "He was the playwright who made me realize that drama could be poetry!" And, then and there, he recited the longest speech of the play.

I went on to speak of the possibility of my directing *The Lark* (Christopher Fry's translation of *L'Alouette*), but I pointed out that Julie Harris, who was to star in it, could not wait till I was finished with *Tiger*. "Let her wait," Anouilh said. "You are the right man for it."

"But, Monsieur Anouilh," I interjected, "you never even saw my production of *Colombe*. Besides, it was a failure."

"That doesn't matter. You did it well, according to my correspondents in New York."

There was something remarkable to me in this. Playwrights whose plays flop almost always blame the producer, the director, the actors, the sets. In this respect, Anouilh, reputed to be wily, shifty, and sharp, was an exception, as was the angelic Christopher Fry; when my production of Giraudoux's *Judith* failed in London, Fry, who had translated the play, went out of his way to reassure me that it had had merit.

Short and delicately thoughtful, with his beautiful face, gentle voice, and smiling eyes, Fry was the perfect playwright for a director to work with—a man of exquisite, unaffected manner, modest and witty withal. It is true that on the occasion of my collaboration, he was the translator, not the author, though at one point he behaved as if he were the author. When I suggested some slight alterations in the text of *Tiger,* he protested in Giraudoux's name. His compromise on this score was to permit me to make the changes, but when he had his translation published, he was faithful to Giraudoux's text and only made a note of my amendments.

Unlike most other artists I have known, Fry is a good family man. When I casually suggested one day that I thought husbands and wives would do well to take occasional holidays from each other, he gently rejected the notion. There was for him something profoundly salutary in what he deemed the permanent and indestructible physical closeness of marriage. Old-fashioned though such a sentiment may sound and be, there was no trace of puritan rigor in Fry's adherence to it, but, rather, a genuine purity of feeling. It was for me a clue to his real nature, and it inspired in me something more than respect.

When I left London, I put Fry in charge of the production from the author's or spectator's viewpoint, and I made Michael Redgrave, who played Hector, responsible for maintaining stage discipline and calling rehearsals if necessary. Fry wrote me a witty report on the state of the production, in which he said that "Wyndham Goldie's pauses [in the role of Busiris] are no longer pregnant, they are in labor." He made equally amusing and pertinent remarks in person, always in a small, unemphatic voice without ever a note of malice or grievance. Indeed, he once thought of retiring to a rectory. I'm glad he didn't: the roughhouse of the theatre needs such a man.

I was fortunate with the London cast of *Tiger at the Gates.* Besides Michael Redgrave, we had the enchanting Diane Cilento, whom Kenneth Tynan had recommended to me, as Helen of Troy, Barbara Jefford as Andromache, Walter Fitzgerald as Ulysses, Leueen MacGrath as Cassandra, and Robert Shaw, suggested by Fry, in a small part.

Michael Redgrave is so intelligent he destroys all by himself the silly notion that actors are or ought to be stupid. It is not even true that they should not be schooled, though someone has said that a university education polishes dull students and dulls bright ones. That actors are often childlike is certainly true, but that is not to be counted against them: the child in all of us is to be cherished.

Even before it was announced that I was to direct Giraudoux's play and that Christopher Fry was to translate it, Redgrave had written me that it was a play he very much wished to act in. I was astonished at the first company reading of the play to see that he got everything right, anticipated my every desire. Even most good actors need time to seize the dramatic pattern of a role. But Redgrave got better with every performance, though like several other first-rate actors, he is a "slow study."

An analyst interested in actors' behavior might well ponder the following item: after five weeks on tour without a mishap, Redgrave, in his first entrance on opening night in London, fell. A special platform, more than five feet above stage level, had been built to make his first appearance as the Trojan hero especially impressive. Since Redgrave is six foot four, his fall on the elevated platform was, to say the least, resounding.

Neither Robert Joseph nor I was in the house at the time; we were both pacing outside the theatre awaiting the first-act curtain. When we went backstage, I sensed at once that something out of the ordinary had happened. Redgrave stood surrounded by the entire cast; they were all laughing, and I heard Redgrave say, "Don't tell Harold!"

The audience—bless them—had not laughed. "What did you think of when you were down?" I asked Redgrave. "I thought I'd better get up," he said. The evening was a success.

At rehearsal one day, I asked Redgrave to read a speech as he imagined Louis Jouvet, the original Hector in Paris, had read it (I meant dryly). I saw that he was furious. A long pause followed my request. Later, in his dressing room, he told Bob Joseph, "Imagine such a direction! But I *was* better when I tried to comply with it."

During the New York run, I noticed that the humor in Redgrave's performance was becoming ever more pronounced. To "milk" laughs is a great temptation. When the company assembled to hear my reactions to the evening's performance I said to Redgrave, "Michael, you're pushing the jokes a bit too hard. You are not funny. Your own humor is a matter of intelligence; you are not a comedian by nature. You understand the jokes, but you mustn't try to make them." He remained silent. But in his dressing room, he said to Bob Joseph, "If Harold comes in here now, I'll run him through with this sword." Then he added casually, "I won't have to; I'll get Stella to do it."

Catherine Lacey, the Hecuba of the company, thought it was wrong of me to speak as I did to a great star like Redgrave in the presence of the whole company. Diana Boddington, stage manager of the English production, had remarked to me in London, "You and Tony Guthrie are the only directors who speak to stars as you do to every other member of the cast."

Redgrave is a strikingly handsome man, and I could see that he wished to remain so. I noticed that his make-up grew lighter (less "Asiatic") the longer the play ran, and his hair style rather more attractive. He is shy and easily hurt and eager to be loved. But it was just these childlike qualities that endeared him to me.

He is a devoted father and justly proud of all his children. Vanessa was a theatre-school student at the time of *Tiger*. She and her brother, Corin, attended rehearsals but managed to remain all but invisible. Her sister, Lynn, was too young then to attend, but I came to know her later. After Redgrave left New York, he gave me a subscription to the *New Statesman*. The Redgraves are all left wing—Vanessa, as everyone knows, most actively so.

Most British actors, no matter how "irregular" they really are—and some are very irregular indeed—are nearly always socially correct. They see and know and value the advantage of a respectable public image. Ralph Richardson, whom I directed in *The Waltz of the Toreadors* in New York, is not exactly irregular, but he is sometimes very odd— though always winningly. Ever formal in outward manner and dress, he is tall and massive and instinctively intelligent.

When I visited him in his beautiful house near the Spaniards Inn on Hampstead Heath, I noticed a violin hanging on the wall of his study. "Do you play the violin?" I asked. "No, I just like to look at it," he answered. There was also a microscope on a table. "What do you examine with this?" I asked. *"Things,"* he said. I extended my hand to say good-by to him, and he placed in it a live hamster he kept as a pet.

The late Hugh ("Binkie") Beaumont, the all-powerful London producer, told me how Richardson once invited a group of distinguished guests to a formal dinner and half-way through the evening went to sleep on his living-room floor.

Once, after I had dined with him and his wife at their home, Richardson offered to drive me back to my hotel in his Bentley. Meriel, his wife, sat in the back seat. The road from Hampstead to the Hotel Connaught in Mayfair is all downhill. Richardson stepped on the accelerator; the car rapidly picked up speed; and though the hour was late and few people were about, the ride was becoming perilous. I said nothing, but I felt my body stiffen as we approached eighty miles an hour. Richardson was watching me out of the corner of his eye. When the car began to race even more madly, he cried out like a kid, "I've scared Harold, I've scared Harold!" Reading Richardson's memoirs in the *Observer* a few years later, I learned that the "trick" he had played on me was exactly the one Laurence Olivier had pulled on him. In his memoirs, Richardson wrote, "I never forgave him."

Richardson has something in him of the perennial boy. He is shy, in a veiled way tender, and ever susceptible to hurt. I asked him if there was any mode of acting he subscribed to. He could think of only one: "The actor must *dream*," he told me, "dream constantly." This may be translated as the need for the actor to stimulate his imagination. But that Richardson does indeed "dream," sometimes unaccountably, I soon had occasion to learn.

During the run of *The Waltz of the Toreadors*, I saw him walk off the stage for a moment at a point where neither the script nor the direction called for an exit. Mildred Natwick, who was playing the scene with him, was quite bewildered. Richardson had meant his exit, during a funny and bitter marital quarrel, to suggest the poor husband's attempt to escape from his harridan wife's onslaught. In the same scene, on another occasion, he expressed the husband's inability to withstand his wife's barbs by retreating behind a velvet window curtain and wrapping himself in it so that he was completely hidden from view. After the performance, I suggested that this might be a bit too much. He removed his felt hat and flung it wrathfully down, and I for my part could not help laughing.

He was superb in his role, though his infected tonsils—which the American doctors proceeded to diagnose incorrectly—prevented him from always performing at his top level. Robert Whitehead, the play's producer, told me that on opening night he had gone into Richardson's dressing room after the first act and, to encourage him, said, "Ralph, it's going marvelously. They're crazy about you." Richardson was violent: "I don't trust them! I don't trust them!" He didn't want to hear anything that might cause him to feel "safe" and to "let down." I could have hugged him.

Sometime after *Waltz*, I visited him in London. I asked

him how he was getting on in the new play he was doing, *The School for Scandal.* "Well enough," he said, "but John [Gielgud] keeps changing his mind. He's worse than you!" One has to love such a man. He reminds me of a character out of Dickens.

During the preproduction work on *Tiger at the Gates,* Sonny Wax introduced me to another of his clients, an ex-actor, Harold Pinter, whose play *The Birthday Party* was about to go into rehearsal. It was a dismal failure: only one critic, Harold Hobson of the London *Times,* approved of it.

On a later visit to London, Wax asked me to introduce him to Roger Stevens, whom he wished to ask to "subsidize" the promising young playwright. Stevens agreed to do so and thereby acquired the rights to Pinter's plays.

The Caretaker was written under this arrangement. I praised it when it was presented in New York. I also wrote an introduction to a collection, *Seven Modern Plays,* which included *The Birthday Party.* But I never really had a chance to speak to Pinter until a party given by the director Robert Lewis in New York, where I asked him a simple question: "At the end of *The Birthday Party,* is Stanley taken away to an insane asylum, or has he incurred the displeasure of some racketeer who wants to get rid of him, or what . . . ?" Pinter's answer was "Any of these are possibilities. The point is, he is being *taken* away."

Wax recommended that I cast Pinter's wife, Vivien Merchant, in the title role in Giraudoux's *Judith.* I did not, because, out of nervousness or pride, she refused to read the part for me. We were both wrong: she would have made a splendid Judith. Later she consented to read for another role in the play and played it extremely well. I also offered Pinter a part! During this period I got to know him.

Unless one is his intimate, he speaks very little. At a table in a night club, after a brief silence, he asked me, "Are you happy?"—a question that totally nonplused me. He told me how Beckett, for whom he has an undisguised admiration, had once tried to help him choose a gift for Vivien. Together, they looked into various shopwindows. "There's something nice," Beckett suggested. It was something altogether cheap and tasteless, Pinter commented.

While rehearsals of *Judith* were in progress, the book editor of the London *Sunday Times* asked me to review John Russell Taylor's *Anger and After,* a book about the young English dramatists, in which Taylor stated that Pinter was the only "great" playwright of the lot. In my review, I suggested that it was perhaps too early to pass any such judgment in regard to new playwrights. Two days later, I received an angry note from Pinter saying that if my previous approval of his plays had been merely "patronizing," he wasn't having any of it.

I wrote back to say that I had certainly not meant to be patronizing, but that I believe the issuing of extravagant encomiums to young artists very early in their careers—such as calling them "great"—is misleading on all counts. If the artist falters later on, adulation might well turn to condemnation: "Well, he was never very good in the first place." This has happened to many actors, dramatists, and novelists —particularly in America. I added that I hoped *The Birthday Party* and a number of shorter plays of his would turn out to be a prelude to work even more remarkable.

When, shortly after *The Homecoming,* of which I wrote two laudatory reviews, I invited Pinter to supper and reminded him of our past misunderstanding, he said that it was silly of him to have been so touchy.

There is in Pinter a marked reluctance to declare himself, to say more than is strictly necessary. This is not an affectation: it is part of his nature as well as of his writing style. But if he is repressed, he is also passionate. He is what his boyhood in the East End of London, infested with Mosley's Blackshirts—the British Fascist toughs of the early forties who beat up Jews—has made him. But, assured of friendliness and praise, he unbends—as much as possible for

him. I told an actress at a party in London after the opening
night of *The Birthday Party* revival that there was something
in Pinter's looks that made me think of Byron. She immediately repeated this to him, and he turned halfway to
me, saluted offhandedly, and turned back to the conversation he was having with some other guests. The night I had
him to supper, he told me he enjoyed reciting verse. He
began a poem by Yeats; when his memory failed him for a
moment, he interjected a "Fuck all" and then continued
with the lyric.

I last saw Pinter in his own lavishly decorated new
home, an eighteenth-century Beau Nash mansion on Re-
gent's Park, at a party he was giving after the opening of
Landscape and *Silence* at the Royal Shakespeare Theatre. As
I ascended the flight of marble steps to the party room, I
murmured to the actress Diane Cilento, "Pinter's pessimism
pays."

Getting back to the promiscuous use of the word "great"
for the work of new artists, I am impelled to cite a talk on
the American theatre I gave in Tokyo, shortly after the successful New York opening of *Who's Afraid of Virginia
Woolf?* The question most often put to me was, "What do
you think of Edward Albee?" My answer was, "Ask me that
ten years from now." And the last line of my review of *Look
Back in Anger* reads: "In ten years Osborne may be as good
as people now say he is." Osborne, who seemed to like me a
lot when we first met, was decidedly cold at our next meeting.

I met Tony (Sir Tyrone) Guthrie in 1945, when he was
directing the Theatre Guild revival of Andreyev's *He Who
Gets Slapped,* in which Stella Adler appeared. I couldn't *not*
like him—Stella had remarked that he was the only director
who dressed worse than I did. Of course, he dressed much
better as time went on. And so did I.

I came to love Tony Guthrie for his laughing fearless-
ness and easy self-assurance. He was able to say anything to

anybody without giving offense. He often said very salty things not only to actors and authors, but to "all-powerful" producers. Yet, together with what might be taken for arrogance or conceit, there was a humble side to him. This is true self-confidence. "Touchy" folk have weak egos. "Nothing exceeds my conceit," I said once, "except my humility." That was the expression of a *strong* ego.

A pretty young actress who was taken up by George Jean Nathan and others of the critical fraternity tried to give Guthrie trouble at rehearsal. "Sit down over there in the corner," he instructed her, "and don't bother me." "Don't question what I'm doing," he told Paddy Chayefsky during rehearsals of *The Tenth Man,* "I'm a genius."

Once, over drinks, Stella and I heard Guthrie tell Terence Rattigan and "Binkie" Beaumont, who were urging him to direct more plays in the West End, the English "Broadway," that he didn't give a damn for the West End, that the West End was generally "tatty," insignificant, worthless, and that these words could also serve to describe most of their own productions. He said all this casually, as if it were so obvious no possible exception could be taken to it.

He did not fear, or apologize for, failure—always a sign of strength. He knew that failure is the norm of the theatre and success the "accident." When I told him that I had directed Konstantin Simonov's *The Russian People* badly and that the only good performance in it had been given by an actor in a secondary role, he said, "Funny, that's exactly what happened with *my* production of it."

Bob Whitehead told me that while he was producing *Tamburlaine the Great,* which Guthrie directed, he dropped into rehearsal one afternoon and heard this exchange: on stage, Tony Quayle as Tamburlaine was delivering a long, impassioned speech bemoaning his misfortunes; surrounding him was a crowd of noisy supernumeraries. Quayle stopped abruptly and called out, "Tony, if all these people carry on this way, not a word I say will be heard. Doesn't it matter?" Quick as a flash, Guthrie, out front, called back, "Not a bit. Carry on!"

Perhaps not surprisingly, many English stars who admired Guthrie did not care to be in his productions, and he, in turn, was not eager to cast stars. Redgrave summed up the paradox: "Guthrie is a great director. But if I'm playing the king and have an important entrance, I don't like to have a brace of monkeys holding my regal robes behind me."

"Guthrie understands the value of emotion in acting," said Beaumont, who also admired him, "but he's afraid of emotion." And this is, if not an accurate, then a sufficient description of Guthrie's limitation as a director. He was especially brilliant with melodrama and satirical comedy.

He told me how he had once got it into his head to produce *A Midsummer Night's Dream* Shakespeare's way: with an all-male cast. "Wonderful," I said. "And how did it go?" "It flopped," he said, without a flicker of complaint or regret.

He often had wild notions of this kind and did not hesitate to act on them. In 1946, when the British mandate in Israel was nearing its end and tension was high because of frequent eruptions of violence between Israeli terrorist groups and British troops, Guthrie happily accepted an invitation from the Habimah Theatre to direct *Oedipus Rex* in Tel Aviv. The following winter he directed the same play in Helsinki, Finland. He would have accepted an assignment at the North Pole if someone had offered it. He established the Shakespeare Festival Theatre in Stratford, Ontario, and the Guthrie Theatre in Minneapolis. Once he tried to persuade that bold entrepreneur Roger Stevens to do Shakespeare's *King John* on a ferryboat or a barge, but the ever-prudent Bob Whitehead intervened in time to warn Stevens that the idea was foolhardy.

Though his expenses would have been paid at the best hotel, Guthrie always chose the least fashionable place to stay in during a play's road tryout. He didn't like the constraints a "proper" hotel would have imposed on him. In London, he lived for a long time in a tiny apartment in Lincoln Fields Inn, a historically important address, where the ceilings were so low that he and his wife, who were both well over six feet tall, could not stand erect. Ralph Richardson reported that one evening when he and his wife had dinner at the Guthries', they ate the entire meal with the laundry hanging from a trestle over their heads. There was never anything the least bit grim about Tony. He was full of quiet fun, endless energy, and, long before it became fashionable, a throw-away vocabulary of Anglo-Saxon obscenities.

Toward the end of his life, he was appointed chancellor of the University of Belfast, and, later still, ran a jam factory for some "utopian" purpose. He was about to accept a visiting professorship at Hunter College when he died. A theatrical traditionalist, he would have knocked all the "artiness" out of the students' heads. His own art was above all lusty and boisterous.

The last time I saw him was backstage at a rehearsal of his production of *Dinner at Eight*. "Tony," I said, "I have a feeling I'll have to pan the hell out of you on this one." "You can pan me any time you like!" he said. He meant it.

He did a play in London with Robert Morley and Ruth Gordon. After the curtain came down on the opening night, he said: "I had thought it a funny play. It isn't. The audience didn't laugh." What a brave and honest man he was. What a rarity in the theatre.

One of the experiences I shared with Guthrie was the staging of plays in Israel.

For all its internal and external problems, Israel remains one of the few countries of Western orientation that is humanly vital. It bustles and buzzes, having achieved unity within dissension. As Chaim Weizmann is supposed to have said to Truman, "You are the president of a hundred fifty million people; I am the president of a million and a half presidents." Israel thrives on controversy of every sort. But every brush appears to end with a smile.

Israelis enjoy and suffer from a superiority-inferiority syndrome. They are at once proud of and annoyed with themselves. They are in large part an immigrant people, happy to be in the promised land and yet impatient with its physical limitations. I heard a taxi driver—a new immigrant —protest the arrogance of his recently encountered compatriots by saying, "After all, the whole country is only as big as a yawn."

When, during a rehearsal of *Montserrat* at the Habimah Theatre, I said something to the effect that all wars are wretched and unjustified, the queenly actress Hanna Rovina added, "Except ours." Even an American Zionist could parody the worshipful tribute Israelis pay their new-found home by asking me, "Do you think any other country has so beautiful a moon?" And the cultural activity! In relation to its population, there is greater attendance at concerts and theatre in Israel than anywhere else on earth. Virtually every town, village, and kibbutz has its own art museum. It is a sign of Ben Gurion's humorous wisdom that, apprised of such civic blights as prostitution and thievery, he commented, "At last we've become a real nation—like all the others!"

CHAPTER

12

The Sorrows
of Writers

Heavy drinking is not the only vice common among artists, who are of course just like other people. Think of Dostoevski's gambling, Tolstoi's fornications. Stendhal often made a fool of himself; Balzac did too much of everything.

It is certainly not true, as some would have it, that such men became artists because of their vices, though they are often quite skillful at wringing virtues from them. The artist puts the best of himself into his work. It is petty to dwell on the negative aspects of an artist's nature, though journalists and biographers have long profited by doing so.

The question of where the artist derives his basic material and inspiration from has given rise to a multitude of theories. Critics like Taine, Sainte-Beuve, and Edmund Wilson explain an artist's work by examining his environment and life history. Others take the work as the man.

When I was at the artists' colony Yaddo, in Saratoga Springs, New York, I grew impatient with its director, Elizabeth Ames, who could think of no higher praise for a novelist, a painter, or a composer than to say, "So-and-so is such a gentleman." When she had issued this accolade for the umpteenth time, I could not refrain from interjecting, "Being a gentleman isn't what makes an artist."

On the other hand, it is a convenient ploy among scriblers more adept at publicity than at the depiction of character to present their models sunny side up. Dorothy Parker and George Kaufman, for example, are often refracted to us through their witticisms. Dorothy Parker, whose play *The Ladies of the Corridor,* written in collaboration with Arnaud d'Usseau, I directed, was an unhappy woman whose tears were mixed with acid, and she was seldom far from hysteria.

The powerhouses of Broadway, more often than not, are extremely fragile. Kaufman was mortified by his infrequent failures. I invited him to a party at my house in honor of Michael Redgrave. Most of the guests were prominent stage folk. He didn't show up. I invited him to another party at which he did appear, but he did not utter a word all evening.

"Your guests are mostly musicians," he explained, "and I know nothing about music." I asked him why he hadn't come to the last party, where the guests were all theatre people. "Well," he answered gloomily, "my last play was a flop." "But that," I said in amazement, "was long before the party." "Yes," he went on, "but I had not yet recovered." Seeing me off to London to direct *Tiger at the Gates* immediately after my smash hit *Bus Stop,* he said, "I admire your business-like attitude." He had assumed I would be staying on in New York to bask in my success.

Sinclair Lewis and William Faulkner were certainly heavy drinkers. Nevertheless, I found much tenderness in "Red" Lewis, and nobility in Faulkner.

Odets based a scene in his unproduced play *The Silent Partner* on a story about Lewis I told him which Waldo Frank had told me. One morning, Lewis phoned Waldo at his home in Truro, on Cape Cod, and said he was eager to speak to him and would come by early that afternoon.

At the appointed hour, Lewis's limousine pulled up. Waldo came out to greet him. The chauffeur got out and said, "I need your help." Inside the car sat Lewis, in a state of drunken insensibility. The two men lifted the inert writer from the car, carried him into the house, and set him on a bed. The "guardians" waited patiently for the ill effects of Lewis's drinking to wear off. But at six o'clock, Lewis was still in a stupor. Waldo and the chauffeur lifted him from the bed and carried him back to his car, and away it went. That was the end of the important event. (In his play Odets wished to dramatize the unreliability of the "intellectual" in moments of crisis.) So, the flaws of notable men are common to all humankind; it is their genius that is individual.

I myself never saw Lewis drunk. What I chiefly observed in him was reticence and humility. I introduced him to Bill

Saroyan. Lewis was the "old man" of the twenties and Saroyan was the up-and-coming writer of the thirties; Lewis was a Midwestern Protestant and Saroyan a second-generation small-town Californian of Armenian descent. Saroyan was intent on proving that the differences between them were all to his advantage, that he, in short, was the "new America." He grew ebullient, boastful, and finally loudmouthed, as was his wont. "Look at the football teams," Saroyan trumpeted. "More than half of the players have foreign names—Czech, Yugoslavian, Polish, Scandinavian, and so on. These fellows are *more* American than the Anglo-Saxon boys." Lewis smiled and nodded reflectively: he showed no disposition to debate the issue. He understood why Saroyan had to assert himself.

Although Saroyan throws himself about a lot, his conceit has something playful and joyous in it. A woman once told me how, in an attempt to seduce her, he stripped to the skin in front of her. I wonder if he was surprised to discover that his exhibition provoked only laughter. Perhaps he himself thought it funny. His braggadocio and clowning are an act.

When I last met Saroyan, at a Met dress rehearsal of *Fidelio,* he asked me, "Is this for people?" "Lots of people enjoy it," I said. "Well," he assented, "I guess that's the answer."

Speaking of conceit in artists, Kenneth Tynan told me that Laurence Olivier had said of a certain member of the British National Theatre Company, "He's a very good actor, but he'll never become a star; he's not a big enough shit!" So many artists insist they are "the best, the foremost, the greatest," that I am always a bit surprised to find that they rarely have the self-confidence of a good shoemaker. I still wonder why they are not satisfied to be just themselves. If they were constantly to compare themselves with the giants, as Hemingway did all the time, all artistic creation would cease and most of those embarked upon it would be tempted to destroy themselves. (I remember Irwin Shaw's embarrassment when his publisher or his agent announced *The Young Lions* as "the best war novel since *War and Peace*.")

Faulkner was the soul of sobriety every time I met him. Yet the first story I ever heard about him had him lying dead drunk in a Paris street and being picked up by the police. When documents on his person revealed his identity, the officer in charge had him deposited at his hotel without further ado; there were more Faulkner devotees in France in the early days of his career than among us.

Jean Stein, daughter of the former ophthalmologist, jazz musician, artists' representative, film magnate, and centimillionaire Jules Stein, introduced me to Faulkner. Jean collected celebrities, from New York, Chicago, and Los Angeles to Paris, Venice, and Rome. She had a nose for people worth knowing, and Faulkner had an eye for good-looking girls. (When he was being honored at an official dinner in Paris by a group of great literary figures, he insisted on having my pretty stepdaughter Ellen Adler at his side.)

Stella invited him with Jean to our home. At first, Stella had been rather reluctant to do so, because on the occasion of a party elsewhere Faulkner had remained mute throughout the evening, and she thought this rude. But Jean assured Stella that he was not always so grouchy.

Indeed, he was not at all so at our dinner. I made sure he wouldn't be by sounding off on life and art, to which I felt sure he would add his own comments. As the evening progressed, he appeared ever more at ease.

After the excellent dessert, Faulkner rose from the table and headed straight toward the kitchen. "I want to congratulate the cook," he said.

In preparing for the production of Tennessee Williams's *Orpheus Descending* in 1957, I thought it a good idea to travel in Mississippi to acquaint myself with the play's locale. I flew to Memphis, hired a car, and called Faulkner to ask him what hotel to stop at while in Oxford. "At the Faulkner Hotel, my home," he answered. After an hour's drive, I reached the house, in what I took to be deep woods. (I am so entirely city-bred that Gadge [Elia] Kazan once said of me, "Harold thinks the only things that come out of the ground are snakes.")

Faulkner received me with utmost civility; his wife was not at home. The first thing I noticed as I entered the living room was a photo of a Confederate officer I supposed to be Robert E. Lee. It was a picture of Faulkner's grandfather.

After a pleasant dinner, at which Faulkner sat at the head of the table in a formally erect, somewhat military posture, we repaired to a small study. The whole evening lay before us. I took advantage of our solitude to ply him with questions in a manner that, under other circumstances, might have been construed as an interview. I am disposed to engage in conversation with people I don't know by asking a great many questions. This was a habit that particularly irritated Stella.

"What do the people in this town think of your novels?" I began. "They don't read them," he answered. "They know I'm some sort of writer. They consider me a good hunter, a fairly competent farmer, and know my family as long-time residents."

I questioned him about his attitude toward the decision on civil rights that the Supreme Court had not long before handed down. He believed it a mistake. After the War Between the States, he explained, Southerners felt victimized by the North. With time, the old antagonisms had all but vanished. But now he saw the Supreme Court ruling as reviving the conviction that the North was still bent on destroying the South.

"I understand," I said, "but to begin with, the blacks had to have legal assurance that genuine freedom and equality would follow." Faulkner said that he thought such freedom and equality would have followed of themselves, without the intervention of the Court. I remembered how ten years back, in Hollywood, before I had been formally introduced to him, I heard him say that he had learned a certain song from "the niggers." (I heard a good story about Faulkner in Hollywood. After he had contracted to write a screenplay, he came to the producer's office and explained he couldn't work in the writer's cabin that had been provided for him on the studio lot. He could work only at home, he said, and asked leave to do so. The request was readily granted. For the producer, "home" meant some house in the vicinity of the studio. For Faulkner, it meant Mississippi, which he wasted no time in repairing to.)

It was difficult for many of us at that time to comprehend just how extreme the situation was in the South. In places like Atlanta, one could attend a banquet, as I did, at which blacks and whites discussed the theatre and at which prizes for achievement in writing and acting were awarded to blacks as well as whites. But fifty miles from Atlanta . . . ! When, after leaving Faulkner, I visited Hodding Carter, a newspaper editor, at his home in Greenville, Mississippi, I found that he was carrying a gun in his belt. His life was threatened frequently on account of his liberal views.

The first evening of my stay with Faulkner, his stepson came in to ask his "pappy's" advice. (The young man never referred to the writer in any other way; it was always "pappy.") I no longer recall the issue on which the writer's counsel was being asked, but I do remember the answer, delivered by Faulkner with grave judiciousness: "The question is not one of morality but of ethics. They're not the same thing," he said.

The next morning Faulkner's wife joined us for a silent breakfast; I could see that he had returned to his preoccupations. His eyes were fixed on some distant horizon. I took advantage of his "faraway" mood to visit the campus of "Ole Miss" and then to drive around the town with his stepson. I was especially curious to see the quarters "reserved" for the blacks, which turned out to be not as extensive as in some other parts of the state. While on our way to our destination, I ignorantly and perhaps foolishly asked if there had been any lynchings of blacks there in recent years. "Oh, no," said the young man, "but if there had been, Pappy and I would have gone out and lynched the lynchers."

I wanted to visit the Mississippi village where the Kazan-Williams film *Baby Doll* had been shot. I especially wished to find a black man called "Uncle Pleasant" whose celebrated eerie shout, called the "Cherokee cry," Williams had heard and introduced into *Orpheus,* which I was about to direct. To find him and to get out to his place safely, I had to enlist the aid of the town mayor, who, typically, also owned the general store.

He asked me to follow him to a cluster of wooden shacks on dusty soil, where it was plain the people subsisted on the barest minimum. Yet no one looked miserable; in fact, there was a certain liveliness about the place. As I advanced to the center of the settlement, I was stared at as a curiosity. The mayor called out, "Where's Uncle Pleasant?" The old man soon strode down to where we stood and asked what we wanted. The mayor told him I wanted him to do the Cherokee cry. He complied at once. The mayor whispered to me, "Give him something." I gave him a dollar, and he walked rapidly away.

I went back with the mayor to the general store. He asked about the play by Mr. Williams that I was going to stage. "Mr. Williams and Mr. Kazan are nice gentlemen," he said. Then, smiling, he added, "But they don't understand things down here."

I met Carl Sandburg in Hollywood, where everyone seems to have touched down at one time or another. Like everyone else, I was struck by his tall, powerful figure, his fluid, stentorian voice, his shock of snow-white hair, a lock of which drooped mischievously over one side of his forehead. Without immodesty, he appeared very self-assured.

We talked a good deal about Lincoln, who was ever on his mind. When I asked what he thought of Edgar Lee Masters's little-known book on Lincoln, he snapped, "Masters is a copperhead"—as was, for Sandburg, anyone who doubted Lincoln's absolute integrity. (I met Masters with Mencken once at the old Lafayette Hotel on University Place in New York. He had a sour, shut-in, saturnine look, so that it was difficult not to think of the unhappy creatures in *Spoon River,* whereas Mencken was all bounce, laughter, and impertinence —a jovial, beer-swilling, broad-faced boy given to taunting everyone he assumed to be his inferior. I couldn't help remembering that when a journalist suggested Mencken write an article on Aaron Copland for the *American Mercury,* he asked, "Is the fellow worth it?" Mencken thought he knew a lot about music, but I suspect he believed, with George Jean Nathan, that no music of any merit had been composed since Richard Strauss.)

Odets and some other friends and I invited Sandburg to dinner at Romanoff's in Beverly Hills, where he was handed one of the establishment's encyclopedic menus. He put it down abruptly. "Serve whatever you like," he ordered. "I'm a farm boy. When Ma plunked something down on the table, we asked no questions, we just ate."

Theodore Dreiser too was in Hollywood, and I met him at Odets's. He was a bushy-browed bear of a man, as tall as he was stocky, and slightly stooped, as if his great weight bore him earthward. He was no longer read much—the young critics thought his prose as ungainly as his body—but I admired him enormously. I considered *Sister Carrie*—particularly the pages describing Hurstwood's decline—a masterpiece. Dreiser had dug to the root of and expressed *the* American tragedy as perhaps no other novelist of his time had been able to.

After the publication, in 1925, of his first best seller—

he had been writing novels since 1900—he was lionized every-where. He had been more or less neglected till Mencken's revealing essay in *Prejudices*. . . . At one of the parties given for Dreiser, Aaron Copland, who was also just becoming a "star," told me that Dreiser kept harping on how he had always been underestimated on account of his style. Balzac was a great novelist, he asserted vehemently, but no one ever maintained that he was a "stylist."

I had just heard a typical Hollywood anecdote which touched on Dreiser. When the story editor for MGM recom-mended that the studio make a film of *Sister Carrie*, no one had paid any attention. In desperation, he wrote a detailed summary of the plot and sent it directly to Louis B. Mayer himself, along with a letter pleading with him to read the out-line. "I didn't ask him to read the book itself," the editor told me. "He never read anything."

In due time the story editor was summoned to the boss's office. When he entered Mayer's lair, the old lion looked up at him and snarled, "You want me to make a picture about a *hoor*. You're fired." (The movie, called *Carrie*, was eventu-ally made by Paramount. Laurence Olivier played Hurst-wood; Jennifer Jones, Carrie.)

Dreiser was touched by Odets's and my attention and by the long essay on *Sister Carrie* Odets had written and read aloud to him.

Odets's behavior did not surprise me. He had always wished to ingratiate himself with the famous; he had sent copies of his first six plays to Bernard Shaw, declaring him-self his "disciple."

Dreiser had his sullen prejudices: against the English, for example. I thought this odd, as the English had been the first to recognize his merit. He was a limited man, and one of the towering talents of our literature.

What I found most sympathetic was his sad, doomed pas-sion for young women. His books give indication enough of his intense sexual appetite. He was seventy when I met him, and had become enamored of a young married woman, Stella Adler's niece Lulla Rosenfeld, whom he used to meet at Odets's get-togethers. She described to me the complete commitment of his embraces, how he devoured her with desperate kisses. There was something splendid as well as pathetic in this, because Dreiser was, by his own confession, impotent.

At our first meeting, I recognized William Inge's hypersensitivity. He was more withdrawn than any dramatist I had ever met, and excessively modest about his work. At our first discussion of *Bus Stop,* he asked if I wanted any revisions in the script. After the first out-of-town performances, I insisted that he substitute something for the joke that ended the second act, since it had nothing to do with the plot or theme, and he complied.

Inge was not afflicted with the acute vanity I had found in so many other writers. But on opening night in Philadelphia, when a TV commentator who had just reviewed *Bus Stop* in less than lukewarm fashion, came into the very restaurant where we had just heard his review, Inge averted his face like a whipped child before an unkind father. On another occasion, he lashed out at a waitress in a delicatessen who insisted on putting his hat on a hanger after he had placed it on a chair beside him. "I want it *there,*" he shouted, as if the waitress's act were an infringement of a basic liberty. His emotion was far in excess of the waitress's "crime." Inge was a gentle man, but at that moment I could see there was much in him that was repressed.

He had been an alcoholic, and through psychoanalysis he had overcome this. He rarely mentioned analysis and the help it had been to him, but its influence was everywhere in his plays. For him, analysis had been a light in the dark. Bill could not reconcile himself to his homosexuality, and I often heard him say that homosexuality was a form of arrested adolescence, an evasion of responsibility.

He offered me his next play, *The Dark at the Top of*

the Stairs, which needed work, but I was just about to leave for Europe—the worst time to approach me on any business, as I am always in spiritual flight from New York and especially from Broadway.

While I was abroad someone wrote me that Inge kept asking, "When will Harold be back?" Yet when I got back, I learned that he had turned the play over to Kazan. I had no quarrel with him on this account, yet when Bob Joseph invited us both to a party, Inge called him and asked, "Is it all right for me to come? Harold might be sore at me."

At the party, I greeted him with all the friendliness I felt toward him. I saw how relieved he was by my cordiality, and when my review appeared, he called to say he liked it.

Highbrow critics denigrated all of Inge's plays. They seemed to resent their success. Though Inge was certainly not a major talent, I believe he has been underestimated. His later plays, beginning with *A Loss of Roses* and *Natural Affection,* were too violent and unhappy for wide audience acceptance, and they all failed. (I directed *Natural Affection* in an Arizona tryout, but refused to go on with it unless he revised it drastically. Its final revisions made the play, directed by Tony Richardson, even more savage than it had originally been.) But there were vestigial elements of creative power and social relevance in these plays.

Inge gave up his New York apartment, on the walls of which were fine examples of the best contemporary American artists as well as paintings by Giacometti, and bought a house on a quiet Hollywood hill. Here he wrote a prize-winning film, *Splendor in the Grass,* which Kazan directed; several plays, of which all but two were never produced; and two novels, neither of them seriously reviewed. For a time he taught drama at the University of California at Irvine and at the Actors and Directors Workshop in Hollywood. With the exception of one light comedy, *Where's Daddy?,* a failure I directed in New York, Inge's last plays were fierce. They dealt with the havoc resulting from the suppression of instinctual drives, and our alienation from a society becoming ever more bewildering and cruel.

Even the poorest of Inge's later plays merited a hearing. In certain respects, they marked an advance over his earlier ones. They were less sentimental, less ameliorative. Technically unsteady and psychologically sketchy, they still testified to the burdens of our time. They are honest statements wrought from subjective knowledge and steady observation. Similar plays written by French or German dramatists would surely be produced in their countries.

Innumerable European poets, novelists, playwrights, and composers of secondary importance are still remembered and discussed with respect. We not only forget our lesser talents but neglect many of our masters. When, in 1949, I offered to write a biography of Eugene O'Neill, several publishers asked me, "Who cares about him today?"

I was in Europe in June, 1973, when Inge killed himself. I was deeply sorry. He was a lonely man, ill at ease everywhere. For him, living must have been a constant ache. Only work and acceptance of that work could have saved him. By "acceptance" I do not mean box-office success or even critical acclaim, but simply the opportunity to be heard, to be vouchsafed a platform.

I could not bear to read the various articles devoted to Inge at his death, but a phrase from one of them was quoted to me. "After *The Dark at the Top of the Stairs*," the article read, Inge's talent was "for all practical purposes" exhausted. But talent is not a matter of "practical purposes." That it is so measured, especially today, is deplorable and tragic. The fearful dependence on success is crippling to creation.

CHAPTER 13

Politicos!

Though I have known people in all walks of life, except farmers, I have had almost no direct contact with political figures. Or at least, on the occasions when I did encounter them, our meetings had nothing to do with politics; they were and remained private citizens to me.

John Lindsay was the most readily and pleasantly available of mayors. I was personally prejudiced in his favor; when he was a congressman, he was asked to speak at one of the yearly Obie (off-Broadway) theatre award parties, and in his speech he mentioned *Tiger at the Gates* as one of the three plays he had been most impressed by.

Once, after he had been elected to a second term as mayor, I drove with him to Gracie Mansion and told him why I had voted for him. "Since politics is a dishonest business," he said, "your dishonest reason for voting for me is in keeping with it." I thought that a handsome statement.

Lindsay is a theatre buff. He very often turns up at Betty Comden and her husband Steven Kyle's New Year's Day parties, where theatre personalities abound. One such party happened to coincide with Lindsay's second inauguration, and he arrived late. Almost the first thing he said to gentle Leonard Lyons—everyone's friend—was "I made the usual inaugural address, but what I wanted to say was 'I've been taking your shit for four years and now that I've been re-elected, you can all go fuck yourselves!'"

Such forthrightness should endear a public official to his constituency. But the contrary is probably the case. Franklin D. Roosevelt's occasional spells of levity—for instance, the mention of his dog Fala in one of his campaign addresses—struck the likes of Tom Dewey as wholly improper. And some people felt that Adlai Stevenson's "comedy" was an indication of "unreliability." The great are expected to be solemn. One thing is certain: Lindsay is not solemn.

I had dinner one evening with Stevenson when he was our ambassador to the UN. I was more than usually talkative. He agreed when I said that it was impossible for people to love anyone if they did not love themselves. . . . I neglected to say that to love is one of the most difficult things in the world to do. It requires enormous self-discipline! The dinner was interrupted by a phone call from the White House, probably from Arthur Schlesinger; this was just before President Kennedy's fatal trip to Dallas, which Stevenson had warned him not to make. While Stevenson was on the phone, Marietta Tree, a member of the U.S. delegation to the UN, who, besides Mercedes McCambridge, was the only other guest, suggested that I address our host as "Governor" rather than "Mr." Stevenson. She also said she thought the phrase "philosopher-king," which I had used, might well be applied metaphorically to Governor Stevenson.

Some time after President Kennedy's death, I met the fabled Jacqueline, at her own Fifth Avenue apartment. Roger Stevens had arranged a meeting there to discuss plans for the construction of the Kennedy Center for the Performing Arts in Washington. This led to the setting up of a committee to nominate a director for the center. I was appointed to that committee, and at several of those meetings I saw Mrs. Kennedy again.

Also present that first day were Arthur Schlesinger and Robert Kennedy, the latter dressed in a rich tweed fabric well suited to his rugged elegance. In his somewhat halting manner (Robert Lowell is reputed to have said that Stevens speaks English as though he hated the language), Stevens outlined the aims and wide scope of the project—characteristically, with tentative confidence and hopefulness.

Robert Kennedy was not at all sanguine about the center's chances of success. He pointed out that residents of Washington were not likely to attend such an institution in great numbers, and that visitors from other parts of the country do not come to Washington for plays, concerts, opera, ballet, or films. His head lowered, he spoke in a subdued voice, reflectively but firmly. His seemed the last and most convincingly discouraging word. But Stevens would not have it so. "I disagree with you, Senator," he said, with equally quiet assertiveness. But the Senator was not to be budged. He repeated his first contention almost word for word in the same neutral tone, as if no one else were present, and indeed no one joined the discussion on either side. But the Kennedy Center is now a fact—largely, I believe, due to Stevens's unremitting efforts, old-time American optimism, and grit.

The committee meetings that followed were all fun. That is generally the chief reason I go to such gatherings. I follow them as if I were at a show, a stage director taking note of the actors' performances. (Andrew Sarris noticed this at the sessions of the National Society of Film Critics, of which I was a member for a while. "You're not here as a participant," he remarked, "but as a spectator.") Oliver Smith, who was supposed to serve as an architectural consultant, especially in connection with what came to be known as the Eisenhower Theater, found that there was not much consulting for him to do. He therefore assumed very much the same attitude as mine. Still, we both tried to contribute something —besides laughs.

Mrs. Kennedy made several suggestions as to the possible director. Her first choice was Leonard Bernstein. At one point she asked, "What do you think Lenny will do when he has retired from the Philharmonic?" "Conduct," I answered.

Some reasonable nominations were vetoed on the grounds that the nominees were homosexual. The committee itself had no objections on this score, but Congress, we were informed, would never approve a known homosexual. When Justice Abe Fortas was called in ex-officio for advice, I asked him about this embargo on homosexuals, pointing out that two of the men being seriously considered were notorious womanizers. "Oh," said Fortas, "Congress won't mind that."

Even before the actual construction of the center had

begun, there was a slight hitch. The site the center was to occupy was also coveted by the Catholic hierarchy (in Rome, presumably). "That's rather naughty of the Pope," Mrs. Kennedy said, with a twinkle in her eyes I can only describe as cute. There was something of the little girl about her.

When I asked if she would like to accompany me to the theatre some evening, she unhesitatingly answered, "Certainly." I asked when and she said, "Any time. I'm always free."

I invited her to see Arthur Miller's *Incident at Vichy,* which I had directed. She said no, Miller was in her bad books because in *After the Fall* he had been so "horrid to Marilyn." When I suggested that we see *Tartuffe* instead, she readily accepted: she feels a special affinity with everything French.

At her apartment house on Fifth Avenue, I was checked by two secret service men seated in a cubicle at the rear of the lobby. In the apartment itself, I was checked—or received —by John Jr., who had a very Kennedy face, except that it had an almost too sensitive or high-strung aspect. The lad's dog growled at me, and little John reprimanded him with a stern, "Quiet! Naughty dog!"

Mrs. Kennedy and I drove down to the theatre in her limousine. As we stepped out of it, we were photographed, much to my embarrassment. She appeared to enjoy the play, but when a scene was staged showing the hypocritical Tartuffe conducting a sort of house-Mass (the invention of the director, Bill Ball), she whispered, "That's impossible."

During the intermission, there was a moment that brought out in her both the little girl and the first lady she had been. She said something about the inconsequentiality of *Hello, Dolly!* and voiced distress that such a piece should be so successful. When I rejoined that shows of that sort had always been extremely popular, a fact that was no cause for either surprise or indignation, she flushed, seeming to take my comment as reproof. Her reaction was that of a child being called down by a teacher, and I could tell that she resented anyone assuming a tone of superiority with her: one does not point out a *faux pas* to royalty.

After the performance, as we rode uptown to Sardi's East, I casually mentioned that though I had been eager to get to know her better, I had also felt some resistance to the prospect. "Why?" she asked. "Because I don't like to go out with the FBI," I said.

I studied her closely in the car. Her mouth is too wide, her lips too thin, her hands a little heavy, her eyes "out of drawing," yet the total effect is one of considerable attractiveness. She certainly smoked a good deal. "Since I was fifteen," she said. "They allowed girls to smoke at boarding school?" I asked. "Oh," she laughed, "we didn't do it on the grounds."

At supper, she was amused when I quoted Sam Behrman as having said about Robert Dowling, the late real-estate tycoon and occasional Broadway angel: "If you put a horse under him, he'd be a statue." I hesitated to say anything about her late husband, but she spoke of him. She mentioned a time he had asked her why she had scowled all evening long at a certain senator. "He said such dreadful things about you last week," she explained. "Oh," said the President, "he'll be nice enough next week when he wants me to do something for him."

We had dismissed her limousine, so when we left the restaurant I hailed a taxi. The driver turned immediately to her and very simply inquired, "Are you . . . ?" She nodded. He didn't turn back for a single other look during the rest of the ride. I remarked in French that this sort of thing must be wearisome. *"Oui,"* she said, *"c'est un fardeau. Mais cet homme est gentil."*

She was genuinely interested in educating herself, in exploring what her life as the President's wife and her early upbringing had not permitted her. She had always been on the fringe of such knowledge but never before had she been free to immerse herself in it. So, after the assassination, she sought out the learned, who in turn were flattered by her interest and eager to know someone who had lived so close to the center of power, from which they were usually cut off.

I was somewhat disquieted by the way in which Jackie chose to acquire the "education" she felt she had missed. More personal enlightenment is afforded, I thought, by an innocent wandering among the books, music, and art one truly enjoys than through selective guidance by "authorities." Most artists and connoisseurs are in their own way narrow, often even snobbishly exclusive. One's own taste is formed in time. Adventures along mistaken paths, freedom in error, may prove more nourishing in the end than instruction from the Brahmins of culture. When the unfledged try to fit themselves into molds of correct opinion, whether it be traditional or avant-garde, more often than not an absurd confusion results, and I imagine that Jackie's ascent into the realms of higher thought in the company of the sophisticated did not benefit her as much as she might have wished.

When she married Onassis, I sent her a note wishing her well. She replied, thanking me for my kindness. At a meeting of the Film Critics Society, I asked Arthur Schlesinger, who was then, among other things, covering movies for *Vogue,* if he had ever met Onassis. Schlesinger made a highly uncomplimentary remark about the man; he had not seen Jackie since the marriage. Why then did she marry him? "For security," Schlesinger said. Well, I thought, at least it was not for *national* security.

We can really know very little about people's motivations except through long intimacy with them. Perhaps the power of an Onassis can in the final reckoning provide the little girl of baffled soul who was our first lady and our intelligentsia's adopted darling with the freedom and support that had been denied her in the worlds of society and politics, in which she had moved for so long.

• • •

And now a story about someone who had fallen from grace.

One day, long ago, I received a message from the *Nation* that Alger Hiss, who had recently been released from prison, had expressed a desire to meet me. Would I call him? I phoned Carey McWilliams, the *Nation*'s editor, to make certain it would be all right with him if I, the magazine's theatre critic, contacted Hiss. One could not be sure of anything in those unsettling days.

Hiss and I lunched at a small restaurant on Twenty-seventh Street. He was tall, lean, sandy-haired, and his face surprisingly betrayed no trace of suffering. He looked, in brief, an unremarkable WASP.

He had been reading my monthly pieces on the arts in *Tomorrow* and was troubled that I, who seemed to him from my articles, a positive, life-affirming person, should find so "negative" a writer as Camus sympathetic. I explained that in my view Camus was by no means a nihilist, that, on the contrary, his philosophy was a rebellion against the depressing evidence that existence so consistently presents. To live, Camus says, humankind must pit itself against the enduring absurdity or tragedy of life. I promised to send him my review of *The Plague,* which, along with my discussions of the still untranslated plays of Sartre, I called "The Testament of Paris." He was not convinced.

After this literary or philosophical exchange I rather gingerly ventured to question him about his case. "I really know very little about it; I have no preconceptions," I explained. He was ready, he said, to answer anything I wished to ask.

I asked if he considered himself a religious man. I had once asked Paul Scofield the same question. In both instances the answer was yes—more unreservedly so with Hiss. He added that he was an Episcopalian, "the most liberal," he said, "of religious denominations."

I then asked if he had suffered abuse from people who recognized him in public. At the time we met he was employed in a lackluster capacity in a comb-manufacturing company. He had been shouted at derisively, he told me, by the driver of a passing truck, and once a man in the subway had called out to him viciously, "Why don't you tell the truth?" He had wanted to answer, but the man had disappeared.

I had just read a review in the *New Statesman* of his book, which had been published shortly after his release from jail. The book was a strictly legal argument to prove how improperly his trial had been conducted. The English reviewer noted that, while Hiss's exposition of the patent insufficiency of the evidence produced against him, and of other distortions of judicial procedure that had occurred, was well reasoned and impressive, he (the reviewer) missed what for him was one indispensable statement: an absolute denial of guilt. Why, I asked Hiss, had he failed to make such a statement? After a second's hesitation he answered, "It was perhaps a matter of pride."

In a moment of despondency about the deterioration of the quality of life in our country, I said to Justice William Douglas, "America is a fossilized infant." He responded calmly, "America is a nation difficult to judge. There is no precedent for it in history."

CHAPTER

14

Snapshots, Brief En-
counters, Stray Moments

When Brendan Gill, Broadway theatre critic for the *New Yorker* and ubiquitous guest at the city's best parties, heard that I was setting out to write this book, he suggested that I call it "Seeing Shelley Plain." (Gill is the only theatre critic who still attends opening nights in a dinner jacket. This was customary with nearly all theatre critics before the twenties. According to Kelsey Allen, who for many years reviewed plays for *Women's Wear,* theatre critics were given their jobs because at the time they were the only reporters who owned evening dress. The maverick Heywood Broun, originally a sports writer, dressed with exemplary sloppiness. He was also his paper's book reviewer. He always came to the theatre carrying a book under his arm—and would read it when he found a play dull.) I understood what prompted Gill's suggestion: the fact that I had known or seen many quasi-historical characters "in the flesh." I also remembered reading James Huneker's account of how, in his student days in Paris, he had caught sight of Flaubert and what awe the vision had inspired in him. But I had no intention of doing that sort of book.

Still, there have to be exceptions. One of the indelible memories of my student days is that of Sergei Diaghilev walking along from the Place de l'Opéra toward the Madeleine. He walked with ponderous gravity, masterfully, monumentally, as an ancient Oriental potentate might walk. He was of swarthy complexion, tall, massive, and altogether splendid. He had the look of a person who owned everything he beheld. He seemed to be in a state of profound cogitation, probing his own unconscious. Here is a man, I thought, of crushing, imperious will, yet endowed with exquisite aesthetic sensibility. He might be suspected of "decadence," but I could see him only as a creator on a grandiose scale, a czar of both real and magic spheres.

And as I set down this recollection of my frequent strolls along the *grands boulevards* of those days, there comes to mind, in grotesque association, another image: that of a very pretty one-legged whore who was always there at night, working the streets on crutches.

I met and listened to Stravinsky on a number of occasions. I say I "listened" because in his old age those who did not know him intimately rarely conversed with him; they just asked questions. He always answered very simply and to the point. (Stravinsky paid me the indirect compliment of saying to Copland that he had seen nothing better acted or directed in Russia than my production of *The Member of the Wedding.*) But the most vivid impression I had of him was the time I first saw him dashing along a street in Paris in 1922. He was forty then. A short man with reddish hair, a lean, agile body, sharp features, and penetrating eyes, he could have been mistaken for a crooked lawyer or an international spy.

Shortly afterward, I was much amused to hear Nadia Boulanger tell Copland that Stravinsky had said to her of a publisher who was trying to make an unfavorable deal with him: "He can't cheat me; I am a better businessman than he."

Remarks of this kind and the many artists' letters I've read are what made me say at a lecture years later, "Artists are dreamers . . . and what they dream about is money." One of the funniest sections of *Virgil Thomson* by Virgil Thomson is the correspondence between Gertrude Stein and himself, full of close argument as to the percentage of the receipts each might claim from the production of *Four Saints in Three Acts.*

Among the actresses I have directed, my personal favorites are Julie Harris, Maureen Stapleton, Kim Stanley, the staunch Uta Hagen, and Lois Smith of poetic and upright spirit. And I mourn the untimely death of the talented, hard-working, intrepid Betty Field.

I once called Julie Harris "a Sister of the theatre." She appears to have no life outside of it. Off stage she is private to the point of anonymity. . . . Kim Stanley's idealistic thirst for perfection—impossible of realization—on and off stage, is the source of the intense anguish and anger in her.

Maureen Stapleton's "fishwife" vocabulary—"an impediment of speech," Neil Simon wittily called it—makes it difficult to give credence to the fact that she is a constant reader of Keats and Yeats. But it is so. She must have been a victim in her early life of some nameless wound; to heal it she requires the escape of acting, the solace of close embrace and constant companionable reassurance. "Don't I always compliment you?" I once asked her. "Not enough," she countered. Nothing will ever be enough.

Each of these fascinating women deserves at least a chapter. So does Diane Cilento, the entrancing Helen of *Tiger at the Gates,* a bright and wild roughrider from a distinguished Italo-Australian family of physicians.

Of the writers whose plays I have directed or produced, perhaps the youngest was Arthur Laurents, in whom sensibility and a defensive aggressiveness are combined in precarious balance. The slightest rebuff, or what he suspects is one, makes him bitterly antagonistic; praise, encouragement, and affection melt him.

The oldest was Maxwell Anderson, whose ambition it was to emulate the dramatic masters of the past. Though gifted with humor, he tended to gloom. He was a thoroughly honest, moral, generous man, with a strong sense of justice and great compassion for the distressed. There was withal a softness that caused him to reel more than one commonly expects under the blows of misfortune and the weight of destiny. Every setback to his idealism—in regard to America, for instance—made him morose. When the first sputnik orbited the earth, he seemed personally hurt. He very nearly wept. "We are no longer the first." And he was utterly romantic—or sentimental—about the relation between the sexes.

When I met Carson McCullers for the first time she was already an invalid. She had suffered a stroke, which rendered one hand useless and left her with a limp. Sallow in complexion, she was tall, thin, the muscles of her face rather slack. Her hair was cut short; she nearly always wore trousers. Yet for all her debility, I sensed a stubborn will in her, resolution, and, above all, self-esteem. Like many people who are disabled, she was fiercely self-centered.

I remember her lying in bed in a Paris hotel—she was probably resting on doctor's orders. During the course of our conversation she asked me if I had read her novel *The Heart Is a Lonely Hunter*. I hadn't. "You must. It's one of the finest novels of the century." I smiled. "Why are you smiling?" she asked. "It's just what I said it is."

She knew next to nothing about the theatre: she hadn't seen more than a half-dozen plays in all her life. Despite the aura of illness that enveloped her, she sometimes burst into long peals of girlish laughter. This occurred, for example, when I told her that working with Ethel Waters in *The Member of the Wedding* had been more like training a bear than directing an actress.

I've already talked about charming, warm, witty, worldly Sam Behrman. One of the most remarkable things about him was that, debonair as he was, he was terrified of life. He had a Hebraic respect for the written word, an endearing worship of culture heroes, whose foibles and eccentricities made them especially fascinating to him. Born poor, he hankered for the world of wealth, elegance, and luxury, but his heart was always with the humble. He was a marvelous conversationalist. Once when we were at a restaurant with Robert Whitehead, his wife, Virginia, and our stage manager, Jimmie Gelb, Sam was talking a brilliant blue streak. Suddenly he stopped and exclaimed, "My Lord! I've been gassing from the moment we sat down. But what's the alternative? Harold will take over."

The Israelis call their native-born *sabras,* or cactuses, because they are tough outside and sweet inside. The description applies equally well to Lillian Hellman. Her probity is unrelenting. One of its finest manifestations was the letter she addressed to the inquisitors in Washington, in which she declared herself ready to answer any questions related to her own associations and beliefs, but unwilling to testify about others'.

On a more personal level, I have always admired her admission that a speech I requested she write for the final moment of her play *The Autumn Garden* and which she could not produce to either her or my satisfaction was supplied by Dashiell Hammett. And I'll never forget her response to my comment that Chekhov's characters, for all their foolish bumbling, were lovable, while hers were much less so: "But Harold," she said, "I'm not as good as Chekhov."

Tennessee Williams has a penchant for confession. He is tormented by a puritan obsession with sin that is largely relieved by pity and a sense of the ridiculous. If there is a vein of cruelty in him, there is a greater vein of commiseration. He is in quest of a God he cannot find. If he did not write, which he never ceases to do, he would go mad, he says, and I believe him.

Arthur Miller, earnest and upright, is sustained by a sense of mission. It is the deep-seated heritage of his forebears. He gains strength from this, which, like most virtues, has its pitfalls. For all his unbending seriousness and a certain coldness of manner, there is more humor in him than is generally supposed. He is much less rigid now than he is said to have been in his younger days, when he put people off.

His shining hour came when he refused to name the persons present at what might have been a Communist cell meeting; his position was upheld by the Supreme Court. Miller practices what he preaches.

Irwin Shaw, a long-cherished friend, is a man of good will, convivial, generous. I first met him just after he wrote

Bury the Dead. I asked him his age. "Twenty-three," he said. "Your trouble," I told him, "is that you're not twenty-four!" I meant he had to grow up. He has—rather painfully. (He laughingly tells our mutual friends that I still speak to him as if he were twenty-three. But time is always the present for me. I keep thinking of people as I knew them at our first meeting.)

He played football in college and to this day skis and plays tennis regularly. In the early days of his writing career, I thought of him as a "Hemingway boy." There were a number of young writers in the forties who adopted a Hemingway "stance." They were all athletic, sought adventure and engaged in acts of physical daring. They were all at once "tough" and soft, wholly American with dashes of cosmopolitan sauce. I was rather suspicious of this indirect Hemingway influence. (I once heard David Rockefeller say, "Travel is a substitute for action and action a substitute for thought.")

I always supposed—it was probably only an illusion— that I led Shaw, who is an omnivorous reader, to European literature by recommending Balzac's *Cousin Bette* to him. When he wrote *Retreat to Pleasure,* the Group Theatre's last production (1941), I admonished him for his preoccupation with success, quoting Cocteau: "A young man should not invest in safe securities." To do so was indeed a retreat. I don't imagine he appreciated my little sermon.

It was my love of Paris that inspired him to pay the city a brief visit. He has lived in Europe (mostly in Paris and in the Swiss town of Klosters) for the greater part of the intervening years. In Paris one day I was rather taken aback to hear him say that from childhood he was bent on success and *knew* he would succeed. I'm not sure why this should have troubled me, except that I had never thought much about success. He did succeed, and, cordial as he is to everyone, he prefers the company of the successful.

He has suffered, I imagine, because people no longer speak of him with the high regard that greeted the publication of his first stories. He did not realize what I always seem to have known: that in our country the mortality rate in reputations is higher than anywhere else.

I admire Shaw's working habits. He writes incessantly, still turns out best sellers, and has remained as likable as ever. He drinks to the point of ulceration and, as the final chapter of his recent *Evening in Byzantium* reveals, he is resigned to drink, come hell or high water. For all the sadness and regret in him, he retains his enormous gusto and capacity for laughter.

Others of whom I have had fleeting glimpses or with whom I have had brief encounters pass before my mind's eye as if I had photographed them and then assembled them in a film of unpredictable sequence.

When I was fifteen, my father took me to hear Sholom Aleichem read some of his wonderful short stories at Carnegie Hall, where the intellectual senior of the Yiddish-speaking community had assembled to honor the great humorist, newly arrived in New York.

It was not sufficient for the organizing committee simply to allow their guest to do what the audience had come for; each of the committee members had to make a speech extolling the writer's genius. The salutations began at eight-thirty and went on for three hours. Bogged down with panegyrics, the hapless writer began reading. He had reached the middle of the first story when the ushers, exasperated by the inordinate duration of the festivity, took to shouting in unison, "All out! All out!" and opened all the exit doors. "Close those doors!" the chairman of the evening bellowed. But the doors were not closed and the "All out! All out!" resounded more commandingly until the audience and finally Sholom Aleichem himself rose and meekly traipsed out.

My father also took me as a boy to hear John Galsworthy read one of his essays at the old Aeolian Hall on West Forty-second Street. I recall his long black Edwardian coat, his discreet smile as he acknowledged the laughter that greeted his occasional quips. That, and how he tipped his hat to the admiring ladies waiting outside the hall to get a closer view of him. They gazed at him adoringly: he was tall, spare, handsome, with perfect features, very much the educated English gentleman, whom they knew enough not to trouble for an autograph.

Shortly after World War I, I heard Frank Harris talk about Bernard Shaw at the Rand School, a Socialist establishment on East Twelfth Street. (Oscar Wilde said of Harris that he had been invited to all the best houses in England—*once*.) One of Harris's anecdotes about the Irish playwright related to Mrs. Shaw, who arranged the seating of her guests in a box at the theatre by saying, "Mr. A will sit here; Mr. B will sit there; and the genius [Shaw], here."

Harris spoke contemptuously of little Belgium, which had been invaded by the German army—I gathered he thought the invasion entirely justified—and promised to deliver his next talk on "a greater man than Shaw, Thomas Carlyle." I did not care to hear Harris a second time. With his long black mustache—dyed, no doubt—he resembled a Junker.

I was rather put off by T. S. Eliot when I heard him read parts of *The Waste Land* and others of his poems at the New School for Social Research in the early thirties. He had fine, regular features, he was tall and thin, wore a long black frock coat, and was strikingly pale-faced. There was something condescending, almost mocking, in his attitude toward the audience. He intoned the verse, a disagreeable mode of reading common among poets and especially wrong for Eliot's poetry. He looked for all the world like a highly bred Anglican cleric.

Another and very different poet I heard *speak* his verse was Robert Frost. It was only a few weeks before his death. The committee in support of the MacDowell Colony for musicians, artists, and writers, of which Copland was the chairman, had arranged an evening to honor Frost. The hall was packed with men and women in evening dress. When Frost, engagingly venerable, appeared, the audience rose and gave him an ovation the likes of which I have heard only one other time—when Chaplin appeared in New York on his return from "exile." When the ovation subsided, Frost said, "If only my mother could see me now."

Sitting opposite me in a Paris bus in 1923 was a superbly handsome, very well dressed, gray-haired man whose face was somehow vaguely familiar. As I rarely forget a face, even if I have never seen it before except in a photograph, I puzzled over my inability to "place" this one. Is this man, I wondered, a former actor out of the past, or is he an eminent statesman . . . ? Suddenly it came to me: he was Maurice Maeterlinck. He had written *The Life of the Bee* in 1901 and his popular play *The Blue Bird* in 1909. I had thought him long dead. He was only sixty-one when I saw him. I was naturally interested in him as a pioneer in symbolist drama, but I had another, special, reason for "studying" him. Just a few days earlier, a classmate at the Sorbonne had quoted a line from one of Maeterlinck's writings. The professor, André Le Breton, a smooth-tongued reactionary, informed the student that quoting Maeterlinck was out of order in papers written for the university because "he is not a classic and he is not French."

Sometime during the war, Maeterlinck, a refugee in New York, together with his much younger wife, was a dinner guest at my home. He was close to eighty at the time, and his white, tissue-thin skin seemed transparent. His face bore the imprint of tired, aged wisdom.

Maeterlinck brings to mind another artist whom I met in the forties and who I felt certain was then on the verge of death. A man of enormous bulk and height, speaking with a pronounced German accent, appeared at the door of my apartment asking for Stella Adler, who was out. As I was expecting her, I asked him to wait. It was Otto Klemperer.

He terrified me. He had just recovered from a brain operation and his speech had been affected; it hurt to listen to him. Surely, I thought, this giant was not long for this world. But he lived on for many years, to achieve his greatest triumphs as conductor of London's Philharmonia Orchestra.

In all of his musical life, Copland has hissed a composition only once—a piece by Carl Orff. And only once did I hear him emit a semiarticulate cry signifying "Bravo!" This was at a recital of Gabriel Fauré's songs. When the aged composer was called to the stage, Aaron could not contain his enthusiasm, because Fauré had not come into his own—that is, his personal style had not completely evolved—until he was past sixty.

Aaron has never been given to adulation of those he respects. But when he recognized Ravel at a concert in 1922, he pointed him out to me with something like reverence. Ravel's face would be remembered as very special in any gathering. There was a quality in it of exquisitely civilized sensibility which reminded me of certain wonderfully arresting eighteenth-century portraits.

I cannot efface from my memory the vision of Somerset Maugham literally falling on his face in Romanoff's restaurant in Beverly Hills. A tall, burly companion (secretary or attendant?) lifted him from the floor and bore his body to the men's room.

Graham Greene's somewhat bloodshot yet peculiarly watery blue eyes mesmerized me. I met him at one of the "Sunday afternoons" Donald Ogden Stewart and his wife, Ella Winter, used to hold in their large London house, which had once been the residence of Ramsay MacDonald. Stewart, a famous humorist in the twenties, went "radical"

in the thirties. In part, this shift was a result of Ella's infence (she was Lincoln Steffens's widow), but, more than th..,
it was a response to the winds of dissent that were sweeping
through Hollywood "intellectual" circles at the time.

Stewart, who had been a friend of Hemingway's and
Fitzgerald's, belonged to the Algonquin set: Dorothy Parker,
Heywood Broun, Franklin P. Adams, George Kaufman, and
others. (Sam Behrman told me that Oscar Levant, that devilish and bedeviled jester, who was an occasional guest at the
Algonquin revels, once blurted out that for all the public
acclaim bestowed on these "stars," they were all artistically
and intellectually second-rate. Levant was never again invited
to join them. There was something reminiscent of Molière's
Misanthrope in this.) "We lived for fun," Stewart said. It was
perhaps inevitable that following the Depression this Columbus, Ohio, Protestant should have been converted to radical
views. He was still as keen as ever, and his bright good humor
 remained untarnished, but he had become *serious*. He no
longer sent huge baskets of flowers to the women he courted,
or permitted himself to buy jewels for them. There was a
strong vein of austerity in the radicalism of the thirties, and
the puritan that had always dwelt within Stewart emerged,
with a force all the greater for its long suppression. He once
made a speech in which he declared that "Communism may
not need us, but we need Communism."

After he turned to the left, Stewart wrote a play about
the threat immanent in the misuse of atomic power. Its failure on Broadway very nearly shattered him. Being a professional humorist now seemed to him the height of frivolity,
and he was not qualified to become a serious writer of any
note. What I once said to Brooks Atkinson about Philip
Barry probably applied to Stewart as well: "We should encourage him to remain superficial." Barry's religious propensities impelled him to attempt plays more "weighty" than
The Philadelphia Story, just as Stewart's radicalism led him

to renounce the entertaining things he had written and to try to write "important" drama.

At the Stewarts', Graham Greene, his eyes vacant, spoke very little. He appeared to be concentrating on some inner object, trying to elicit an answer to a query lurking in the depths of his conscience. I was determined to get him to talk. I asked if it was true that a number of Catholic clergymen in the United States had requested our State Department to deny him an entry visa on the grounds that he at one time had been a Communist—though he had since embraced Catholicism. "Yes, there was opposition," he answered, and after a pause he added, smiling, "I don't understand the Catholics in your country. They're a peculiar lot."

I was introduced to Anita Björk, whom I had seen in a Swedish film of Strindberg's *Miss Julie*. She was very close to Greene then and had come to England especially to visit him. I asked if I might call on her when I got to Stockholm. "Please do," she answered. A year later, after a performance of *Look Back in Anger* at Stockholm's Royal Dramatic Theatre, I took her to supper and asked her whether Greene really believed in God. Her reply paralleled Stewart's statement on Communism. Greene, she said, had told her that God did not need him, but that he needed God.

I got to know Stewart well when I directed a play of his called *The Kidders* at the Brattle Theatre in Cambridge, Massachusetts. (It was never done in New York, but later had a moderately successful run in London.) When he took up permanent residence in London, I visited him frequently, especially on those Sunday afternoons, where one could often find the likes of Penelope Gilliatt; Kenneth Tynan; Joe Losey; Benn Levy and his lovely wife, Constance Cummings; Isaac Deutscher; Mrs. Sean O'Casey; Charles and Oona Chaplin; and Dr. Spock.

I also remember Stewart in connection with a party Chaplin gave at "21" after the first New York showing of

Monsieur Verdoux. Many movie notables were there, Mary Pickford for one, and most of Charlie's local friends. And yet the atmosphere was chilly; the "friends" had apparently not cared much for the picture and were letting Charlie know it.

All first-night parties are dreadful ordeals unless the play or picture they are designed to celebrate is an unmistakable hit. If the morning notices are not exuberantly favorable, the air becomes glacial. This was more or less the case that night. I felt that many of the guests were not merely disappointed with *Monsieur Verdoux,* but very nearly rejoiced in what they assumed to be a setback for Charlie. Stewart, who was truly fond of Chaplin, whispered to me, "We're going to slip away with Charlie. He needs us; the rest of the gang here are hostile bastards."

The Europeans have always admired *Monsieur Verdoux.* The Italian writer Carlo Levi, author of *Christ Stopped at Eboli,* who attended a showing of the film, answered my "Did you like it?" with an emphatic *yes.* At a recent (1973) showing I noticed that the young folk in the audience were delighted with the film's "message" and applauded enthusiastically.

Sometime during 1973, I read a tribute to Paul Robeson in the New York *Times.* I had not heard anything about him for a long time, and I was glad to learn that he was still among the living. He had been living in the Soviet Union, where he had been treated very well. I remembered a conversation we had had at a party in the thirties. He had been a college football hero, an admired singer, and an imposing actor, yet just before our talk that day, at a reception in his own honor at one of New York's most fashionable hotels, he had been asked to go through the servants' entrance. He said to me at the party, "I don't know why we [blacks] take it—I don't believe we shall much longer."

Richard Wright was also there that day. There was anger in his books, but when I met him later, self-exiled in Paris, his manner was soft, melancholy, and defeated.

I am generally receptive to most avant-garde manifestations in the arts, even when I do not altogether follow their drift. My forbearance is strained only when their representatives or partisans seek to demolish the reputations of their more traditional predecessors. Robbe-Grillet defining the theory of the new novel captures my earnest attention, but when he speaks as if Balzac were a duffer or as if the "Balzacian" novel can no longer be relevant to us, I become restive.

For this reason, when John Cage, at the home of a mutual friend, spoke mockingly of nearly all music that immediately preceded his own and Morton Feldman's (with the possible exception of Ives's, Cowell's and Varèse's), I did my best to conceal my impatience. For Cage and Feldman, the only "masters" were Schönberg and Webern. Cage, and Feldman, who was also present, spoke as if Aaron Copland obstructed their path. I asked Cage to define his aesthetic. Mild in manner, charming, and very intelligent, he said pertinent things about the absurdities of American civilization: its lack of coherence, of continuity, and of tradition; how its only constant trait is lack of permanence; how America consumes itself, demolishes itself every day and how any expression that fails to reflect America's anarchy is not merely old-time, but fraudulent.

"Wasn't that very much the position of the Dadaists in the twenties?" I asked. Cage conceded that this was so, but after a thoughtful pause, he added: "But the Dadaists were still related to art; we are *against* art."

"That is shit, just shit," I yelled, and bobbed around the room as if it had been lifted by a ground swell. "Expression employing any of the media, no matter how subversive of accepted modes and the premises of earlier creative work, still pertains to art. There is always some effort to communicate something, even when that 'something' is presumed to make a hash of everything or mirror universal breakdown or madness."

More amused than offended, Cage "kept his cool." With some hauteur, he said, "The elegant fashion with which you have enunciated your thoughts does not alter the fact that . . . " etc., etc. I finally let the argument drop, but only because I was ashamed of my unseemly outburst; my views remained unshaken. It still makes me angry to hear a playwright call something he writes for the stage *antitheatre*. Joyce did not call *Finnegans Wake* antiliterature.

I have since concluded that the inner drive motivating Cage's lifework is religious. The last time I saw him he was sitting in a box, adding "fun" to a Merce Cunningham recital by interjecting delightful *non sequiturs* at random intervals. . . . I also think it fair to note that ever since Copland invited Cage to address his composition students at Tanglewood, he has treated Copland with increasing friend liness. Cage has won his little "battle"; he need not make progress through assault.

In all my years of playgoing I have never seen an American actor more richly endowed than John Barrymore. Yet, like a number of other greatly gifted actors, Barrymore was contemptuous of the stage. He wanted desperately to be a painter, but he had come to realize he would never be a good one. Whether it was this or deeper psychological causes that were at the root of his self-destructive bent I cannot say, but it was clear that in his last years he was intent on degrading himself. Still, there was always an air of grandeur about him. Wallowing in the mire, he was nevertheless, and unmistakably, a prince.

I watched him once during the shooting of a film. (I saw him much more often on stage.) He had difficulty remembering his lines. Every time he "blew" a line, his speech trailed

off to a "Kiss my ass" or to some other more colorful im-
propriety. When I was given the opportunity to sit beside
him at lunch in the Paramount dining room, I was all fascinated attention. Rapt in grim meditation, he said little; his
answers to the casual questions addressed to him were short
and rather sullen. He was not, I felt sure, thinking about his
role or the movie in which he was engaged.

The waitress serving us asked him what he would like.
He noticed that I smiled at his answer. "What're you smiling
at?" he barked.

"I observe," I answered, "that you have one tone of
voice when you speak to a man and quite another when you
speak to a woman."

"Nat-u-rally," he said, elongating the word in heroic
sonority.

I kept staring at him, and, in mock irritation, he snarled,
"What're you gaping at?"

Calmly, I replied, "Mr. Barrymore, you always look as if
you are about to come forth with a devastating curse or an
earth-shattering laugh."

"Some look, eh!" he muttered, his eyes flashing, and
turned back to his meal.

Though I have had pleasant and rewarding experiences
with actors, there are few I care to write about except profes-
sionally. There are many kind things I could say about the
affable, disciplined, and woman-galvanized Fredric March;
the reasonable, liberal, humorous Melvyn Douglas; the
rough, good-natured Walter Matthau; the blithe Larry Bly-
den; the sweet Eli Wallach; the intense, pure, and noble
Joseph Wiseman. But the actor with whom I have had the
longest and most intimate contact is Marlon Brando.

He was Stella Adler's student. On my return to New
York after a prolonged stay in Hollywood, I found that he
was going out with her daughter Ellen. I cast him in his first

adult part in Maxwell Anderson's *Truckline Café*. (His only other part on Broadway had been in John van Druten's *I Remember Mama*.) *Truckline Café* was a total flop, but the audience acclaimed him, a fact most of the reviewers failed to take note of. They did not perceive that the twenty-two-year-old youth was an actor of extraordinary talent. Professional theatre people who were lucky enough to see Brando during the play's nine-day run were profoundly impressed. On the other hand, a talent scout for one of the major picture companies asked me if Brando wasn't overacting. I thought: Would that all actors could "overact" that way!

Guthrie McClintic engaged him to play Marchbanks in Katharine Cornell's revival of *Candida*. Brando has never forgotten, though I hope he has forgiven, what I said when I went backstage to see him after the performance: "Good try, Marlon!" Marchbanks was a type utterly alien to him.

Brando's indirect and introspective approach to a part, the seemingly interminable time he took to prepare to act ("project") it, baffled and sometimes alienated producers, directors, and other actors. He did not get along with Tallulah Bankhead at rehearsals of Cocteau's *The Eagle Has Two Heads* and was dismissed. Shortly after this came his brilliant Stanley Kowalski in *A Streetcar Named Desire,* and his enduring stay in Hollywood.

Brando is a "deep one." When he played Kowalski he was frequently taken for the character: a half-articulate roughneck, gross, bluff, and brutal. A closer look would have revealed the wounded sensibility that informed the performance. As Brando played him, Kowalski appeared to be a victim of Blanche DuBois's neurotic contrivance. The characterization might, without exaggeration, have been described as Dostoevskian.

Brando is not only acutely perceptive, but articulate as well. He has a good ear, a feeling for language—though perhaps not Shakespeare's! Abroad he quickly picks up foreign tongues and intonations. He "assimilates" people with his whole body. His verbal reactions to people are brief, cryptic, and astonishingly perspicacious. He is never glib.

There is something in him that *resents* acting. Yet he cannot help being an actor. He thinks acting "sickly"; he'd rather "do something for the world"—a social service, perhaps. There is nothing pretentious or phony in this: it expresses a wholly authentic impulse.

Brando's mother was a fine, well-bred woman, but a hopeless alcoholic. He suffered untold misery because of her condition, and the soul-searing pain of his childhood has lodged itself in some deep recess of his being. He cannot readily speak of what lies buried there: he hardly knows himself what it is. He has developed a mask, a "front" that sometimes makes him take to lying, pretending, teasing, and perpetrating practical jokes. Did he not once enter a plane and order the stewardess "To Havana!" for which, much to his consternation, he was detained at the airport and made to explain his "request"? The nameless "complex" that possesses him occasionally induces an impenetrable sullenness. He cannot voice the deepest part of himself: it hurts too much. That, in part, is the cause of his "mumbling." His innermost core—secret, I say, even to himself—can find its outlet only through acting. And it is precisely because his acting has its source in suffering, the display of which he unwittingly resists, that it acquires its enormous power. Acting of this sort is instinct with the stuff of humanity: it is not illustrative, it is creative.

Brando is all "tied up in knots." He is not, never has been, nor ever will be, satisfied with himself. Shortly after *Truckline Café* he sorrowfully confessed to me that he had smoked pot. With similar overtones of guilt, he admitted to sexual promiscuity. What to me were little more than peccadilloes haunted him as sin. With some trepidation, he delves into himself, seeking his own meaning. The search is scrupulously honest, forgoing any resort to banal psychoanalytic recipes.

Because he is not sure he can ever be as good as he would like to be, he wants to help others. I used to suspect that his declared intention to make films for the UN or to devote himself to humanitarian causes was a rationalization for not returning to the stage, which I used to plead with him to do. I was wrong. Whether his social views are sound or not, he is always thoroughly sincere about them. He has a hunger for purification.

Brando has often done films more worthy in intention than in execution, and a few of very little merit. A "veteran" film critic said to me, "You see, these great [theatre] actors are no good in pictures. They're poison at the box office." Soon after this, Brando did *The Godfather* and *Last Tango in Paris*. So much for expert opinion.

American show folk—even the educated ones—tend to view theatre history and aesthetics solely from a Broadway basis. Lillian Hellman, Robert Sherwood, and I were guests one evening at the home of George Kaufman and his wife, Leueen MacGrath. Sherwood deplored the hardships, of our profession, especially the terrible pressure under which playwrights work: a play, he said, must please immediately or be doomed forever. I disagreed, citing plays by Chekhov, Shaw, and Ibsen as proof that Sherwood's contention was historically incorrect. When Ibsen was living in Rome he was notified that *A Doll's House* and *Hedda Gabler,* which had opened in Copenhagen and Munich respectively, had both been hissed; he wrote back that "if they had not been hissed, there would have been no point in writing them." But Chekhov, Shaw, and Ibsen are dead, and, besides, it happened in another country.

On my first postwar visit to Berlin I was invited to supper with the managing staff of West Berlin's city-subsidized theatre. Its *dramaturg*—literary consultant—asked me if I knew George Kaufman. I told him I did. "We should like to

produce several of his plays here. But he won't deal with us—
no doubt because of Hitler, the Nazis, and so forth. Please
tell Mr. Kaufman we were never Nazis. Look, there is Erwin
Kalser, an honored member of our company, and he is a Jew."

I relayed the message to Kaufman. "No," he said, "I
shan't let them have any of my plays. It gives me pleasure to
refuse."

Ionesco is a melancholy "foxy grandma." His face droops
as if he were unalterably discontented and perpetually on the
verge of tears. At the 1963 Edinburgh drama conference he
made a brief speech that everyone thought very funny, and
he looked so sad.

Ionesco speaks slowly, without emphasis, in a low, husky
voice, as though he were a condemned man. When *The
Wipe-Out Game* had just been given its first—thus far its only
—American production, in Washington, D.C., I asked him if
he was satisfied with the way it had been done. "No," he said.
"They stylized it. My plays should not be stylized. No matter
how fanciful, extravagant, or absurd they may seem, they are
matters of fact." The play shows crowds in the streets slaugh-
tering one another.

Jean Genet came backstage with the distinguished scene
designer Georges Wakhévitch to congratulate Peter Brook on
his direction at the premiere of *Titus Andronicus* at the
Théâtre des Nations in Paris. Wakhévitch said to Brook,
"You have come into your own. With this play, you have
found your true *métier,* your own form." Genet, who is small,
stocky, and bald and looks a bit like a thug, fairly leaped out
of his skin and fumed as if he had been personally insulted.
"Never tell an artist such a thing. An artist must keep reaching, try new paths, never become fixed in his 'personality.'
Whatever an artist undertakes is a step toward an unknown
destination."

Natasha Parry, Peter Brook's wife, told me that Genet, an avowed homosexual, can be very tender with women: he had sat at her feet and held her hand most lovingly.

In the middle and late forties I directed two adaptations of plays by Konstantin Simonov: *The Russian People* and *The Whole World Over.* Immediately after the war Simonov visited the United States and was invited to speak at a meeting to promote Soviet-American friendship. In response to the audience's welcome he said, "Thank you for your applause, which I appreciate and deserve." No one laughed. I quoted him on my own behalf when I accepted my Légion d'Honneur decoration at the French consulate in New York. This time the audience did laugh—no one more heartily than the consul himself.

I met Billy Rose through Odets. Billy envied people he considered artistic and well educated. "I'm just a saloon-keeper," I heard him say at a Group Theatre gathering. (At a preview of my production of Shaw's *Heartbreak House,* shown at the Billy Rose Theatre, he whispered to me, "This is a play for people who wash every day.") Billy was eager to have "real artists" visit him at his country house. Arthur Miller and his wife, Inge Morath, accepted his invitation. They described it as a disastrously dull occasion. Billy was a rich and lonely man, a self-declared "four-time loser" in marriage.

He bedecked himself with culture. He bought old masters and impressionist paintings by the carload. When I came to see the Rose collection with Odets he treated us to the following tidbit. One day when he brought home and was about to hang a new Renoir, his wife, the swimming champion Eleanor Holm, threatened: "If you hammer one more nail into the wall, I'll divorce you."

When I left the Rose mansion Odets asked me what I

thought of what I had seen and heard. "Rose makes me think of a man," I said, "who would boast of his fecundity by announcing, 'I've adopted two hundred children.' "

In Rome last year I read with horror of Brandon de Wilde's death in an automobile accident at the age of thirty-one. I recalled the enchanting boy he had been when I directed him in *The Member of the Wedding*. He was seven then.

He had never before entered a theatre. I shall never forget his excitement, as if he were witnessing a fairy-tale miracle, when he saw the curtain rise at the initial dress rehearsal. On opening night in Philadelphia, when Brandon, on stage behind the curtain, heard the rumble of the audience, he showed signs of panic. As I entered his dressing room, his father (our assistant stage manager) said, "Brandon is scared." This scared *me*. "No, you're not, you're not!" I cried out. What else can I say? I thought in a sweat. Shall I tell him, "If you goof tonight I'll ruin your career?" But it was Ethel Waters who faltered that night; Brandon was perfect.

It is difficult to know what periods or social conditions foster creativity. Rome was ridden with beggary, starvation, murder, rape, and pillage when Michelangelo was at work there and numerous architectural masterpieces emblematic of the glorious eventide of the Renaissance were being built. When Copland shared an apartment with me temporarily vacated by Odets during the worst days of the Depression, he told me it was a tough time to compose music. But his *Piano Variations,* his ballet *Billy the Kid,* his children's opera *The Second Hurricane,* his *El Salon Mexico,* his *Statements for Orchestra,* and his *Short Symphony* all date from that period.

In 1940, walking on Broadway, already on its way to

becoming the shambles it is at present, Odets asked me, "Is it possible for anything good to come out of such an environment?" I could only reply, "What do you think Russia was like when Chekhov was writing his plays?" When I repeated this conversation to Max Lerner, he refuted the implication of my rejoinder to Odets by saying, "Oh, but Russia was 'building' then, it was on the rise." Perhaps so. Broadway's aspect today, to put it mildly, is far less reassuring than it was in 1940. But of this contradiction, and my attitude to the future, to which so many of us look with fear and trembling and others refuse to look at all, I shall have more to say later on.

For me, at any rate, the Depression was a time of elation. It struck me only recently that I, who have sometimes been referred to as "a man of the thirties," did most of my direction and nearly all my writing in the later years. The hard times of the thirties served many of us as an incubator. And perhaps the times, like the stars, have less to do with the nature and deeds of men than we suppose.

In Nadia Boulanger's salon in the twenties I met the young son of the world-renowned pianist Alexander Siloti. The youth had lived through the early years of the Russian revolution. "There were times in those days," he said, "when one had to choose between eating and going to the opera or a concert. It is a wonder to me now how often I chose the opera or a concert rather than a meal."

During the Spanish civil war, when I read with anguish of the bombing of Madrid, I had a dream that reminded me of Siloti's reflection on the painful choice he had had to make in the Russia of 1917–19. In my dream I found myself asserting: "It is in such times that it is imperative to endure and create."

I also recalled the character in Renoir's *Grand Illusion* who, between battles and in a prison camp, keeps reading

Pindar. His buddies "ride" him for it. Exasperated by their derision, he exclaims, "There's nothing in the world more important than Pindar!"—by which he means poetry.

The only Soviet diplomat I ever met was Ambassador Maxim Litvinov. It was at the opening night of Simonov's *The Russian People* in Washington, in 1942. As Litvinov entered his box at the National Theatre, the audience gave him a standing ovation. After the show the Theatre Guild management, which had produced the play, invited him to a party. A friendly atmosphere prevailed. Even a Republican senator, though he was displeased when I told him he was handsome enough to go on the stage, loosened up a little.

Litvinov considered the play "too serious" for the American public! He was quite obviously charmed by our leading lady, Elizabeth Fraser, who, he said, could easily be taken for a Russian girl. She was chubby, very blonde, and as American as sweet potatoes. I doubt whether she had ever heard of a balalaika or, before our production, of any of the Russian folk songs we used as incidental music.

The ambassador was short and homey and wore old-fashioned spectacles; his face was sweetened by an honestly benevolent smile—everybody's uncle! He invited the cast and all the others associated with the play to a cocktail-and-champagne party at the Soviet embassy later in the week. All things considered, it was a rather dull party; not a word about the war or politics was uttered.

I might have forgotten all about the affair had I not run into Elizabeth Fraser in Paris sometime in the fifties. I asked her what progress she had made in her acting career. She had done well, she said, except for one hitch. She had contracted to appear in a Hollywood movie. Just before she was to go before the cameras, her agent called to say the contract had been canceled. No explanation. She asked her agent to inquire into the matter. A vigilant investigator had come upon a photograph of her in the company of the Soviet ambassador. It had been taken on the pleasant occasion of that opening night in Washington.

The only foreign ruler I ever saw (except for Queen Elizabeth passing in her carriage on a quiet London street, and the Prince of Wales, later Edward VIII, walking incognito along the Boulevard de la Madeleine in 1922) was General Franco. On my way home from Rome in 1949 I stopped off at Madrid to see the paintings at the Prado and my first bullfight, which Christopher Fry, then working in Rome on the film of *Quo Vadis?*, said he hoped I would dislike. At the arena, as the *corrida* was about to begin, Franco appeared in the royal box. The entire crowd—twenty-three thousand or more—rose. I alone remained seated. I half expected that someone would lift me up by the scruff of the neck. I was disappointed: no one paid the slightest attention.

In London, I was told that a young actress of my hostess's acquaintance wanted to meet me because I knew Chaplin. The young lady had been tested for *Limelight* and wished to know if Chaplin had said anything to me about her. The actress's name was Claire Bloom. We chatted for a bit. Chaplin had not mentioned the test. "But," I added, "I'm sure you'll get the part." "Why do you say that?" she asked. "Because you have a virginal look," I answered. Miss Bloom blushed. . . . Chaplin was unconsciously distrustful of any girl who didn't have that look.

During my visit to Lake George in 1930, both Stieglitz and Strand photographed me within ten minutes of each other. Stieglitz's photograph shows me receptive, smiling, kindly, and soft. Strand's photo has me stern, ready for battle, indomitably prepared for every terrible eventuality and ready to cry "Forward!" The first is a picture of Stieglitz, the second a picture of Strand. Each of these two artists had done his self-portrait. I learned something about photography as an art.

Henry Kahnweiler, Picasso's lifelong sponsor and friend, on a visit to New York, spoke at Meyer Schapiro's class at Columbia. Kahnweiler described the time—1910—when he became interested in the cubists Picasso, Georges Braque, and, a little later, Juan Gris. It was a time when a painter who sold a canvas for a hundred francs (about nineteen dollars) could live comfortably for a month. One of the students in the class asked, "Didn't you find it discouraging to sponsor painters most people thought either crazy or fakers?" (Renoir, on seeing one of Picasso's paintings, had called it *"merde."*) "No," Kahnweiler answered. "We were sure we'd win in the end." This brought tears to Schapiro's eyes.

Kahnweiler went on to describe how Gris brought in a new painting. When Kahnweiler congratulated him on it, praising its many technical merits, its invention, and so on, Gris worriedly queried, "Yes, but is it a *picture?*"

Robert Whitehead and I were eager to produce *Long Day's Journey into Night,* which I had read and reviewed for the *Nation* when it was first published. After long negotiations with O'Neill's widow, we were informed that she had decided to have Jose Quintero direct the play under another management. This scandalized Whitehead, since he had been the first to ask for the play, had revived *Desire Under the Elms* for Broadway, etc., etc. Impressed by Whitehead's sincerity, Mrs. O'Neill told him that there was still another unproduced O'Neill play, *A Touch of the Poet,* to which she would grant him production rights.

As we went into rehearsal, she warned us that we were not to cut a line, even a word. If we did she would immediately detect the omission. She had typed the play herself, four times, there was a part in it written for her, and so forth. To the actors' dismay, I immediately set about cutting thirty minutes from the script.

There was alarm when Mrs. O'Neill came to see the first run-through. She liked what she saw and left the rehearsal satisfied that we had done well. The play was a hit. Some days after the opening, she telephoned Whitehead to protest the cuts, which O'Neill's agent had brought to her attention.

Whitehead handled the situation neatly. "What is supposed to have been cut?" he asked. Mrs. O'Neill mentioned one item. "It's still there," he assured her. She referred to another item, then another. "But they are all in the production," Whitehead honestly averred. Mrs. O'Neill expressed relief. What she didn't realize was that O'Neill repeated every salient point in the play at least ten times; in cutting five or six of the repetitions, everything O'Neill had written was "still there."

While serving as a playreader for the Theatre Guild (1929–31) I wrote letters to various novelists and poets asking if they had written or were planning to write a play. Hemingway answered: "You ask me if I've written a play. Who the hell hasn't?" Hemingway's play *The Fifth Column* was produced several years later by the Theatre Guild and directed by Lee Strasberg.

My happiest experience in reading plays occurred during the Group Theatre days. A script had been submitted which began: *"Act One:* Ten thousand years before the creation of man. *Act Two:* Two weeks later."

My father was often tactless. A woman he questioned about her symptoms said, "I'm perfectly all right, doctor. But whenever I eat rhubarb I get a stomach ache." "Don't eat rhubarb," my father advised. No wonder he lost her as a patient—she wanted him to prescribe something. The story taught me the danger of common sense.

• • •

"La vie est une lutte"—life is a struggle—is not a particularly original thought. But when Carlos Chavez, the Mexican composer, said it in my depleted apartment on West Fifty-eighth Street in 1932, it reinforced me in my struggle to keep the Group going.

I realize now that it was not the words which fortified me, but the man who spoke them. Chavez, like most of the great Mexicans, looks more Indian than Spanish, with his dense and massive torso, his leonine head—the look, in short, of a piece of ancient sculpture of formidable gravity. He himself is a warrior. With quiet resolution he did battle with the phalanxes of the Mexican political, social, and musical bureaucracy. He was out of favor in his country and living in poverty somewhere in Greenwich Village at the time of our early acquaintance. But there was no question in my mind that he too would win in the end.

At one of his lectures, Camus tried to disabuse his audience of their superannuated notions of what a "typical" French gentleman looked like: "A man with a goatee, who wears a pompous frock coat with a decoration in its lapel." He paused, turned aside for a moment, and there, seated on his left, was a Frenchman answering to just that description.

He found this so amusing that he chose to recount this incident at a later talk in Algiers. He began: "Something very droll occurred during my visit to the United States. I was addressing a gathering in which I described the conventional picture of a Frenchman: goatee, frock coat, decoration, et cetera"—and was about to laugh at his story when, once again, he saw exactly such a Frenchman seated on his right. He was so thrown by the coincidence that he sat down and, spluttering, asked for *"de la vin"* instead of *du vin*.

Waldo Frank introduced me to André Gide, whose apartment on the Rue Vaneau he had sublet. Gide stepped in for a minute, coming from the adjoining apartment, which he had retained. When Waldo told him that I was a man of the theatre, Gide remarked, "The problem in the theatre is to find good plays." "The problem in the theatre," I rejoined, "is to create a Theatre."

Jealousy is often the tribute artists pay one another. "Why do they resent me so?" Odets asked me at the height of his career. "They resent you," I answered, "with what is *best* in them."

It is a fact that artists never forget even the least significant of unfavorable reviews. The converse is frequently also true. In 1946 I wrote admiringly for the limited circulation of *Tomorrow* magazine about a David Smith exhibition. Ten years later he greeted me on Madison Avenue —we had never met—and thanked me heartily, as if he had just read the review and was still as little known as he had been in 1946.

George Grosz, whose savage drawings of Berlin in the twenties were as redolent of those days as Marlene Dietrich's repertoire or Brecht's early plays, often engaged me in conversation. But "conversation" is in this instance a misnomer. Grosz rarely conversed: he rasped and roared, he choked with exasperation. One could barely understand what he was saying, in German or in English. In New York, as in Berlin, he always painted what he scorned—even in landscape. His art was all indignation. He died four days after his return to Germany. Was that the purpose of his return?

At a party given by Lee Strasberg and his wife, I was introduced to Neil Simon's business manager. "You'll be interested to know," I told him, "that I've just written an article called 'In Defense of Neil Simon.'" "Wonderful," he replied, "I look forward to reading it." Half an hour later, while I was talking to other guests, the business manager came up to me and said, "I don't understand why a man who earns forty thousand dollars a week requires a defense."

If Eddie Cantor was funny on stage, off stage he was witty. Stella and I were invited by the retired and once famous American entertainer Borah Minnewitch to a small estate outside Paris. Cantor, who, with his wife, Ida, was the only other guest, never stopped talking. At one point his wife interrupted with a convincing "Shut up!" to which, quick as a flash, he replied, "If I shut up, you'd starve to death."

Cantor told us that Ida's father had refused to consent to their marriage. "If he wants to be an actor," he maintained, "he's a bum." Cantor proposed that he be given a year to prove that he could earn a good living in the theatre. "Papa" agreed. Cantor did very well that year, and permission to marry was granted.

Years later Cantor invited his father-in-law to lunch at Sardi's. Everyone greeted Cantor with affection and great respect. This made no special impression on the old man. After lunch Cantor said, "Let's go for a walk uptown." When the two men reached Broadway and Fiftieth Street, the younger one pointed to a sign over the Rivoli Theatre and said, "Look, Pop." Cantor's name was blazoned there as the star of a new Goldwyn picture. The old man looked up and nodded, but said nothing. Then Cantor guided his father-in-law across the street to the Capitol Theatre, where an MGM picture was showing and his name was even more prominently displayed. "Papa's" reaction remained the same. Undaunted, Cantor said, "Now let's walk downtown." On Broadway at Forty-second Street stood the Rialto Theatre, which housed another Cantor picture, with all the attendant publicity. Once again "Papa" nodded, but then said, "Now let me show you something downtown."

When they got to Thirty-fourth Street "Papa" pointed

with conviction to a sign reading "Macy's." "That name will be there *forever.*"

In Paris I attended the *vernissage* of a small retrospective show of Utrillo's paintings. The artist, short, frail, and "pickled," was held erect by a buxom woman I took to be his wife, though she may have been his nurse. (She was probably both.) She kept handing him glasses of red wine. He mumbled his thanks to the many guests queuing to congratulate him, among them Camille Bombois, whose paintings of circus artists may be seen in reproduction in many American hotels, offices, and homes. He looked like a burly, red-faced butcher's apprentice who had taken to dressing like one of the artists in *La Bohème.* When he reached Utrillo, he literally shook with joyous and adoring veneration. Among connoisseurs, Bombois is considered a *naïf,* a primitive. Just then, he was a darling.

"Laymen" always think it behooves them to talk about art when they meet an artist. Of a composer, they ask questions about music; of directors, questions about plays and actors. Artists frequently profess, and to a degree actually experience, overpowering boredom when they are spoken to casually about their work. I heard a woman Willem de Kooning brought to dinner at my stepdaughter Ellen's home ask him about painting. "Please," he said, rather curtly, "don't speak to me about painting. Anything you like, but not painting."

Of Vienna, that now retarded city, Anna Marie Durringer, a former acting student of mine and five years ago a member of the (national) Burgtheater company there, said, "The setting is fine, but the cast is bad."

Leo Lania, a sometime collaborator on various projects with Brecht, also spoke sadly of Vienna's decline. "What's wrong with it?" I asked. "No more Jews" was his answer.

Dimitri Mitropoulos told Copland the same thing about the violin section of German orchestras after the war.

As an associate producer at Columbia Pictures (I produced nothing) I was expected, along with the other associates, to attend a weekly meeting with Harry Cohn, the Boss. At one of these meetings a remake of *Of Human Bondage,* the picture in which Bette Davis came to sensational notice in "the business," was suggested. Cohn, oddly enough, had never seen it. He said that he would do so and announce his decision at the next meeting.

His reaction was sharply negative. "What's the matter with you fellows—trying to make me do such a stupid story. Who'll believe that an educated, intelligent guy like Leslie Howard would fall crazy in love with such a dirty bitch as that waitress?" Silence. Then I murmured rather apologetically, "It's probably happened to everyone in this room." The Boss didn't laugh.

At another meeting, the representative of the Breen office—then Hollywood's instrument for self-censorship—let Cohn and the rest of us know that, according to the new "code," adultery might be shown on the screen so long as it was never condoned. Those guilty of breaking the Fifth Commandment had to be shown to suffer for it. This was in tune with the Hollywood temper of those days. What I found hilarious—and this was perhaps ingenuous of me—was that the discussion following the announcement was couched in language filthy enough to bring a blush to a jockey's cheek.

In a flighty mood at a Hollywood restaurant, I denounced the gossip columns of the *Hollywood Reporter* and other movie-industry journals. They were all fabrications, I maintained, yet everyone believed them. ("We are thrilled by the notices we pay for," Sam Briskin, then in charge of production at Columbia Pictures, told me.) Someone challenged me to prove my contention. I wagered that I could place an item in the *Reporter* intimating that I was "squiring" Greta Garbo! I knew a young woman who, as a freelance scout, picked up rumors about Hollywood notables and slipped them to the movie mags. I asked her to please release the news about my "going out" with Garbo. In due course, the item appeared in the *Reporter*.

At the next producers' meeting, Cohn asked if what he had read about Garbo and me was true. I kept mum. This seemed to confirm the report. "I've been out here—the head of a studio—for twenty-two years," Cohn expostulated, "and I never even met Garbo—and this *momser* takes her out!"

Lion Feuchtwanger, whose novels were best sellers in the late thirties and early forties, lived and worked happily in Hollywood. He was a veritable manufacturer of literature; he worked by the clock. He once boasted that he had reached page three hundred of a new novel within a planned period of time. I was tempted to repeat what Alceste, in *The Misanthrope*, says about the writing of a poem: "Time has nothing to do with it."

In 1946 or 1947, when life in Paris was austere, Stella Adler paraded her splendid wardrobe everywhere. Her hats —very few Frenchwomen wore or possessed them then—were especially eye-catching: they looked like the hats of stage stars prior to World War I. One afternoon as Stella walked past the Deux Magots, applause sounded from the *terrasse,* together with shouts of *"Bravo, chapeau!"*

In Moscow in 1934, a little girl of ten or less kept following us about. She had learned the exact time we left our hotel each day, and she trailed along everywhere. It was Stella in her gorgeous attire—the like of which was nowhere visible in Moscow at the time—that so fascinated her. When, finally, Stella turned to indicate, through a gesture and a smile, her appreciation of the girl's silent homage, she fled as fast as her fleet little legs could carry her.

On the other hand, when the husky women building the Moscow subway, who were dressed in overalls caked with cement, beheld Stella in her fine dress, they giggled uncontrollably.

In 1963 I was asked to address a group of Moscow drama critics, teachers, and "theoreticians" on the subject of the American theatre. I prefaced my remarks by saying that, though I would be severely critical of the economic and social organization of our theatre, I believed that America possessed as many talented artists as any other country in the world.

During the question period that followed, someone asked why I had spoken favorably of Beckett and Ionesco when they were such "negative" playwrights. I explained that they reflected a state of mind broadly characteristic of contemporary Western sentiment, and that what was "negative" in them had, to some extent, the force of protest. I added that such "negative" playwrights aroused the "optimist" in me, while the optimistic plays I had seen in the Soviet Union worried me. I expected a harsh response, but many of the listeners laughed, and a few applauded.

Someone wanted to know if our critics were corrupt. I replied that I did not understand the question. The man made a gesture implying the taking of bribes and murmured something about "Wall Street." "Oh, no," I replied casually, "our critics come by their stupidity quite honestly."

CHAPTER

15

Reluctant
to Be Born

"Nowadays every writer seems riddled with anxiety to find out what young people think of him," Camus said in his *Notebooks,* "when the only interesting thing would be to know what he really thinks of them."

Camus's epigram set me to questioning myself as to what I feel about our youth today. Up to the age of forty I was chiefly interested in people older than myself. I supposed that the experience of knowing my elders would be enriching. But after forty I became more concerned with the experience of knowing the "inexperienced" young. To say that the young are forecasts of history is not quite the same as believing that they are wiser or more perceptive than we are, or understand the world any better.

I was a very young man up to the age of forty! Though I began organizing the Group Theatre when I was twenty-eight, and was directing *Awake and Sing!* (my first independent job as a director) when I was thirty-four, till forty I felt myself a kid and in many respects behaved like one. (Copland thought so, and he ought to know, having been born mature.) Maybe I still am, and maybe it is nice that I am. A mother of several grown children in Dostoevski's *The Idiot* says, "What children we still are and how nice it is we are such children."

Unlike Jewish boys who at thirteen conventionally begin their *bar mitzvah* speeches with the words "Today I am a man," most Americans cannot claim the same distinction till they are safely past forty. (I know a great many women who agree with this judgment.)

My main sources of knowledge now about contemporary youth are the actress Juleen Compton, and a friend I shall refer to simply as Amy, in addition to the vast number of my students at Hunter College and at universities and private seminars all over the world. Generalizations in this area are notoriously unreliable, but it may also be pusillanimous to avoid them.

I don't have to generalize about Juleen: she was my

second, and last, wife. I married her in 1960, when I was more than twice her age. We were casually divorced a couple of years later; we "dated" the evening after we decided on the divorce, and I have no papers on the proceedings. To this day we are close friends.

Juleen is the daughter of a well-to-do Mormon family; her great-grandparents trekked across the country from upper New York State, and, after much hardship, settled in Phoenix, Arizona, where Juleen was born. Juleen's mother was a schoolteacher; according to Juleen, she once invited Barry Goldwater to a Phoenix country club, where he was asked to leave because he is one-quarter Jewish. Juleen's father was a rich ne'er-do-well and an alcoholic who was sent packing when she was four.

Juleen's mother wasted no time in taking on a second husband, also a Mormon and also rich, a lawyer involved in land speculation. A big man with one hand cut off at the wrist, he was a fierce Viking and an arrant reactionary. He thoroughly approved of Hitler and laughed gleefully upon hearing of Roosevelt's death. Juleen loathed him. The only thing she ever reported to me in his favor was that he had said, when the fifteen-year-old Juleen slapped his face, "If she can do that, she will go far."

At sixteen—she had completed high school in three years—Juleen left Phoenix, bound for New York, where she enrolled in a dance academy. She had taken only a few lessons when she realized that to become a prima ballerina (and for her, nothing less would do), she should have taken care to be taller than five foot two.

She was engaged to play Little Red Riding Hood at the Children's World Theatre. Because she was paid very little and had a lot of spare time, she looked around for other work. Her captivating good looks—she has the face of a gamine with a slight Oriental cast to her features, which, with her gift for fantasy, she attributed to Mayan ancestry—attracted the attention of men of high standing in politics and commerce. (At eighteen she married, but her husband was no match for her—very few men are—and she soon had the marriage annulled.) Norman Winston, an eminently successful builder, taught her the rudiments of the real-estate business and banking. She has a mind for finance and an unusually developed visual sense, and within two years, at the age of seventeen, she became the head of her own exterior color and material co-ordinating firm. She made a great deal of money decorating army bases all over the country, using colors and textures in exciting ways to relieve the drabness so often typical of military bases. She also undertook the decoration of large apartment-house lobbies, as well as the restoration of town houses. She bought and sold the houses until she had enough money to invest in the stock market. This too she did exceedingly well.

She meanwhile continued to act, playing little-girl parts in summer stock, in road shows, and on Broadway. Vladimir Horowitz befriended her and taught her to appreciate music. She attended acting classes with Uta Hagen, Joseph Anthony, and Lee Strasberg, through whom she met Odets, who helped her to understand literature and painting. It was the Strasbergs who suggested that she join my professional actors' class.

Days of seeking, of struggle, followed. She was cast in small parts. She began to write, novels at first. They were about girls like herself, without any real home or base or inner security. The novels showed sensibility but lacked skill. They remain unpublished.

She gave dazzling parties in a beautiful house off Fifth Avenue, but she needed to be something more than the wined-and-dined, admired darling of men and women who thought her "extraordinary" but did nothing except entertain her so that they might be entertained in return, or else offer her opportunities to make still more money and give still more dazzling parties. She was simply, to use her words, "teacher's pet." Then, because she loves and knows a lot about antiques, she bought an antique shop and ran it for a while.

Juleen was very much a child of the early fifties. Most such children were, in many respects, half asleep. They showed little interest in anything but their own problems. The critic Fred Dupee told me that most of his English literature students at Columbia were as markedly conservative in their social outlook as in their artistic inclinations. Juleen herself knew next to nothing about politics—then.

She met Senators Warren Magnuson and Joe McCarthy, who were much taken by her. It is typical of Juleen that she went about with them without ever realizing what fearful roles they were playing in the political arena. When she heard from Odets that he was being accused of having been a "red," she asked Senator McCarthy if he could do anything to help. "Why didn't you tell me he was a friend of yours?" he said. "If I had known, he wouldn't have been bothered."

And all the time Juleen was seeking something she couldn't define: a purity, of being and action, which was nowhere to be found among the successful-crowned or the jet set. "I want to believe in something that makes me better for believing in it," she said. She was devoted to artists, but she often became disillusioned with them because they turned out to have the same vices as everybody else.

She was interested, briefly, in a young man who shared in the general "nausea" of the day. He spoke to her of Camus, who was the writer who voiced his own deepest feelings and whom he mistook for a cynic, a prophet of negation. When Juleen asked me about Camus, I told her that her friend misunderstood him. Years later she tried to acquire the film rights to *The Plague,* which she hoped to direct as well as produce. The erstwhile Camus fan had, in the meantime, gone on to become head of one of Hollywood's biggest studios. Today he wouldn't dream of making such a film, no matter who was to direct it.

So she was rich and she was sought after, but she felt

trapped and empty; her very bones, she said, ached. The producer Gilbert Miller's grandson, similarly disoriented, led her to the "beat" world, where the young who refused to be the dupes of a fraudulent society took refuge. Juleen was tempted to settle in among them. She enjoyed their company, smoked grass with them, and floated; after a while, she began to think about retreating to a state of "just being" on some faraway island. Now Norman Winston called her, affectionately, a "Fifth Avenue beatnik."

She knew I did not approve of any of these channels of redemption, yet I never tried to dissuade her from them. When she asked why, I said, "Because I know you'll change your mind yourself." "Everything is so complex," she said; "I don't want to give anything a name." I was right. She had too much creative momentum to content herself with such forms of withdrawal, and she soon became disenchanted with the bohemian life style.

She wrote several plays and took a course in film making; one day she decided to make a picture that would engage all her disparate, little-used talents. She had conceived a story, which she outlined to me.

It was about a small-part actress who envisions herself as a star. She is involved with a young man who won't accept a job in his father's business. He too is seeking answers. They go abroad, where they meet a young, aristocratic, homosexual French painter. Entranced by their yearning, the artist invites them to his grand château on the Loire, which turns out to be ridden with vermin. All three move on to Greece, whose antique beauty they hope will reveal some secret to them. But, though the girl recognizes the grandeur of the ancient ruins, the going world is chiefly the jukebox ambiance pictured in *Never on Sunday*.

A trip they take to Turkey turns out to be even more disappointing. They go back to Greece, and the girl has a brief and meaningless sexual encounter with an illiterate youth who works on a boat that the three "refugees" have hired.

Her American boy friend is totally fed up by now. "There's a place for me in my father's business," he tells her. "Let's go home." "There's no place for me there," she answers. She refuses to give up her quest, says good-by to him at the railroad station, and returns to town to find that her homosexual friend has been "rolled" by toughs. As they drive off together to neither of them knows where, the girl, trying to console the shattered painter, asks, with a sort of desperate hopefulness, "Have you ever been to Egypt?"

I listened to this outline of Juleen's story and all I could say was, "All your characters are *stranded*." This became the title of the picture, which she shot in France and Greece in 1964. She wrote the script, financed, directed, cast it, and acted the main part. At the Cannes Film Festival the picture was awarded the *Semaine de la Critique* prize of the *Cahiers du Cinéma,* which pronounced it one of the best "non-Hollywoodian" films.

In 1962 Juleen went to Paris and succumbed to its caress. She bought a run-down apartment and turned it into a showplace with the same architectural and decorative flair that had transformed several unpromising New York houses into small palaces. She became the "princess" of the *Cahier* group, who pleaded with her to remain in Paris and work with them. She was extremely grateful for their faith in her, but she had come to see that their admiration was disproportionately subjective; she had just happened to make the kind of film they liked best. She looked forward to making films that were more "objective." Their perspective was totally French, and hers, she now realized, was essentially American. So she came home, and in 1967 she decided to try an American picture. She shot it in the Ozarks. Again she produced, financed, and directed it herself, but this time she did not act in it. It was called *The Plastic Dome of Norma Jean* and only allusively related to the other Norma Jean, Marilyn Monroe.

Juleen's Norma Jean is an adolescent country girl in

Arkansas. She is a clairvoyant. She and her loyal friend Vance
are picked up by a young rock combo led by the ambitious
Bobo, who sets up a road show in a plastic dome. It soon
becomes apparent that be-bop will not keep the yokels
coming, and Norma Jean is prodded by Bobo to exploit her
visionary ability; this does wonders at the box office. But the
vital force she expends in the nightly exploitative exhibitions
of her powers soon makes her ill. When her prediction of the
suicide of one of the customers comes true, she collapses, and,
hidden by Vance, tries to escape. But the public does not
wish to give up its thrills; the mayor does not want to forgo
the profit she has brought to the town, nor Bobo his fame
and fortune. They track Norma Jean down and accidentally
kill her.

The Plastic Dome of Norma Jean so fascinated Michel
Le Grand (composer for *The Umbrellas of Cherbourg*) that
he wrote the score for it for nothing. It won Juleen first prize
at an International Film Week in Monte Carlo. It was shown
also at a film festival in San Francisco, but has had no general
release in our country. Both Juleen's pictures appealed to
European *cinéastes,* Lindsay Anderson in particular. But her
subsequent screenplays had the disadvantage of being too
costly for "art films."

Juleen's hardships in Hollywood, where she now lives,
are not as important as what her films tell us about the nature
of her quandary—hers and that of many others of her generation. Her films are about innocence destroyed; her central
characters are forced into conscious compromise or corruption, or, more often, are wiped out by their inability to
accommodate themselves to an aimless world that wastes their
gifts.

Long before I met her, Diego Rivera had painted a portrait of her and Jacob Epstein had sculpted a bust he called
Savage Innocence. Both of them saw in Juleen what I saw, a
pagan with a conscience. She doesn't understand sin except
as ugliness of behavior. She is appalled by lack of sensibility—

common enough everywhere, but capitalized on and enthroned in Hollywood. Strongest of all is her sense of justice. She is romantic without being sentimental. It is impossible for her to be false to her nature, to suppress her idealism. There is in her a yearning for the absolute which the tough-minded maintain has led her astray. She was angry that I did not resign when Bob Whitehead and Sam Behrman refused to cast her in a part I, as the director, wished her to play in *The Cold Wind and the Warm*. Resignation was the gesture she expected of me, and she refused to accept anything short of it.

A long time before there was an organized women's liberation movement, Juleen spoke to me about the need for one. But when the time came, and she tried to join, she felt the hostility of the group. In their view, she was a "loophole" case: she knew how to deal with men, how to take advantage of being attractive to get ahead. Yet she had allowed a top Hollywood producer to tell her, "You've got more talent for direction than nearly all the directors on my lot. I'll accept a screenplay you write, let you produce one if you can package it with stars, but I couldn't get away with having a woman direct for me. The 'drone directors' would have my scalp if I assigned you a picture."

In the August 24, 1973, issue of *Le Monde* there is a long interview with *"Juleen Compton, cinéaste Californienne"* called "Women Take Power." She talks about *Stranded* and then about her activities in Women in Media and Cinewomen, Hollywood film societies devoted to women in film.

Juleen has come through. I do not mean that she has hit the jackpot. She has acquired the discipline and patience needed for achievement; she always had the brains. Though she is as repelled now by Hollywood's synthetic "sugar" as she was by the slaughterhouse of New York, her work now is in California—she likes its peculiar isolation and quiet—and she has come to understand that she "is all about work." Her quest goes on. "The people whose 'pet' I was," she wrote me in a recent letter, "are all waiting for me to 'show' the world; if I'm lucky, someday I'll 'show' myself. I sometimes have the feeling I have let all those down who took such pains to educate me, but, fortunately, you taught me to forgive myself."

A mutual friend introduced me to Amy at a film showing at the Museum of Modern Art. She is only twenty-three. She was born in Paterson, New Jersey, of middle-class parents who are now of the "new poor." She had her A.B. from Barnard, where she majored in communications. She has always been an "A" student. Many of her college classmates turned "radical" before graduation. They were children of the sixties, the time of troubles. Their poet laureate was Bob Dylan, and his nasal plaint "I've got nothin', Ma, to live up to" served as their refrain.

Their radicalism differed from ours of the thirties. It was not purely Marxist; in fact, it didn't espouse any strict ideology. It consisted merely of a belief in "participatory democracy." According to Jack Newfield, a "sympathizer," it looked forward to "community, honesty and freedom. It was generally indifferent to tight organizational discipline or reasoned economic policy. It was soulful without a specific religious stamp, though the religious impulse, I am inclined to believe, was willy-nilly present. It was marked in various proportions by elements of 'anarchism, socialism, pacifism, existentialism, humanism, bohemianism, populism, mysticism, and black nationalism.' "

Amy belonged to the Students for a Democratic Society, but SDS could not cohere as a group; its structure was too loose, and it failed to enunciate any goal beyond "freedom." What were the young people to do, where were they to go, when they were no longer students?

The characteristics of their collaboration in good will toward all but racists, patrioteers, profiteers, and sundry stuffed shirts would endure long after their ties with the group as such dissolved. But after their graduation and the election of 1968, which presented no opportunity for collective activity and aspiration, it was inevitable that their association as a unified body should break down. They were left in abeyance; they would always look back nostalgically to the time of their early enthusiasm.

When I referred to them as idealists, Amy objected. To her, idealism connotes something dreamy, unreal, unproductive. But idealism is either a philosophic system, or it is what we mean by any arduous struggle to achieve a concrete and altruistic end. It is in this sense that Amy is an idealist, as the best of the young always are.

In her rejection of the *word* I see a general and typical significance. Amy is intelligent, warmhearted, and resolutely honest. But being very young she does not yet know how her acute perceptions and sensibilities may best be used, for both herself and others. Stretched out before her are a multitude of possibilities. The prospect of an ordinary career, even a well-paid one, leaves her glum. "What I'm looking for," she says with intensity, "what my work must lead to . . ." The rest is an index finger pointed toward heaven.

Amy is well read and speaks and writes with ease. For all that, I find in her a constriction of vocabulary, the result of her shying away from inflated rhetoric. "They do not believe in words," Joan Didion has said of the young she met in San Francisco. Yet there is, among the educated young, a contradictory recourse to epithet, slogans, and catchwords as obfuscating and in their way as small-minded as the abused and eroded verbiage of the discredited Establishment.

Take the word "liberal," for example. It has been placed on the "Index" of the young. When I used it to describe a recently appointed college president (I meant, of course, that she was reasonable and fair), several students were contemptuous. In a lecture I gave at a university in the Midwest, I said in passing that I was more interested in the opinion of a "judicious" minority than in that of an uninformed majority. "Elitist!" the audience cried, hurling the word at me like a stone to crush me. I was so amazed by the total condemnation their epithet contained that I didn't trouble to point out to them the innovators, revolutionaries, and seers in art, religion, social thought, politics, and science who have also been considered "elitist." Even the expression "generation gap," while certainly convenient, is misleading. Both the young and their elders suffer a loss when they regard themselves as entirely cut off from one another.

These ambiguities and confusions of language and terminology are symptoms that have their consequences in behavior. The gates to a lustrously sane future appear to be shut. The arts today speak mainly of our disarray, of our schizophrenia. To those who seek something other or more than money, business is of meager appeal. Yet what today does not soon become commerce? The official ideologies have been dishonored. Where then shall one turn? Certainly not to the ancient dogmas as embodied in the established institutions, and only the debilitated give themselves to drugs and other cultish panaceas.

How, in these circumstances, does one move forward with confidence? There is a stalemate—transitional, I believe, in the case of Amy—which leads in some instances to a sort of embattled and anarchic arrogance or to something like a restive laziness. Amy, for instance, eats too much, sleeps too much, smokes too much, is not punctual, and is generally negligent in dress. But she is also buoyant, eager, a keen judge of books, plays and films, people, and events. This contradiction gives her and others as potentially valuable as she an air of being suspended—"hung up." They all appear reluctant to be born.

Avoidance of close contact with the poor stifles one's humanity; but the deliberate shunning of those who are not poor leads also to distorted vision. Both are signs of weakness; both set up ghettos of the mind. When I introduced Amy to certain social "luminaries" she reacted as if the momentary connection were not merely a bore but a contamination.

"What do I have to do with *these* people?" she exclaimed. It is reverse snobbery.

Amy, it almost goes without saying, is on rigid guard against male chauvinism. When one day I remarked that the sight of a woman drinking alone at a bar always made me sad, Amy could not restrain herself from interrupting with "That is a sexist statement!" True enough. I wholeheartedly approve of the women's liberation position in its social, its economic, and most of its marital aspects. But, though I cannot give precise definitions of "masculine" and "feminine" traits, I do know that men and women differ psychologically from each other.

Setting aside the question of masculine superiority as irrelevant and false, I still do not believe that all people or all civilizations are the same. I certainly do not desire uniformity in language, customs, manners. The color and zest of the human adventure spring from the differentiation of the species. And this differentiation is an unending source of delight. The drive to make everything and everyone conform to a single monochromatic pattern is the curse of our civilization as it leads to a meaningless perfection, helpful perhaps to everything but blood, flesh, mind, and spirit.

When Amy discovered that I had a housekeeper, she was shocked. I understood how she felt. It is certainly ridiculous that I don't know how to do my own housework. I'm sure I could do it—badly—if I had to. I might of course argue that doing household chores would take time away from work I do better, which is probably more useful to others. I wonder if Amy's shock doesn't somehow imply that housework is low work. In this, she was making the same assumption she finds so reprehensible in the middle-class attitude to menial service. When I was a boy, my father told me that while medicine was undoubtedly a noble calling, much of it involved doing very filthy work.

Amy is also put off by fancy restaurants, not alone because of the cost. On the whole she prefers rough clothes, which are of course more comfortable. But there is also a tribal statement in these apparent fetishes and taboos, a statement many carry to stupid or ugly extremes but which Amy tempers with basic good humor and common sense.

The younger generation's determination to cut itself off from the vocabulary and habits of thought, from the proprieties, conventions, and modes of behavior of the middle class—still the main functioning body of our society—results, ironically, in ever greater dependence on it. There is much pathos and tension in this. Amy has occasionally confessed to me her disappointment that so many of her friends are now attending law school, driving cabs, or taking the kinds of jobs they formerly scorned. But what are they to do? Short of becoming saints or martyrs, they cannot shut themselves off entirely from the world that surrounds and envelops one. All of us who see and suffer the decay around us nevertheless share in it.

If some of those who were rebels in the sixties have now turned to the law or to other professions, we can hope that they will turn their skills to the service of a more humane community. Those who wish to free themselves from what is noxious and stultifying should take care to remember that even confrontation requires expertise.

All is not lost! Amy and her friends will find their way. They will come to understand that their very complaints about the absence of sound values are based on the same values that have inspired the most enlightening works of art and literature, including religious scripture, as well as the most seminal works of social thought.

I confess that I was thrilled to hear Amy say that she still believed in that millennial concept, the soul. As R. D. Laing has written, "Who could be so superstitious as to suppose that because one cannot see one's soul at the end of a microscope, it does not exist?"

The dilemma we all face worried Chekhov long ago. "As long as our boys and girls are still students," he wrote in a letter, "they are still honest and good, they're our hope, [our] future; but as soon as those students have to stand on their own and grow up our future goes up in smoke, and all that's left of the future are cottage-owning doctors, rapacious public officials, and thieving engineers."

It would surely prove historically disastrous if the generation with a will to change society were to cool off into a neurotic complacency or into the quiet desperation Thoreau spoke of. I ask my students to bank their fires and to clean their weapons of language and thought and use them for something more than parade.

I have spoken of Juleen and Amy because, while they differ in age and temperament and background, they are alike in their blazing intelligence and fierce independence. Juleen has succeeded in establishing a kind of equilibrium for herself, and Amy, I am confident, will in her own way soon do the same. Both are the best of our youth, "the hope of the future."

There are others about whom it is much more difficult to predict anything. But in the middle rung of the student body, the so-called average, particularly in the big city colleges with their free admissions system, I find a strange mixture of both the heartening and the dismaying.

What is best in the student body as a whole is a spirit of questioning and inquiry that does not confine itself to the bare data of instruction but seeks to know what connection there is between it and "real life."

The majority attend college for practical reasons: nowadays a B.A. is indispensable for a decent job. These are the students who do just enough to get by. Many of them ape the insurgence characteristic of their generation, wherein phraseology substitutes for thought and action, and attitudinizing masquerades as passion. I heard a girl say of me as I passed through a thicket of hippies queuing up for a rock concert at the Fillmore East: "I could kill a man like that." She had her reasons: I was wearing a felt hat and sporting a cane.

The young people in my classes do very little reading apart from the books assigned by the curriculum. They "specialize" in issues or personalities picked up from the talk of the town. A theatre major who had never seen a Grotowski production undertook to write a thesis on his importance and influence. He was "the latest thing."

Many of my students had never heard of Alfred Lunt or read many plays written before 1945; what did not bear directly upon current Broadway or off-Broadway theatre they felt it was safe to ignore. When students in a graduate class in theatre studies were urged to read certain signal literary works, at the very least novels by Melville, Hardy, Dickens, Tolstoi, and Flaubert, they laughed.

These students lack a cultural family. They wish to bypass history. They want to begin from scratch with movies, television, ads, and slang. But people who cut themselves off entirely from the past have no future.

Such infections of the student body could be cured if they did not spread to many of the teachers, some of whom are permissive to the point of self-effacement, or, worse, assent to and fortify the students' mental blocks and blanks.

An instructor in the theatre department of a reputable New York college challenged my suggestion that students ought to acquaint themselves with dramatic masterpieces written before the twentieth century (with Shakespeare, for instance) on the grounds that the students were far in advance of and more intelligent than Aristotle or Machiavelli (his examples): didn't Aristotle accept slavery, didn't Machiavelli consider women inferior?!

I left the conference at which this revelation took place with an incident from my Sorbonne days tantalizingly vivid before me. André Le Breton, the professor who found it improper to quote Maeterlinck, scoffed at an English girl for having written in a paper that Chateaubriand had learned a great deal from the study of English literature: Le Breton was an impassioned Anglophobe. "You yourself, mademoiselle," he declared, "don't write very well—though English," and cackled at his own barb. When the girl attempted to reply, Le Breton cut her off with "I don't propose to debate anything with *you*." Those professors at the Sorbonne did not brook any sort of "back talk" from their students.

Of course I thoroughly disapprove of academic tyranny. But I wonder if in the long run it isn't much more salutary than the sort of voluntary abandonment of authority some of our college teachers now feel obliged to indulge in as a "modern" tactic. A teacher occupies his position because, supposedly, he knows more than the student does. If this is not the case, the teacher should be disqualified or the student should not be in his class. Asking questions of a professor is the best means of testing him, getting the most out of him. There are some students who want to *tell*, to instruct their teachers, as if their very youth rendered them superior and closer to the truth.

The permissiveness today in education is not a sign of a society in the process of examining itself but of a society tired and hopeless of itself. The students at the Sorbonne were by no means as passive or as cowed as one might suppose. On leaving Le Breton's class, more than half a century ago, I heard one student say to another, "That man is truly insufferable." Though I agreed, I had to admit that I had learned a lot from him, for he knew what he knew.

Bobby Lewis, a stage director who is also a teacher, not long ago said to the opening session of a new class, "I want you to know that anybody under thirty bores me." It was his amusing way of letting them all know that the first thing he expected of them was attention, the ability to listen. I begin my own seminars by asking the students, as a favor to me, to refrain from smoking in class. Education, I explain to them, ought to be painful!

My students are on the whole pleased with this attitude. They are relieved and glad to encounter *some* conviction in a teacher. Whether they know it or not, they are looking for someone who is ready to affirm *something*. They are sick of merely being discontented with a world that, as the saying goes, they never made. The best among them will learn that waiting for Godot need be neither a static position nor a fight. It is a search.

CHAPTER

16

All People
Are Famous

Walking with Waldo Frank in Paris one spring day in 1923, I saw Picasso having a drink on the *terrasse* of the Café Flore. "Would you like me to introduce you to him?" Waldo asked. "No," I answered, without hesitation.

I didn't wish to meet Picasso because the contact would in no way have constituted a meeting. What would I have said to him? "Monsieur Picasso, it's a great honor; I've always admired your work!" He would have been a name, a face, not a *person*.

Getting to know people, whoever they may be, is what's important; life, after all, is just one person and another. This may be an odd statement for me to make in a book where so many famous people have appeared. For one thing, some of these people were "unknown" when I met them. For another thing, all the famous people taken all together would occupy only a corner of my personal hall of fame.

But then, what is fame? Copland sat in a café in the Paris of 1938 with Sanford Meisner, who had come over for a weekend from London, where he was acting as Kazan's understudy in *Golden Boy*. Someone who had known Copland as a boy in Brooklyn happened along, greeted him, and sat down at the table. Soon Meisner left for an appointment, and the man who had joined Copland asked, "Who was that fellow?"

"Sanford Meisner," Copland said.

"Never heard of him. What's he do?"

"He's an actor," Copland replied.

"Never heard of him," the man repeated.

Copland added, hopefully, "He's a member of the Group Theatre company."

"Never heard of it."

"Well," said Copland, "you must have heard of Clifford Odets."

"Odets, sure!" the man exploded with delight. "He was the junior counselor at our boys' camp."

So too some of the personalities in these pages are

bound to be "strangers" to a good many. Ernst Toller, for instance, is still remembered in Germany, but he has been forgotten by most theatre people here. Hanns Eisler is now a culture hero in Germany, but only a few Americans know who he is. To Mencken and George Jean Nathan, James Huneker was a model critic, but now he is a subject for college theses—if that. To many of my theatre students, Nathan himself as well as Stark Young are figures out of prehistory!

Some of my closest friends are relatively obscure outside their professional circles—for example, Jimmie Gelb, one of the best stage managers in the theatre, whom I met through Kazan and engaged for *Truckline Café*. He was too poor to go to college. But he had a good mind and managed to learn more about the theatre than most of the producers he worked for. He is also an exceptionally good judge of people. He is clearheaded and kindly, tenderhearted and at the same time unsentimental—actors love him. He could have been a fine director, but because of something like excessive humility, or the compulsion to serve rather than to be served, he never sought to attain that position. What I value most highly in him are his integrity and loyalty, rare qualities anywhere, but especially rare in the unstable realm of the theatre.

A former student in my acting classes and at Hunter, Constance Clark, charms me by a covert Irish canniness that expresses itself in unexpected remarks, such as, "I don't want to sell out—I want to buy in"; or, as an apology for being insufficiently resolute in political action, "It isn't that I lack courage; I lack the conviction." These statements are not wholly true, and have something to do with the loss of her Catholic faith. While a lack of self-confidence and self-assertion need not follow such a loss, there is a tendency for those whose binding religious belief has been sundered to become uncertain in other regards as well; this is more or less true of ex-radicals. But Connie's sweetness and wit remain undiminished.

I am touched by Pamela Tiffin's struggle to find herself. Because she is so strikingly attractive, she was thrust into commercial modeling when she was sixteen, and then virtually forced into the movies. Through her marriage to Clay Felker, now editor and publisher of *New York* magazine, she was plunged into the company of wheeler-dealers in the newspaper, political, and financial whirlpools. But what she really wanted all along was to study and learn. Between modeling engagements she took college classes in Latin poetry, and in Rome, where she has done most of her film work, she took courses at Loyola in art, history, and Irish and European literature.

At present, Pamela is working toward a degree in literature at Columbia. When I remarked that a degree has very little to do with education, she said, "I know that. But it means something to me." Nearly everyone is striving to attain something more than a material goal in life, and study and learning seem to many, as certainly they seem to Pamela, a means of reaching such a goal. To her, every good teacher is sacred.

When I was wretchedly poor, in the most trying of the Group Theatre days, Martin Gabel, who later married the charming Arlene Francis, asked me if I needed money, and I said no. Ever since he has looked at me with an eye both critical and affectionate. He sent me a beautiful leather-bound copy of *The Fervent Years* long after it was published. "With one stroke," I wrote him, "you've made my book a 'classic'!"

Ira Lewis, the author of *The Sponsor*, was acting in Jack Gelber's *The Connection* when I re-encountered him. I subsequently cast him in *Incident at Vichy*. And when, still later, I told him that I was going to cast him in my "demonstration" production of *Long Day's Journey into Night* in Tokyo, he fell upon my neck and kissed me. This was a tribute to what he considered my "disinterested generosity," which is the basic theme of his play. He is all devotion to goodness wherever he finds it and by the same token fiercely indignant wherever he detects the slightest evidence of injustice, ingratitude, or moral insensibility.

I have a special regard for the noble Edwin Denby, the best dance critic in America, who refuses to publish any more, although he still attends almost every ballet or dance recital and is the author of the libretto to Copland's little opera *The Second Hurricane* and writes very good poetry as well.

Other valued friends are the eminent literary critic Irving Howe and his profoundly beautiful wife, Arien, professor of psychology at the New School for Social Research; and Robert Hatch, the admirable film critic and executive editor of the *Nation* whose wife, Ruth, a high school art teacher, always makes me think of the American pioneer woman. It has been said of me that I always identify men by the women they have chosen. Just the other day I failed for an instant to recognize Paul Newman, whom I know well, until I saw his wife, Joanne Woodward, beside him.

It may be thought from these passing acknowledgments to a few of my friends that I move exclusively among artists. This supposition would seem to be borne out by the fact that even among those in "trade," I turn chiefly to people who are artists by nature. For example, in the shoe business my friend Seymour Troy, volatile and explosive on every subject, is undoubtedly an artist in the designing of women's footwear.

When I think back to my first years in Hollywood, the name of Bess Taffel, a screenwriter now married to Bob Boyle, an art director in films, gleams brightly. She braved the Los Angeles political inquisition and then severe illness, but the fortitude and calm for which I honor her are recognizable in her most casual moments as well. Chaplin, when I visited him at his home in Switzerland, asked after her affectionately.

I was proud to know the late Nicolà Chiaramonte, a fighting humanist, a refugee from Mussolini, an anti-Fascist soldier in Spain, a man of letters in Paris and New York, and finally a critic in Rome of books, films, and plays. He was a man of vast learning, of deep feeling, and of great breadth of vision; I am pleased that three volumes of his essays on politics, literature, and the theatre are now being prepared for publication.

In Rome too, Paolo Milano, Chiaramonte's friend and successor as literary critic for *L'Espresso,* has long been a valued companion. How moved I was—and what awe I felt—when he told me that as young men he and Chiaramonte spent hours together reading the classics in Greek and Latin.

Slightly stooped, serious, but smiling, Milano speaks of himself as a "moderate terrorist"! He asked the late Palmiro Togliatti, leader of the Italian Communist party, "How are we going to make a revolution in Italy? We are all of the same family!" And just a few days ago in Rome I heard him say a wonderful thing: "After reading all of French literature, I have come to the conclusion that it is all the work of one person!" . . . From him I learned, to my astonishment, that Rome has produced only one first-rate poet (Giuseppe Belli, 1791–1863), no distinguished statesman, no great pope, no great novelist. "But Paolo," I protested, "you are a Roman, and, what's more, a Roman from one of the oldest families." "Oh, I'm exceptional," he said, and he laughed. But he truly is.

In Paris and New York I enjoy the company and conversation of Stefan Hessel, the only German-born member of the French foreign ministry. He was involved in the French resistance, was captured by the Nazis, and was thrillingly rescued from a concentration camp by his companions in the resistance. He and his wife, Vitia, who translates from French, English, and Russian (and back again) at conferences among heads of states, are among the "larks," to use Anouilh's pretty metaphor, in the Gallic firmament. When Vitia, who also writes novels, was asked what her racial origin is, she answered, *"Juive russe, comme tout le monde!"* ("Russian Jewish, like everyone else!")

Michel Gordey, for many years a foreign correspondent with *Paris-Soir* and now with *L'Express,* the man who first broke the news of Khrushchev's denunciation of Stalin at the Twentieth Congress of the Communist party in 1956, belongs to the same galaxy of "larks." A French citizen, Gordey was born in Russia; he speaks English, German, Russian, and some Italian. He used to be married to Chagall's daughter, Bella; now he is married to an attractive girl from Denver, who is Doubleday's representative in Europe.

Gordey has won several awards in journalism, for his book *Visa to Moscow* in particular. What touches me in him is his passionate lament for France. "In America you speak openly about 'Watergate,' " he said when we last met. "We don't talk of such things in France, because our 'Watergates' are a constant occurrence."

In Israel, I greatly admire Joshua (Shaika) Weinberg, formerly a computer expert, which he claims was good training for his present job as managing director of the Cameri Theatre in Tel Aviv. Well educated, diplomatic, and modest, he is one of the most intelligent of the Israeli "doves."

The world-embracing Meyer Weisgal is *my* "favorite character outside of fiction." He is chairman of the Weizmann Institute of Science in Rehovot, and an occasional theatre producer (Reinhardt's *The Eternal Road*) as well as a journalist. He wrote his splendid autobiography, *Meyer Weisgal Thus Far,* at age seventy-five, when he was chronically ill and death was striking, unanswered, at his door. He is a man whom everyone should know, as indeed many have, the world over. I love him for his raucous Rabelaisianism, his generosity, his aesthetic sensibility, his regard for talent and learning, his ability to wring eleemosynary contributions out of rocks, but most of all for his refusal, *with respect,* to regard anybody, no matter how highly placed, as anything but ordinary, like himself.

Conscientiousness and geniality were the qualities that attracted me to the late Sidney Kaye, proprietor of the Russian Tea Room, on West Fifty-seventh Street. He created such a friendly atmosphere that his restaurant became a favorite meeting place—a European-style café—for musicians, actors, professors, purveyors of the arts.

He appreciated everyone in whom he could find the light of good nature, warmth, or talent. He could even laugh at jokes made at his own expense. After he returned from his honeymoon with pretty Faith Burwell, I asked him, "How's Faith?" "Oh, Harold," he said, "I can't tell you how happy I am." "I didn't ask how happy *you* are," I snapped back. "What I want to know is, is *she* happy?" This convulsed him with laughter. I remember too how he laughed when I asked him how he spelled his name, meaning "Kay" or "Kaye." "You see, Harold," he began to explain, "my real name is Kalmanowitch—" "Oh," I interrupted, "I know how to spell Kalmanowitch. I want to know how you spell *Kaye*." He rushed to the phone to favor Leonard Lyons with the "story."

I was awed by the gallantry with which he faced his death from cancer. When he told me and Jimmie Gelb that he was doomed, he spoke as casually as if he were referring to a cold. He prepared himself and his wife with stoic calm and trained her to take over and run the Tea Room. In him I found confirmation for my belief that a person is mature only if he is able to accept the prospect of death.

Little Max Asnas, the "Corned-beef Sage" and former owner of the Stage Delicatessen, another rendezvous for the comics, pugilists, gamblers, secretaries, and seers, also charmed me by the "Jewish daddy" familiarity with which he addressed all his customers—and the police. Once, in my "bad years," when a check I'd paid him with bounced, he told me so with an almost apologetic smile of commiseration.

Vincent Sardi, Sr., who opened his restaurant on West Forty-fourth Street during the Depression, was a man of memorable graciousness. He had the simplicity of the true aristocrat, a stalwart and easy forbearance that made Sardi's the most famous meeting and eating place of the theatrical profession and its fellow travelers. He extended credit to actors in need; he built his establishment on trust.

And here, very much at home, is Viola Ford, my housekeeper, who has shown me that, as Miguel de Unamuno has said, "Goodness is the best source of spiritual clearsightedness."

A student in a seminar I was giving at the University of Minnesota a few years ago came to New York seeking stage fame. She was nineteen. She enrolled in one of my acting classes and later worked briefly in a summer stock company in New Hampshire run by friends John Vari and Alfred Christie. She was a tall, sensuous brunette with deep dark eyes. But she could find only modeling work and, in 1962, when the first of the James Bond pictures was released here, a job as Sean Connery's escort during the campaign to put him over with American audiences.

I took her to the theatre; I introduced her to my "circle." When she complained that she wasn't getting anywhere, I told her to be patient, This, of course, had little effect. She would not be satisfied, she said, with just "getting by" as an actress, she had to be a star. She deliberately starved herself, though she already had a perfect figure, for work in films. She told me that if she did not realize her dream by the time she was twenty-one, she would kill herself. When I came back from one of my trips to Europe, I was told that she had died that summer from an overdose of sleeping pills.

I always think of her when some young person complains about not having "made it." Only a few weeks ago, a twenty-seven-year-old woman doing a doctoral thesis on some phase of medieval history came to seek my advice, or perhaps only a healing "message." I asked, "What's the matter?" and she said, "I'm a failure." It was by no means the first time I had heard the same sorry phrase from someone under thirty.

The sentiment that prompted her to speak of herself to me like that must not be confused with humility. I was outraged by her self-abasement. For me, the blessing of life is in living it. Life's sorrows are not accidents, they are part of the process and texture of existence. It is natural to fear pain, though it is not always good to avoid it. We should not be afraid to die, though it is right that we seek to postpone death as long as possible. If life is a struggle, it is nevertheless one we must engage in with ardor. At worst, my own nature echoes the Jewish proverb "A man should go on living, if only to satisfy his curiosity."

This, however, is not exactly what I tell visitors like the young woman with the thesis. I tell them about those who have "made it" comparatively late in life. I warn them first against the American mania of instantly "making it"— everyone wants to get everything so *fast*. They should realize, these impatient ones, that often what one gathers on the *path* to accomplishment is more rewarding than the goal itself.

The girl from Minnesota was so fixed on stardom that she couldn't even find any satisfaction in her own beauty. Her fixation on success—it might be called the *dementia Americana*—rendered her virtually asexual and became a destructive tension. It stemmed from blindness to the fact that all people are famous.

We are all chips off the same block. Our separateness is the definition, the proof, of our livingness. As individuals we are the heirs of eons of life; we are inextricably enmeshed in every part of it. We are bits of the ineffably mysterious and magnificent universe. We have only to strive to live as completely as our endowments permit (in doing so, we increase them) and to take pleasure and pride in them. We are all great, *i.e.*, wonderful, "famous," because we are products of and partners in the world's grandeur. Even the inevitable suffering of life, implicit in our being separate from the all, must be embraced not with resignation, but with joy. Living is its own reason.

Kenneth Tynan told me that his aim as a critic was to celebrate and foster genius. If I were to set down a parallel intention as a man, I would say that I hope to sustain other people in their *selves*. I recently heard my friend Robert Bak, the eminent psychoanalyst, say, "We are all footnotes in history." True, but hardly *humanly* useful. The earth itself is only a footnote, an infinitesimal speck of dust in the cosmos. But we are still related to its grandeur. It is that sense of participation in the universal that animates the greatest works of art and all the world's religions, and we must take care to preserve it in ourselves.

We can shape our daily lives and spirits the way the artist shapes his memory and imagination and creates his work from them. Enjoying or enduring the present, preparing for the future, we should also look back, far back. Our experience is part of the wider experience of our day, of bygone ages. How can we be "small" in such company! We are all historical figures.

Certain people boast of their egotism. But most often such boasts are merely symptoms of an injured ego. For the ego, once injured, becomes swollen and sick. The true self is enhanced and fortified through its embrace of others, and thus fashions its own "fame." The all is greater than the one, but the one cannot be conceived except as part of the all. Without this realization, which is the path to self-respect and humility, we are only latent human beings. "Each and every creature exists for the perfection of the entire universe," wrote Thomas Aquinas. And Unamuno said: "There is nothing more universal than the individual, for what is the property of each is the property of all."

Recently I came late to a party at which Vladimir Horowitz and several other accomplished people were gathered. I felt I had interrupted something—a game, perhaps. I asked what was going on. "Each of us," I was told, "is naming the period in history when he or she would have preferred to live." Some spoke of fifth-century Athens, others of the Middle Ages, the time of absolute faith, still others of the *ancien régime* in France, which Talleyrand, whose life spanned several eras, thought the most delightful of all. When called upon to name my best time, I answered, "Right now." "Why?" I was asked, with almost as much surprise as skepticism. "Because *we're* here," I answered.

It is true that since Hiroshima many of us have come to regard our time as the worst of times, the most disruptive. This accounts to some extent for the restlessness of the young, their desire to live fast, or, on the contrary, to remove themselves as far as possible from the follies of the world. Generally, I am inclined to feel as Chekhov did when he wrote in a letter, "I cannot accept the idea of our 'nervous age,' because people have been nervous in all ages. Anyone who is afraid of being nervous should turn himself into a sturgeon or a smelt." Because he died in 1904, Chekhov may be thought to reflect the still prevalent optimism of the nineteenth century, which, however, began to wane after the initial triumphs of the Industrial Revolution. Before Chekhov, Emerson championed "the equivalence of all times" and maintained that "the disadvantages of any epoch exist only for the faint-hearted." But when all is said and done it may be Macaulay who was right when he wrote in *The History of England* that "there is constant improvement precisely because there is constant discontent. It is natural that being dissatisfied with the present, we should form too favorable an estimate of the past."

The debates on this score are to a large degree futile. We live now—it is our eternity—and doing so, we must struggle as people at all times have struggled against adversity. Optimism is foolish, pessimism is mad, and both are finally irrelevant. There exists today a *fashionable* pessimism: studied, preached, extolled as a sign of superior understanding. All striving is said to be in vain.. But we strive because we must: living dictates it. In his humane wisdom, Chekhov also said: "Anyone who sincerely thinks that a man has no more need of lofty, remote goals than do cows, and that those goals cause 'all our troubles' can do nothing more than eat, drink, or, when he's had his fill, take a flying leap and bash his head against the corner of a trunk."

Many do just that or advise others to do it. It's a pity. But they are a tiny minority composed in the main of people who are busy lying to themselves. Most of us wish to live, and most of us will fight to live, and not for "remote goals," either. All goals, whether or not we believe them possible of fulfillment, are felt as present needs. The idealist is a realist. The theatre manager Max Gordon's prescription for success was "keep the store open," and this applies to nothing so much as to life itself.

A student in my class responded to my capacity for enthusiasm by saying, "Men of your day"—he meant the thirties—"had ideals. What ideals can we cling to today?" Nonplused for the moment, I said something like, "Nonsense! Start with breakfast! You won't eat rotten eggs, you won't drink sour milk, just as you won't eat spoiled fish or decaying meat for dinner. Work up from there. Everything in life is just as real as food!" The answer wasn't altogether dumb.

People who overcome life's "slings and arrows" have always been my special heroes. In 1938 Thelma Schnee gave a brilliant performance as the hussy in *The Corn Is Green*. She had no luck as an actress after that. Undaunted, she learned Russian by reading all of *War and Peace* with the aid of a dictionary and proceeded to adapt Simonov's *The Whole World Over*, which I directed in 1947 starring Uta Hagen and Joseph Buloff. This was her last critical success. Her devoted and still young husband died suddenly. A brother, a playwright and successful film producer, committed suicide shortly afterward. She began to suffer from insomnia, depression, sexual frigidity. Psychoanalysis did not help. . . . But after the age of thirty-five, through force of will and unusual intelligence, she was able to earn a doctorate in experimental psychology. Under a pseudonym, she wrote a book, *Myself and I,* which describes the process of her cure through the use, under medical supervision, of LSD. She is now an assistant professor of medical psychology at UCLA and staff psychologist at the Neuro-Psychiatric Institute in Los Angeles.

I trust the "ordinary" man, who is never altogether "ordinary." There is perhaps no such thing as a dull life or a totally uninteresting person. Though, in theatre circles at least, I am occasionally described as an "intellectual," I have always been wary of people who are thought of as intellectual or who think of themselves as intellectual. I am reminded of an aphorism in a song by Brecht: "The only thing that can live on the head is a louse!" One can't wholly understand a philosophy, or even a mere thought, if one isn't aware of the individual behind it. There is, as the Russians say, enough stupidity in every wise man. That "stupidity" is to be rejoiced in, rather than despaired of, because there can be no true wisdom that is not well rooted in what is common to us all, or "ordinary." I have often observed how "official" intellectuals cut themselves off from one another by a hostility that is either competitive or snobbish or both. To pride oneself solely on mind, or even talent, is sinful.

When I am asked which of my various occupations I like best—directing, writing, teaching, lecturing—I am obliged to confess that I take a certain pleasure in them all. (This sometimes makes me say by way of semiserious paradox that I have never done a day's work in my life.) Retrospectively, at any rate, I sometimes harbor a sneaky suspicion that I have even taken a peculiar pleasure in some of my sufferings: poverty, jealousy, surgery, and other "flops"! I love to travel, but I am also happy to return. I disapprove of much, but I enjoy almost everything. I find that my chief aim at all times has been to manifest my *self* in every way within my power.

In Odets's diary, I found the following judgment of me: "Harold has turned his every weakness into an asset." It's true: I was lazy, so I forced myself to become active; I was very shy, so I taught myself to be bold.

Berthold Viertel, in his *Hudson Review* article on *The Fervent Years,* said of me: "He is a philosopher without a system." Despite my lack of a "system," I wish to meet Viertel's challenge. I believe that life is essentially irrational, but I also believe that human beings must use their reason—with due recognition of its limitations. I believe that men and women may not be perfectible, but that they must act as if they were. I believe that although we may not possess free will, we must behave as if we did. I believe life terrible and glorious.

Plays Directed by Harold Clurman

Index

1935–36	*Awake and Sing!* by Clifford Odets
1935–36	*Paradise Lost* by Clifford Odets
1937–38	*Golden Boy* by Clifford Odets
1938–39	*Rocket to the Moon* by Clifford Odets
1938–39	*Awake and Sing!* by Clifford Odets (revival)
1938–39	*The Gentle People* by Irwin Shaw
1939–40	*Night Music* by Clifford Odets
1940–41	*Retreat to Pleasure* by Irwin Shaw
1942–43	*The Russian People* by Konstantin Simonov, adapted by Clifford Odets
1945–46	*Beggars Are Coming to Town* by Theodore Reeves
1945–46	*Truckline Café by* Maxwell Anderson (also coproduced)
1946–47	*The Whole World Over* by Konstantin Simonov, adapted by Thelma Schnee
1948–49	*The Young and Fair* by Richard Nash
1949	*Montserrat* by Emmanuel Roblès (Tel Aviv)
1949–50	*The Bird Cage* by Arthur Laurents
1949–50	*The Member of the Wedding* by Carson McCullers
1950–51	*The Autumn Garden* by Lillian Hellman
1951–52	*Desire Under the Elms* by Eugene O'Neill (revival)
1952–53	*The Time of the Cuckoo* by Arthur Laurents

1952–53	*The Emperor's Clothes* by George Tabori
1953–54	*The Ladies of the Corridor* by Dorothy Parker and Arnaud d'Usseau
1953–54	*Mademoiselle Colombe* by Jean Anouilh
1954–55	*Bus Stop* by William Inge
1955–56	*Tiger at the Gates* by Jean Giraudoux, translated by Christopher Fry (London and New York)
1955–56	*Pipe Dream* by Richard Rodgers and Oscar Hammerstein
1956–57	*The Waltz of the Toreadors* by Jean Anouilh
1956–57	*Orpheus Descending* by Tennessee Williams
1957–58	*The Day the Money Stopped* by Maxwell Anderson and Brendan Gill
1957–58	*The Waltz of the Toreadors* by Jean Anouilh (revival)
1958–59	*The Cold Wind and the Warm* by S. N. Behrman
1958–59	*A Touch of the Poet* by Eugene O'Neill
1959	*Caesar and Cleopatra* by George Bernard Shaw (Tel Aviv)
1959–60	*Jeannette* by Jean Anouilh
1959–60	*Heartbreak House* by George Bernard Shaw (revival)
1961–62	*A Shot in the Dark* by Harry Kurnitz and Marcel Achard
1961–62	*Judith* by Jean Giraudoux, translated by Christopher Fry (London)
1965	*Incident at Vichy* by Arthur Miller
1965	*Long's Day's Journey into Night* by Eugene O'Neill (Tokyo)
1966	*Where's Daddy?* by William Inge
1968	*The Iceman Cometh* by Eugene O'Neill (Tokyo)
1969	*Uncle Vanya* by Anton Chekhov (Los Angeles)